"This book provides fascinating and timely insights into alternative forms of management education as pioneered and developed on the University of Hertfordshire's Doctor of Management programme, which provides a person-centred approach that takes account of the complexity of human interaction and feeling in organisations. The chapters, written by staff and graduates from the programme, remind us of the significance of paying attention to the intersections of subjective, organisational and political levels of experience in the world of work, whilst at the same time, raising important moral questions about the importance of kindness in the life of contemporary organisations that are often beset by the ethos of individualism and competition."

Candida Yates, *Professor of Culture and Communication, Bournemouth University, UK*

"We come into the world as humans, living beings, and we leave the world in the same way. In between, curiously, we spend large spells thinking of ourselves as 'workers', 'managers', 'leaders', 'executives' – categories in which it somehow seems important to deny the humanness not only of ourselves but of others, too. This book shows what – and how – we might learn when we scratch the thin veneer of those categories, and does so from a deeply informed, rigorous academic perspective, from a tradition dedicated to taking experience seriously. Therefore it's important for business, for public service, and for all of us who seek to build the capacity to think more humanly about experience."

Benjamin Taylor, *Chief Executive, the Public Service Transformation Academy, UK*

"This book draws on the authors' outstanding reputation, alongside the long-standing ambition of the University of Hertfordshire's Doctor of Management programme, to reinstate management inquiry as an applied discipline. It's a core resource for managers, scholars, methodologists and educators in management education who want to understand management practice through the prism of human complexity. The authors make a compelling case for challenging orthodoxy, and more than that, provide accessible means and methods for engaging critically with the managerialist paradigm through reflexivity and creativity, providing honest accounts of journeying from innovators in this space."

Hannah Hesselgreaves, *Professor in Organisational Learning, Northumbria University, UK*

COMPLEXITY AND ORGANISATIONS

Virtually everyone accepts that workplaces are complex, but there is little insight into how we might engage with complexity more skilfully. If complexity isn't something that managers can control and leaders cannot harness, then what does a complexity perspective offer?

This fourth book in the complexity series describes how taking complexity seriously can inform approaches to understanding organisations. It focuses on the ways that managers and researchers can engage with their own histories to better understand their working lives, how they may be participating in maintaining the very processes they are trying to change and how research methods can shed light on politics of working together. The chapter authors work in a wide variety of sectors and draw on their experience to produce vibrant writing which will resonate with managers and leaders who want to explore how they might understand their working lives differently, and to students who are using first-person reflexive research methodologies.

Drawn from contemporary research in a wide variety of organisations, this book makes a valuable contribution to manager-researchers wanting to think differently about their intractable and enduring everyday dilemmas.

Kiran Chauhan is an organisational consultant at The King's Fund, a health and care policy think tank in the UK. He is also a visiting lecturer at Hertfordshire Business School, University of Hertfordshire.

Chris Mowles is Professor of Complexity and Management at Hertfordshire Business School, University of Hertfordshire.

Complexity and Management

Series Editor: Chris Mowles, University of Hertfordshire, UK

The Complexity of Consultancy
Exploring Breakdowns within Consultancy Practice
Edited by Nicholas Sarra, Karina Solsø and Chris Mowles

Complexity and Leadership
Edited by Kiran Chauhan, Emma Crewe and Chris Mowles

Complexity and the Public Sector
Edited by Chris Mowles and Karen Norman

Complexity and Organisations
Researching Practice
Edited by Kiran Chauhan and Chris Mowles

For more information about this series, please visit: www.routledge.com/Complexity-and-Management/book-series/CM

COMPLEXITY AND ORGANISATIONS

Researching Practice

Edited by Kiran Chauhan and Chris Mowles

Routledge
Taylor & Francis Group
LONDON AND NEW YORK

Designed cover Image: Getty Images

First published 2025
by Routledge
4 Park Square, Milton Park, Abingdon, Oxon OX14 4RN

and by Routledge
605 Third Avenue, New York, NY 10158

Routledge is an imprint of the Taylor & Francis Group, an informa business

British Library Cataloguing-in-Publication Data
A catalogue record for this book is available from the British Library

ISBN: 978-1-032-53138-0 (hbk)
ISBN: 978-1-032-53139-7 (pbk)
ISBN: 978-1-003-41052-2 (ebk)

DOI: 10.4324/9781003410522

Typeset in Joanna
by codeMantra

For Product Safety Concerns and Information please contact our EU representative:
GPSR@taylorandfrancis.com
Taylor & Francis Verlag GmbH, Kaufingerstraße 24, 80331 München, Germany.

CONTENTS

CONTRIBUTORS

Maj Karin Askeland is a senior consultant at AFF where she co-directs the Headmaster Program run in cooperation with the Norwegian School of Economics and is a member of staff at the renowned Solstrand Programme for senior executives. She is an associate fellow at the Oxford Saïd Business School and tutor at their programme for Strategic Leadership.

Mikkel Haugsted Brahm is a strategic leader in the Group Architecture unit of Nordea, a Nordic bank. He graduated as Doctor of Management from the University of Hertfordshire in 2017.

Tobit Emmens is the associate director of research & development at Devon Partnership NHS Trust, a mental health and learning disabilities healthcare organisation in the UK. He is also the lead for mental health research in the National Institute of Health Research Clinical Research Network – South West Peninsula and an honorary senior research fellow at the University of Exeter.

Sune Bjørn Larsen is a self-employed organisational consultant. He works primarily in the public sector in Denmark where he draws on his educational background as a psychologist and Doctor of Management along with his experience as a manager, consultant and researcher.

Jannie Rasmussen is an organisational consultant in the Danish consultancy company UKON. She works with leadership and organisational development. She is also a visiting lecturer at Copenhagen Business School, Denmark.

Karina Solsø is a self-employed organisational consultant in Denmark working on organisational change and leadership development. She is also a visiting lecturer at Aalborg University, Denmark and at Hertfordshire Business School, University of Hertfordshire, UK.

Helle Therkelsen Stoltz is a senior social scientist and team leader at Sweco, an international architectural and engineering consultancy company, and is based in Denmark. She works with social, gender and labour aspects of international development projects.

Sophie Wong has a background in business and neuroscience and is a trained therapist/volunteer social worker in mental health services. She served on the board of a neuroscience research institute in Australia.

PREFACE TO THE COMPLEXITY AND MANAGEMENT SERIES

The Key Ideas of Complex Responsive Processes of Relating and their Recent Development

CHRIS MOWLES

Our experience at work tells us that we make plans but they rarely turn out as we intended. We communicate as clearly as we can, but we are still often misunderstood. Even when acting with the best of intentions we can cause harm. Sometimes leaders and managers become brutally aware that they may be in charge, but they are not always in control because work life has the quality of being predictably unpredictable. Management training and education has become much more widespread in the last 30 years yet still largely relies on assumptions of predictability and control. Often dealing with abstractions and idealisations, the majority management discourse rests on assumptions of an orderly world where leaders and managers propose and dispose using tools and techniques of technical rationality (Stacey, 2012).

The minority disciplines within the natural sciences, the sciences of complexity, have been an alternative source domain for thinking differently about the stable instability of organisational life for more than 30 years. Even so, management as a tradition finds it hard to shake off old habits. Just as it is now widely accepted that organisations are sites of complex activity, so there are tendencies within organisational scholarship that assume that even complexity can be managed, putting the manager back in control. For example, it may be assumed that the manager can decide whether a situation is simple, complicated or complex, thus determining whether a 'complexity approach' is needed or not. Alternatively, it may be suggested that a manager can 'unleash/embrace/encourage' complexity, as though complexity is always good and is at the manager's command, thus reinstating managerial control.

Uniquely, then, the books, articles and teaching which has emerged from the faculty group at the University of Hertfordshire (UH), and graduates of the Doctor of Management (DMan) programme there, have taken up insights from the complexity sciences but have tried at the same time to cleave to their radical implications. It has been a decades-long experiment working with the idea that ultimately the social world is uncontrollable, but that we need to find ways to go on together anyway. This is not the same as saying that there is nothing to be done. Rather, the perspective developed at UH, termed complex responsive processes of relating, takes management seriously as a contingent group activity that requires highly reflective and reflexive individuals to negotiate and improvise, particularly in situations of high uncertainty. It assumes that some ways of managing are more helpful than others, and that with practice, it is possible to become more skilful.

Between 2000 and 2008, Routledge produced a series of volumes, both single author and curated books of chapters written by faculty and graduates from the DMan programme, which set out this perspective (Stacey, 2005; Stacey and Griffin, 2005a, 2005b, 2008; Shaw and Stacey, 2006). The foundational volume was the jointly authored book by Ralph Stacey, Doug Griffin and Patricia Shaw entitled *Complexity and Management: Fad or Radical Challenge to Systems Thinking* (2000). In it, the authors interpreted the complexity sciences by analogy and drew on the social sciences to locate it as a resource for social science thinking and research. It marked a radical departure for organisational theory and was a pioneering attempt to mobilise complexity theory to understand organisational life. The subsequent series of edited volumes was entitled *Complexity and the Experience of Organizing* and comprised titles on research, managing and leading in the public sector, emergence, improvisation, values and leadership. These volumes evolved out of the research work undertaken by students on the DMan, which had become an experiential doctorate run along psychodynamic lines. The volumes had wide appeal and demonstrated the importance of taking everyday complex experience seriously, inquiring into it as a participant rather than from an assumed independent position.

This current series reimagines the experience of 20 years ago with the programme under the Directorship of Chris Mowles and faculty colleagues, Nick Sarra, Karen Norman, Emma Crewe, Karina Solsø and Kiran Chauhan. To date, 80 DMan students have successfully completed their doctorates. Over recent years, the graduates in the programme have drawn on a wider and wider variety of scholars and ideas to illuminate their work, including anthropology, social psychology, political economy, feminism, intersectionality and critical organisational theory.

This is the fourth volume in the series, bringing together a group of vibrant, engaged researchers to inquire into complex phenomena at work, and write about the insights they have gained as a way of provoking resonance, recognition and insight in the reader. This is very different from more orthodox entity-based research which is more typical in business schools, or research which is undertaken to increase the effectiveness or efficiency of organisations, or to test some tool or technique of management. Rather, the research in this volume is driven by doubt and curiosity to draw out the plurality of everyday interactions in organisations. Aimed at producing complex knowledge, it is governed simply by paying attention to what is going on, and what sense people are making of it, including the researcher. The generalisability of the findings, their usefulness if you like, is to be found in the extent to which the reader finds this resonant, provoking, insightful and wise. There are no tools, techniques of stepwise methods to be found here.

Readers of the original Routledge series may be interested in comparing and contrasting methods and references from the previous publications to judge how thinking has changed. But first it is worth going back over some of the original scholarship which shaped the thinking of the founding of the DMan and the perspective it embodied, which I do briefly now as a way of providing some context for the chapters which follow. This review does not do justice to the wide variety of sources which students and graduates now draw on for their research, but it may help frame the key tenets of thinking which pervade the chapters in this volume.

Theoretical and practical origins

At the beginning of the millennium, three colleagues at the UH, Ralph Stacey, Doug Griffin and Patricia Shaw, decided to start a new professional doctorate. The trio's aim was to combine all that was productive, if sometimes uncomfortable, from their shared experience of group-based pedagogy with an interdisciplinary research perspective combining the natural and social sciences. This perspective was forged in a very close friendship between the three colleagues, a fact consonant with the perspective they were developing, and which highlights the centrality of relationships to understanding social life.

Starting the DMan also marked a theoretical break from Stacey's previous oeuvre and fascination with the complexity sciences. Ralph had been working with researchers in groups for some time, but in his previous publications he had argued that organisations were complex adaptive systems (CAS), or that they were like them, using the complexity sciences as metaphor. CAS are computer-based models comprising multiple interacting agents. He even argued that complexity thinking applied in certain situations and not others, the subject of the still ubiquitous Stacey diagram.[1] After many heated hours of discussion, Stacey, Griffin and Shaw moved from simple metaphor to interpret the CAS by analogy, identifying properties of interest in the models and refracting them to the social domain. In doing so, they tried to hang on to the generative tension of keeping an in-depth understanding of CAS to set alongside a granular interpretation of relevant social theory and argued that complexity applies in all situations and at all degrees of scale.

I explore what the two domains share in common, and what the conceptual implications are later. But the combined perspective these colleagues developed, complex responsive processes of relating, is an example of what the French philosopher Edgar Morin (2005) later expressed as a necessary development in dealing with insights from the complexity sciences. Morin argued that there needed to be a transition from a restricted understanding of complexity to a general understanding. He set out to encourage new ways of thinking that brought the natural and social sciences together. For him, there was further to go than simply collapsing some of the radical implications of taking the complexity sciences seriously into orthodox natural science thinking based on disaggregation, prediction and control:

> The principle of disjunction, of separation (between objects, between disciplines, between notions, between subject and object of knowledge), should be substituted by a principle that maintains the distinction, but that tries to establish the relation.
>
> (Morin, 2005, p7)

Complex responsive processes of relating is an attempt at describing such a new paradigm of thinking, researching and acting which privileges relationships, process and collaboration, uniting the knower and the known in paradoxical tension.

The perspective originally wove together four principal traditions of thought: the complexity sciences, in particular evolutionary CAS; pragmatic philosophy; process sociology, especially Norbert Elias; and group analytic thinking and practice. I briefly explore these four influences sequentially. The purpose of the following paragraphs is to point to some of the key assumptions which inform the work of authors contributing to this volume, so that the reader might better locate their arguments.

Complexity – radically different assumptions about stability and change

More orthodox theories of management often contain assumptions about social life drawing on systems theory, which depend upon spatial metaphors, notions of equilibrium, and consider organisations as entities. Organisations are described as operating at different 'levels', are disaggregated into parts and whole and go through distinct and managed processes of change. There is an assumption that managers are somehow outside the organisation understood as a system and can therefore operate upon it. As an example, in everyday ways of talking about organisations, managers are thought to be able to 'move it in the right direction,' to 'create the right culture,' and to 'drive change.' These assumptions hide in plain sight: they are taken for granted and are therefore often not alluded to or justified, because they are dominant assumptions. This is the way that ideology works. When I present complexity ideas to groups of managers, they often rightly ask me to work hard to justify them, often without acknowledging that their own ideas about stability and change in organisations are informed by a set of ideas that are equally questionable.

The perspective of complex responsive processes of relating interprets CAS in particular as having profound implications for thinking about stability and change in social life (Mowles, 2021). For example, CAS models are never at rest, but iterate, and then reiterate. The implication by analogy is that this is equally true for social life. Assuming this problematises more orthodox theories of management which propose that organisations have to undergo periods of change from an undesired stable state to an ideal stable state; stability is contrasted with change. Instead, to corrupt Churchill's observation about history, from a complexity perspective, we might think that organising is simply one damned thing after another. Even states of stability are dynamically maintained.

Second, in CAS, population-wide patterns of stable instability arise as a result of what all agents are doing together in their local interactions and may change as a result of the amplification of small differences. Cause and effect are in a non-linear relationship. Interpreting this characteristic by analogy challenges thinking about wholesale, often top-down change predicated on linear cause and effect. To transpose this insight to organisations is to assume that whatever happens does so as a combination of managerial framing and employee interpretation in local interactions, which in turn feeds managerial framing. As an example, and to give a complexity perspective on why wholesale organisational change programmes often fail, what everyone is doing together in their local interactions may be precisely to resist the proposed change.

In CAS, agents negotiate conflicting constraints in their local interactions. By analogy, this directs us to think about how people in organisations negotiate their mutual constraints, their power relationships at work. Power and politics are often avoided in contemporary organisations and orthodox organisational scholarship, and when they are we avoid the ethical implications of the negotiation of how to go on together. Fourthly, in CAS, there is no controlling agent or group of agents which direct activity.

Interpreting this characteristic by analogy deflates the common assumption that individual leadership is everything. Thinking about general patterns of influence is not the same as denying the importance of leaders but rather broadens our thinking to consider the exercise of authority as an improvisational group activity.

And lastly, CAS have a paradoxical movement: local interaction creates the global pattern, while at the same time, the global pattern shapes local activity. In organisational life, we can only take up idealisations of global patterns, call them strategies, in local activity. At the same time, our local improvisations produce what we might think of as strategy in practice. In everyday management thinking, contradictions are resolved by splitting them out with the manager able to choose one pole over the other, leaders or followers, transformation or transaction, strategy or implementation. Interpreting insights from the complexity sciences from a complex responsive process perspective implies that there is no splitting and no choosing, and so no escaping the paradox.

Evolutionary CAS interpreted by analogy do offer a different source domain for thinking about what's going on when we're at work trying to get things done with other people. But they only take us so far and are, after all, models which run on computers. In order to develop a more subtle, durable suite of ideas, in a move from a restricted to a general understanding of complexity, complex responsive processes drew on three additional strands of thinking from the social sciences/humanities. In doing so, it sketched out a more comprehensive theory of mind, of action, of identity, of communication, of ethics and of the paradox of stability and change.

Pragmatic philosophy

Complex responsive processes of relating is infused with pragmatic thinking. Pragmatic philosophy, particularly the works of GH Mead (1932, 1934) and John Dewey (1929, 1946, Dewey and Bentley, 1949), directs us to consider the importance of everyday experience. We mobilise our human capacity for doubt, the ability to reflect on what we are doing. If, as the CAS suggest, global patterns arise simply and only from what we are all doing together acting locally, then the pragmatists' preoccupation with experience, which turns on the exploration of what we are doing together, and what sense we make of it, is a useful perspective. Rather than proceeding from abstract ideas, from the idea of systems, pragmatism is concerned with what people are saying and doing in the co-construction of their social worlds. Both Mead and Dewey assume a thoroughly social self, that the body is in the social world and the social world is in the body. We are formed by the social world, just as we form it, the same dynamic of forming and being formed that I drew attention to in CAS.

The perspective of complex responsive processes of relating draws on Mead's complex theory of communication, that in order to understand each other we communicate in shared significant symbols. Equally, the perspective borrows his idea about the predictable unpredictability of conversation, that meaning arises in our gestures towards one another taken together with the responses these provoke, both in ourselves and in others. We may start out by knowing what it is we want to say but change our minds as we hear ourselves speaking, and as we notice and respond to our interlocutors. Consonant with Morin's suggestion that we consider the subject and object of knowledge in relation, so pragmatism works to overcome dualisms, self and other, I, me and we, and reframes them as paradoxes. Both Dewey and Mead were concerned with an emergent theory of ethics which addresses the competing goods in any dynamic situation.

Process sociology

The main sociological informant of the original statement of complex responsive processes of relating is Norbert Elias (1978, 2000, 2001) who also considers the 'I' and 'we' element of our personality structures to be two sides of the same coin. For Elias, the relatively contemporary idea that we are discrete, autonomous individuals cut off from one another is an illusion which doesn't serve us well. Instead, we are highly interdependent, social selves with no 'inside' and no 'outside,' just as there is no outside of social life from which we gain a privileged view. Elias frames the structure/agency discussion at the heart of sociology as a paradox: society is made up of highly social individuals who together create the habitus, the dynamic recognisable patterns of behaviour which we shape and which shape us. Our place in the social network we are born into, and the groups we belong to produce our sense of self: paradoxically, it individualises us.

I argue that this is a shared assumption between Mead, Dewey and Elias and is consonant with the interpretation I made from CAS previously.

Though Elias developed his oeuvre long before there were computers, he developed similar insights about society that I drew by interpretation from CAS. Elias is preoccupied by the fact that language and thinking represents entities at rest much better than it does relationships in motion. Instead, he uses the analogy of the game both to understand the constant change in social life and to frame the role of power and reflective detachment in gaining social advantage. We are interdependent and have need of one another: the greater the need, the greater the power disadvantage. But so too greater power accrues to those who are able to notice their own participation in the game of social life. This too is resonant with the value that Dewey in particular attributes to our human capacity for reflection and thought in the deepening of experience.

Group analytic theory

S.H. Foulkes, the founder of group analytic theory and practice (Foulkes, 1964; Foulkes and Anthony, 1957) had a troubled friendship with his fellow German Jewish refugee, Nobert Elias. Both were concerned with inherent sociality of human beings and shared the insight that we could act more wisely if we gained insight into group dynamics, and our own participation in them. For Foulkes, the best way to find out about a group was to participate in a group, so developed a method of running agenda-less, free-flowing inquiry in groups, where the principal task is to talk about what is going on. This brings to mind the focus of the pragmatists and their interest in what it is we are doing together and how we come to think and talk about it. In the course of inquiry, a variety of perspectives emerge: there is no need for consensus, and no need to take action, except the action of noticing and reflecting. The point is to be together with no particular end in view and to pay attention to relationships. Foulkes called this the development of 'group mindedness,' which we might understand as a form of decentring of the self, or reflexivity.

Experiential groups run in the tradition of Foulkesian thinking are at the heart of the method adopted by the DMan, and every graduate of the programme will have experienced a minimum of 36, one-and-a-half-hour group meetings run without anyone in charge, and without a task except to talk about what the participants have on their minds.

Summary – key ideas which inform the chapters in this volume

All four strands of intellectual tradition thatinform the perspective of complex responsive processes of relating privilege history, sociality and paradox. The social theory which underpins the insights from the complexity sciences weaves together the traditions of Aristotle, Hegel and Darwin to focus on the processual and evolutionary qualities of social life.

All the chapters in this volume borrow from and develop the founding ideas of complex responsive processes and borrow from the intellectual traditions outlined above. They also supplement and deepen them with their own reading. In doing so, they take what is considered a micro-social approach to researching organisations and depend upon narrative and interpretation. The focus on everyday interaction arises from the key insight informing the perspective of complex responsive processes that whatever happens does so as a result of what everyone is doing together. As a set of intellectual assumptions, complex responsive processes is concerned with the structured flux of relationships, power, practical judgement and ethics. It is concerned to complexify our thinking about the social world, but nonetheless to draw distinctions, to generalise, to call out resonance and to provoke.

To be clear that there are no easy answers in working out how to go on together is not the same as giving up and claiming that there is nothing to be done. Rather, the emphasis in the chapters in this volume is to make sense of what the researchers have been doing in the hope of acting more wisely in future, on producing complex and plural ways of thinking more helpful in navigating uncertain times.

Note

1 Stacey abandoned the diagram when he accepted that complexity wasn't a special condition that applied in certain circumstances, but is a quality of all human relating. Additionally, he was concerned that such diagrams, which are ubiquitous in business schools, give false reassurance that managers are still in control.

References

Dewey, J. (1929/2008) *The Quest for Certainty: The Later Works 1925–1953*, Vol. 4, Carbondale: Southern Illinois University Press.

Dewey, J. (1946) *The Public and Its Problems*. New York: Gateway Books.

Dewey, J. and Bentley, A. (1949) *Knowing and the Known*. Boston, MA: Beacon Press.

Elias, N. (1978) *What Is Sociology?* London: Hutchinson and Co.

Elias, N. (2000) *The Civilising Process: Sociogenetic and Psychogenetic Investigations*. Oxford: Blackwell.

Elias, N. (2001) *The Society of Individuals*. London: Continuum Books.

Foulkes, S.H. (1964/2002) *Therapeutic Group Analysis*. London: Karnac Book.

Foulkes, S.H. and Anthony, E.J. (1984 [1957]) *Group Psychotherapy: The Psychoanalytic Approach*. London: Karnac Books.

Mead, G.H. (1932/2002) *The Philosophy of the Present*. New York: Prometheus Books.

Mead, G.H. (1934) *Mind, Self and Society: from the Standpoint of a Social Behaviourist*. Chicago, IL: University of Chicago Press, 2015.

Morin, E. (2005) Restricted complexity, general complexity. Presented at the Colloquium "Intelligence de la complexite: "epistemologie et pragmatique," Cerisy- La- Salle, France, June 26th, 2005." Translated from French by Carlos Gershenson.

Mowles, C. (2021) *Complexity: A Key Idea for Business and Society*. London: Routledge.

Shaw, P. and Stacey, R. (2006) *The Experience of Risk, Spontaneity and Improvization in Organizational Change: Working Live*. London: Routledge.

Stacey, R. (ed.) (2005) *Experiencing Emergence in Organizations: Local Interaction and the Emergence of Global Pattern*. London: Routledge.

Stacey, R. (2012) *The Tools and Techniques of Leadership and Management: Meeting the Challenge of Complexity*. London: Routledge.

Stacey, R. and Griffin, D. (eds.) (2005a) *A Complexity Perspective on Researching Organizations: Taking Experience Seriously*. London: Routledge.

Stacey, R. and Griffin, D. (eds.) (2005b) *Complexity and the Experience of Managing in the Public Sector*. London: Routledge.

Stacey, R. and Griffin, D. (eds.) (2008) *Complexity and the Experience of Values, Conflict and Compromise in Organizations*. London: Routledge.

Stacey, R., Griffin, D. and Shaw, P. (2000) *Complexity and Management: Fad or Radical Challenge to Systems Thinking*. London: Routledge.

1

INTRODUCTION

KIRAN CHAUHAN AND CHRIS MOWLES

The state of management education – why alternatives are needed

There has been a lively debate amongst academics about the purpose of management education, and therefore the role of business schools, over the last two decades. Seminal contributions have suggested that the purpose of business schools has moved away from the task of equipping managers to manage, towards a variety of other aims. These include increasing the prestige of the business schools themselves (e.g. Pfeffer and Fong, 2002) or gaining academic credibility (e.g. Bennis and O'Toole, 2005) animated by an ongoing quest for legitimacy. The basis of this legitimacy has moved with the times and Alajoutsijärvi et al. (2015) identify three key trends: envy of the perceived objectivity of the natural sciences; a move towards the political aims of creating a theoretical hegemony based on neoclassical economics; and, finally, the advent of academic capitalism where universities in general become like private businesses. All three trends arguably reflect

DOI: 10.4324/9781003410522-1

a normative tendency in organisational life that eliminates the differences that make us human, instead aiming to produce pliable and obedient workers, rather than critical and ethically-minded organisational citizens.

One consequence of this evolution is that management education has tended towards being based on abstract models that seek to reduce the complexity of human experience to value-free, scientific, quantifiable and commodifiable knowledge. Arguably, this leaves managers no better equipped to deal with the everyday messiness of trying to get things done with others at work. Perhaps more importantly, the whole issue of moral responsibility that comes from the exercise of everyday judgement in organisational life is avoided (Ghoshal, 2005): if optimisation becomes the end in view, then people in organisations can detach themselves from the outcomes of their labour. Further, the evaluation of treating colleagues kindly or cruelly comes down simply to a question of managerial efficiency.

A range of alternatives have been suggested as ways of resituating management education in the social and temporal relations that constitute the moral world of work (e.g. Statler, 2014; Lancione and Clegg, 2015; Morrell and Learmonth, 2015; Holt, 2020). Emphasising wisdom, judgement, relationality and reflexivity over the production or acquisition of technical knowledge, this means moving from questions of knowledge to questions of meaning as a means of developing thoughtfulness; and replacing the reliance on abstracted empiricism with a comfort with pluralistic abductive logic – the fallible process of coming to good enough theories based on partial and contested understandings about presenting situations to take a next useful step. It also means an ideological turn away from neoclassical economics towards emphasising the prosocial goals of long-term welfare, global citizenship and sustainability (Khilji, 2021; Rocha et al., 2021; Friedland and Jain, 2022).

This volume comes from a research community that was founded over 20 years ago on these kinds of alternative ideas – the authors who have contributed chapters to this book, along with the editors, are all graduates of the Doctor of Management (DMan) programme at the University of Hertfordshire. This programme provides an environment for managers and consultants to make sense of their experience of work using ideas that have come to be known as the perspective of complex responsive processes of relating. As described in the preface, this perspective brings together ideas from the complexity sciences, pragmatist philosophy, process sociology and group analytical theory. The combination of these disciplines offered the DMan's founders an account of experience that felt richer than any single discipline did on its own and was a way of taking seriously the 'blooming, buzzing confusion of experience', as William James put it, drawing on their own histories and interests. Those currently involved in the research group continue to develop and draw on a coherent set of theories – of mind, self, action, communication, power, ethics and stability and change; these ideas inform the chapters in this book.

Researching practice

Remoralising and recontextualising the world of work requires methods which put people and what they say, do and think at the heart of inquiry. Morality can be understood in the abstract through Kant's categorical imperative (to act as you would want all other people to act towards all other people), but the particular ways that ethical choices present themselves, often as competing goods, can only be understood in the concrete particulars. Traditionally this would be understood as opting for qualitative methods, although to adopt a pragmatist position implies caring less about the distinction between quantitative and qualitative, but instead choosing the most appropriate method to untangle the nature and character of the dilemma being inquired into. The key determinant is not an assumed hierarchy of research methods with quantitative at the top, but a systematic and relevant approach to understanding phenomena more deeply.

A spectrum of research methods

Figure 1.1 is a simplified schematic illustrating why one might choose research methods at the right hand of the research spectrum to inquire into social and temporal relations.

We depend upon methods located at the left-hand end of the spectrum for investigating cause-effect relationships, or the prevalence of phenomena, where we are looking for generalisable conclusions which apply to populations and are replicable following the same methods. The most obvious example is the measurement of dose-response in randomised control trials (RCTs) of medicines. In double-blind RCTs, neither the researchers nor the participants in the trial know who is in which group (those

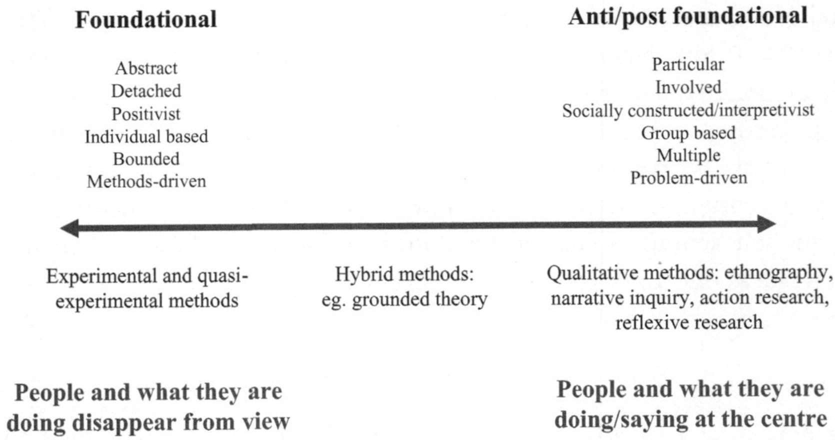

Figure 1.1 A spectrum of research methods

who receive the dose, those who receive a placebo and those who receive nothing). The intention, then, is to remove as far as possible researcher bias and the opinions of participants in the trial – data never interpret themselves, but as far as possible the methods of measurement and statistical assessment are at the heart of the approach. RCTs are sometimes used in social research too where it is possible to isolate variables, such as whether charging a small amount of money for mosquito bed nets increases take-up of anti-malarial measures in East Africa, for example, or whether sending text messages to people facing charges in the small claims courts increases the likelihood of attendance. The work of Nobel Prize winners Banerjee and Duflo (2011) has been widely taken up in international development, for example, to gauge the success of social development interventions in the Global South and is a paradigm of the quest for evidence-based social policy. We understand the intention not just to establish whether a particular intervention has been effective and the money well spent but also to create the basis for acting in the future in similar ways because 'we know what works'.

As in any discipline, there are strong proponents for putting management on a more scientific footing, where the understanding of being scientific is guided by this gold standard of randomisation and abstraction. An argument raged in the Academy of Management in the first decade of the new millennium between those in favour of using more experimental methods and those who pointed to their limitations, which one might understand as an argument between orthodox and critical assumptions about organisational scholarship. The then president of the Academy of Management wanted management scholarship to be like the 'success story' of medicine to promote:

- learning about cause-effect relationships in professional practices;
- isolating the variables that measurably affect desired outcomes;
- creating a culture of evidence-based decision-making and research participation; and
- using information-sharing communities to reduce overuse, underuse and misuse of specific practices (Rousseau, 2006, pp259–260).

However, despite the ambition to build organisational scholarship on natural science-like foundations, attempts to do so have come up short, even for those who most support the idea. For example, in a paper entitled *What's the evidence on evidence-based management?* (Reay et al., 2009), the authors concluded that there isn't very much. RCTs in organisational research tend to be internally consistent but weakly replicable to organisations in other contexts. There are simply too many variables to control for. Following the back-and-forth dialectic of those for and against experimental methods, Briner and Rousseau concluded that evidence could be taken as:

> making decisions through conscientious, explicit, and judicious use of four sources of information: practitioner expertise and judgment, evidence from the local context, a critical evaluation of the best available research evidence, and the perspective of people who might be affected by the decision.
>
> (Briner and Rousseau, 2011)

In other words, a description that most scholars in organisational research would accept without contention when the definition of evidence is construed that broadly. It may be that, just as every human is unique because of their life experience, so too are organisations, even those within the same sector. And while one can say things in general about management and leadership which are weakly generalisable to all organisations when all things are considered equal, it is rarely the case that they can be considered equal. Context, history and the particular managers leading a particular organisation facing particular problems will always be variables which it is impossible to control for. There is no isolating a practice from a practitioner.

Meanwhile, researchers at the right-hand end of the simplified overview of research methods are concerned precisely with context, history and particular people with a particular understanding of the world, and trying to deal with specific dilemmas which are likely to be generalisable in the broadest sense to other contexts, but may not be in detail. In these cases, the research starts with the dilemma first and is thus known as problem-based research. The focus is on precisely how the respondents, including the researcher-manager, co-construct the world which entangles them, how they make sense of it and how they understand, and respond to, their ethical choices. There is no assumed position of neutrality, no god's eye view of what unfolds in organisational life. The research is directed towards illuminating a concrete example of a general dilemma where the steps participants take to go on together are the matter of interest. The point is to produce knowledge from practice, for practice (Eikeland, 2008, p305), with the aim of cultivating 'provisional, tentative models for interpretation and analysis' (Thomas, 2012, p30). This kind of knowledge does not have a law-like quality, but is hedged around by variations, recursions, revisions and contingency, with the assumption that management is a practice and not a science, although it may draw off a background of science as it is implemented in a particular context.

Degrees of criticality

If the motivation of methods derived from the natural sciences is to try to discover things 'as they really are' – facts – then the assumption of qualitative research is often that things could be other than they are. Social facts are made by people and are emergent properties of group life, and as such are shaped by power and politics (Fleck and Trenn, 1992) – so we may even contest what we take to be a fact. Research methods at the right hand of the spectrum are likely to take an interest in the antecedent history to the context under investigation as well as different conceptions of what is actually happening in the here and now. In doing so, they are more or less critical. Most universities claim that they encourage their students to produce critical scholarship, so the concept is worth exploring a bit further to discover if there are degrees of criticality. To do so we borrow and adapt a schematic from the philosopher of science Ian Hacking (1999) as follows:

Position 0	X is taken for granted, X is inevitable
Position 1	X need not have existed or need not be there at all.
Position 2	X is quite bad as it is.
Position 3	We would be much better off if X were done away with or were radically transformed.

We'll use the example of researching leadership to illustrate these positions. **Position 0** we might equate with a natural science position. Even if the research is in service of solving a particular problem, the world is assumed to be as it is, and our research task is simply to discover how it is. If we are interested in leadership, then we might ask what makes a great leader and how do leaders impact upon followers. **Position 1** takes an interest in history and assumes that things could be different depending on what has happened in the past. In our example, it is often a surprise to students in our business school that 35 years ago there was much less focus on leaders and leadership, indeed, very little differentiation between leadership and management, which is something now taken for granted. So as well as inquiring into what makes a great leader, researchers might find themselves asking questions about how leadership has come to be a dominating theme in organisational life or management studies, and what this therefore might tell us about organisations, or society more widely. To inquire further might lead the researcher to **Position 2**, that the theme under investigation is problematic in some or other way. In our example, researchers could become interested in how the preoccupation with leadership, in general and in the particular case or cases in question, might distract away from phenomena which are equally or more important. As Alvesson and colleagues ask (2017), why is it that everything positive in organisations gets associated with leadership and all questions about power and authority in organisations and society are similarly reduced to questions of leadership? This isn't to say it isn't worth exploring leadership, but rather to encourage curiosity about what a focus on leadership illuminates and obscures in relation to other themes in organisational life and whose interests are served and whose are neglected as a result. Finally, researchers may find themselves at **Position 3** whereby the theme at hand is understood to be so problematic that it is worth abandoning. In our example, this may mean agreeing with Learmonth and Morell (2019) that the discourse on leadership is both pervasive and unhelpful and simply amplifies social inequalities which benefit elite groups, creating more heat than light. For Learmonth and Morrell, instead of producing more scholarship about leadership, we should ask different questions about what is going on in organisations. This might include, focussing on the near industrialisation of the leadership discourse to account for its pervasiveness, as the Harvard-based scholar Rakesh Khurana has done (2007).

In this brief and schematic overview of different research methods and degrees of criticality, it is possible to see how a researcher would approach their subject matter and treat it very differently, depending on where they found themselves on the research spectrum, and the degree to which they were critically engaged in the research. So too for managers; even if not constructed in the terminology of research paradigms, the assumptions we make about organisational life will inform how we go about trying to get things done with others. Whether it be solving day-to-day operational problems, trying to agree on a strategic direction or reorganising relationships, Position 0 might lead us to think there are right and wrong ways to do things; whereas taking up Positions 1, 2 or 3 might mean more engagement with the power, politics and contingency of such decisions. How much researchers or managers problematise their subject matter, the existing ideas or theories they use to illuminate it, their own analysis, their relation to the subject matter and the evolution of their thinking about it, is also linked to degrees of reflexivity, a topic taken up in all the chapters in this volume.

The Doctor of Management programme

As mentioned earlier, this volume's contributors are graduates of the DMan programme at the University of Hertfordshire. Students on the programme are usually managers or consultants from a range of countries, sectors and roles who have worked for at least five years. Typically, they'll spend three to four years working in a learning set with up to three other students and their supervisor, as well as the wider research community, producing an 80,000-word written thesis on topics relating to their professional fields.

Unlike the structure common to most doctoral theses (Honan and Bright, 2016), the written component of the doctorate comprises four exploratory projects written over the duration of the programme and a synopsis which articulates the researcher's contributions to theory and practice. The first project is an intellectual autobiography that seeks to bring to light some of the researcher's interpretive and responsive habits and how they have come about through socialisation processes. This begins to identify and problematise the habits they might have long been relying on as they go about their working lives. It also helps to articulate sources of genuine sense of doubt (Peirce, 1877) – in other words, thematic questions about researchers' practice – that are sufficiently moving as to propel them into and sustain an inquiry over several years. These animating questions are then explored in increasing depth through the second, third and fourth projects.

These further projects begin with narrative accounts of events in the researcher's professional life, in which a specific practice problem emerges leaving them in an indeterminate situation that they feel compelled to address. This breakdown in habits can be due to the novelty of the situation, or because it reflects a new awareness of pattern in working life, and typically involves the entanglement of motives, interests and power struggles. These events can be suffused with emotions, making them feel 'hot' compared to organisational life more generally – though the quality of emotion may range from anger, joy, confusion or even boredom. Researchers are encouraged to explore their practice problem both through literature that illuminates what they are grappling with and through conversation with other members of the research group. This exploration has both critical and reflexive aspects: the initial interpretation of an event will involve assumptions which can be analysed both for how they represent wider social patterns or ideological leanings and for how they represent the researcher's own habits.

As researchers become more detached about their involvement, they become more able to inquire into experience with an increasingly complex and sophisticated attitude. Projects are completed sequentially, so each emerges reflexively from the last, and by the fourth project, researchers are typically investigating a niche in the academic discourse relating to their professional field that has emerged from the deepening engagement with their practice. Engagement with literature also becomes increasingly systematic as the research progresses, rather than undertaking a systematic review at the start of the degree. The projects are then re-analysed synoptically to explore the key themes that have emerged over the course of the degree and to articulate the researcher's main arguments and original contributions to knowledge and to practice.

The community's conversations are lively and diverse, as differences in motives, interests, academic training, professional experience and social history come together in unexpected ways. This pluralism brings a richness to the group, and there are gaps which we continue to try to address: for example, the research community is made up predominantly of people from the Global North; the costs of the degree mean that those who lack financial means (personally or through their organisations) cannot attend – this is likely to affect some social groups more than others.

Methods with family resemblances

In describing the outline of the DMan research degree, we are illustrating the core of the research method informed by an understanding of human interaction as complex responsive processes. This comprises:

- beginning with a breakdown in practice
- narrating that event and identifying a practice question that feels compelling to inquire into
- exploring the interpretation of the event through iterative cycles of critical and reflexive analysis, in a community of inquiry and drawing on relevant literature
- offering insights that have been helpful for the researcher's own practice, resonate with other members of the researcher's professional community, and offers a new way of thinking about the original question.

This method shares family resemblances with a range of other qualitative research methods. These include approaches that examine everyday interactions to understand more about wider social patterns, for example ethnography, ethnomethodology (e.g. Garfinkel, 1967), micro-ethnography (e.g. Erickson, 1992), case study (e.g. Flyvbjerg, 2011) and critical realism (e.g. Bhaskar, 1975). The DMan's nearest relatives are methods that engage with first-person accounts of experience: first-person action research, autoethnography and narrative inquiry are examples. Below we offer some observations about the similarities and differences between these three particular methods and research informed by a complex responsive processes perspective.

Action research

Action research covers a range of related methods which, while differing in their onto-epistemological grounding, share some common features (Reason and Bradbury, 2008). Scarlatti et al. (2018) suggest that these include *contextual sensitivity* – dealing with real problems in their originating contexts; *relationality* – understanding knowledge as emerging in social and temporal relations and co-created through participation and polyvocality; a *transformative attitude* – aiming to find practical solutions to pressing problems, encouraging changes in what people think, say and do, with a political orientation towards democracy, social justice and emancipation; and *reflexivity* – expanding the possibilities of the learning process by critical engagement with one's own practices. Scarlatti et al. also suggest that varieties of action research also share common process steps in how the action research question is generated, the role of an advisory board, deciding the research tools, managing the exploratory and dialogue process within the action research group and sharing insights generated at the end of the research process. These steps are often required to be mapped out in quite some detail to ensure that research findings are useful and timely, often aiming to show impact quickly.

Within this broad frame, action research finds various expressions. This can be on epistemological grounds (Cassel and Johnson, 2006): for example, experimental action research is usually located within a positivist paradigm, aiming to ameliorate problems through accumulating objective knowledge about the world that others can put to work. Inductive and participatory forms of action research sit within more of an interpretivist paradigm, emphasising that joint critical engagement with theories-in-use can result in changes in relationships and the practices socially constructed through those relationships. Critical or deconstructive forms of action research aim to problematise discourses, identifying contradictions and dilemmas to provide opportunities for clarification and change; as such these approaches can be seen to sit more within a more pragmatist paradigm, emphasising the intersubjectivity of knowing and pluralism, while also acknowledging the role of power.

Action research methods can also be distinguished based on the nature of the relationship between the research and the researched (Sykes and Treleaven, 2009): first-person action research – as a form of insider research – focusses primarily on the evolution of the researcher's own practice; in second person action research, researchers and participants participate jointly in the learning process so the validity of these methods rest in the extent to which the insights the research process generates are useful for the groups involved in addressing the challenges that occasioned the inquiry. Third-person action research incorporates the focus of first and second person and extends it to creating generalisable conclusions to be shared beyond the action research group itself.

On this basis, research informed by a complex responsive processes perspective could be seen as drawing on a number of strands of action research. Most obviously first-person action research, in so far as researchers inquire into their own practice, but also third-person action research (based on the paradoxical understanding of local interaction and global patterns) as they seek to understand and say something about society at large. Researchers also draw on features of participatory action research based on the importance given to communities of inquiry (the learning set, the wider research community and an encouragement for researchers to share their research insights with people in their professional circles – see Solsø, this volume); and critical/ deconstructive action research given the attention to power, politics and paradox. Differences include the extent to which there is an overt political orientation; while researchers are encouraged to become more aware of and detached about their ideological leanings so they can inquire more expansively into their worlds of work – which may lead to quite significant changes in how they go about their work or lives more generally – there is no requirement to adopt a particular ideological stance, nor to encourage the groups they work with to do the same. Similarly, there is not necessarily an overt action orientation – for some researchers, a change in attitude that may lead to greater capacities to act is as far as they go, though in the interests of gaining their doctorate, whatever they come to must be persuasive to members of their professional communities and their examiners (Rasmussen, this volume). Finally, researchers are encouraged to engage with the emergent nature of their inquiries, rather than planning too much in advance; while there is a set overall structure, the routes researchers take can be quite unpredictable – like life itself – and periods of acceleration or stuckness are all treated as being of sociological interest.

Autoethnography

Ethnography in its broadest sense is usually understood as an approach to the study of a culture or social world. This is typically through participant observation whereby researchers join groups in some capacity, usually for extended periods of time, with the aim of understanding social practices *from the perspective of their study subjects.* Through a deep engagement with the complexities of everyday life, researchers seek to illuminate the logics of practice that are produced and reproduced in local interaction. These aspects of social life often remain underexplored through other research methods, for example direct observation, interviews or questionnaires. Fieldwork involves attending to language, rituals and artefacts (Cunliffe, 2010) as aspects of ongoing social processes, accompanied by 'headwork' to abductively connect observed phenomena to broader societal contexts (Van Maanen, 2011). This 'continuous dialectical tacking between the most local of local detail and the most global of global structure in such a way as to bring both into view simultaneously' (Geertz, 1974, p43) lies at the heart of an ethnographic sensibility, which continuously stays open to new possibilities for meaning and problematises the taken for granted (Ybema et al., 2009). *Organisational ethnography* is defined by its field – the study of processes of formal and informal organising – and is often differentiated from the traditions of social and cultural anthropology by being less immersive and of shorter duration, not least because workers also come and go from their workplaces (Ciuk et al., 2018).

Autoethnography then is the study of a group's habits – including in organisations – by one or more of its own members through inquiring into their own involvement in work. It can be understood as a form of participant observation where the researcher has 'natural access' to their study site, though it is suggested that 'observing participant' offers a better description of the activity (Moeran, 2009) as the researcher doesn't necessarily instrumentalise their enculturation process as traditional ethnographers might. Autoethnography tends to be characterised by the recounting and analysis of deeply personal aspects of experience (Richardson, 2009), often with an encouragement to write evocatively and expose a vulnerable self (Ellis and Bochner, 2000). According to Adams et al. (2022, p4), it (1) foregrounds particular and subjective knowledge, (2) illustrates sense-making processes, often involving reflexive engagement with confusing aspects of very intimate experiences, (3) aims to make contributions to existing research, thereby differentiating it from, for example, autobiography, (4) challenges norms of research practice by reclaiming researcher bias and (5) explicitly engaging and compelling responses from audiences.

Research informed by a complex responsive processes perspective shares many of the features of ethnography, and autoethnography more specifically. It too privileges attending to and writing about everyday, personal experience as a means to understanding social norms more widely; again, this is theoretically grounded in the paradox of the individual and social and usually limited to exploring organisational phenomena. It also emphasises the elaboration of the researcher's reflexive analytical process and engagement with the emotional aspects of experience though with a greater degree of criticality than is typically found in autoethnography. As a process of obtaining a research degree, researchers are working towards making theoretical and practice contributions, and as a method that understands subjectivity as an analytical resource rather than a hindrance to producing insights, it could also be seen as a reclaiming researcher bias. Finally, research informed by a complex responsive processes perspective carries no requirement to try to provoke action amongst others as Adams et al. (2022) suggest; while researchers are encouraged to share their work with their colleagues and professional communities in the hope that audiences find research insights plausible, resonant and useful (Brinkmann, 2012), the analogy of the butterfly effect from the complexity sciences suggests that the outcomes of such engagements will be predictably unpredictable.

Another key difference is the engagement with the plural perspectives of those who react or review the research through critical and reflexive inquiry in various group settings – the learning set and community meetings (see Solsø, this volume). This kind of engagement with difference offers the researcher alternative explanations for what might be going on in their working lives based on the subjectivities of those whom they encounter, something lone autoethnographers may not routinely have access to. This kind of collaboration differs from what is known as collaborative autoethnography (Chang et al., 2013), whereby two or more researchers inquire autoethnographically into a single phenomenon, combining perspectives and conclusions.

Narrative inquiry

Analysing narrative material can form part of many types of qualitative research that aims to inquire into experience, perhaps, because, as many have argued, experience can be understood as having a narrative-like structure (e.g. MacIntyre, 1981; Bruner, 1986; Polkinghorne, 1987). Narrative therefore has the potential to illuminate social life, contextualising what people say to and do in terms of the complex hinterlands of cultural history that may be representing in those encounters and forcing the articulation of assumed causal relations. However, researchers' aims in working with narratives can differ according to their research traditions. In post-positivist traditions, analysing the stories we tell can offer a way to reveal the underlying nature of shared reality that exists independent of our individual minds (e.g. Bhaskar, 1975); researchers try to eliminate the effects of history, enculturation and individual bias to identify enduring mechanisms that link contexts to outcomes. In critical traditions, narratives are more often understood as ideological (e.g. White, 1973) or discursive artefacts (e.g. Foucault, 1970; Lyotard, 1979). Here, 'antenarratives' comprising partial, fragmented and unconnected descriptions of events and times and are transformed (more or less explicitly) into narratives with apparently coherent plots; so, researchers can explore polyvocality and multiple meanings in narratives to illuminate the background connections between knowledge and politics (Boje, 2001), perhaps hoping to make some difference to the communities involved (Czarniawska, 2004).

Narrative inquiry has been identified as a distinct method from the traditions just described by a group of scholars (see, for example, Clandinin and Connelly, 2000; Clandinin and Rosiek, 2007; Clandinin, 2022) who are of particular interest here as they too find their onto-epistemological grounding in pragmatist philosophy. Clandinin and colleagues take John Dewey's theory of experience as the basis for identifying the suitability of narrative for illuminating time, sociality and place, starting with puzzles of personal, practical and social interest, rather than being formally guided by research questions per se (Clandinin, 2022, p26); as such they require a deep exploration of the researcher's personal motivations and involvement in the research processes they undertake (Clandinin, 2022, pp21–22). The research process is then a relational one of getting alongside research participants to enable the retelling of the stories people live and tell, iterative inquiry with participants and academic literature, to enable new possibilities for living – these processes of *living, telling, retelling* and *reliving* (Clandinin, 2022, p19) are key components of narrative inquiry that 'begins and ends with a respect for ordinary lived experience'. As such, these authors try to reclaim the epistemic status they see as degraded in realist or critical traditions that construe narratives as epiphenomenal.

The connections between this formulation of narrative inquiry and research based on a complex responsive processes perspective are easy to see – both involve processes of inquiring into everyday breakdowns in practice that are puzzling; iteratively thickening the accounts of those breakdowns through social and scholarly inquiry and coming to reflexive insights that provide new capacities to act. The complex responsive processes tradition could be seen to differ it's interdisciplinarity, and especially the inspiration it takes from critical management studies, psychodynamic traditions and process sociology. We might put differences relating to criticality down to a relative inattention to issues of power in Dewey's writing; this despite his extensive social activism alongside fellow pragmatists Jane Addams, Mary Parker Follet and George Herbert Mead. However, where Dewey did write about power, one can see a pre-figuring of ideas later articulated by the likes of Michel Foucault: for example, writing about maintaining an epistemic dualism of habit and thought, Dewey argued that it enabled 'those who wish a monopoly of social power … to do the thinking and planning while others remain docile … instruments of execution' (Dewey, 1922, p72). The complex responsive processes theoretical cannon developed from its founders' interests in trying to provide a better account of *organisational life* (Stacey and Griffin, 2005; Stacey, 2012), a context in which power is central but often underacknowledged or underarticulated. We can make a similar argument for attending to group psychodynamics: organisational life tends to be group-based but the everyday affectual politics of human-interrelating are often covered over. Likewise for process sociology: while the pragmatists had a lot to say about temporality in experience, drawing on the likes of Elias (as well as key ideas from the complexity sciences) illuminates the connection between power and history.

The use of group work

Group work is an important aspect of the DMan; however, there is a very little formalisation of method associated with this aspect of the programme, given that it is an improvisational practice of exploration. We find two main themes about how group work is taken up in the management education literature more generally: first, a focus on teamwork in educational settings as experiential preparation for the 'real world' needs of working with others (e.g. Rafferty, 2013; Curşeu et al., 2014; Tosey et al., 2015); second, a focus on how attention can be drawn to the relational aspects of working to enable researchers to develop their reflexive capacities (Cunliffe and Jun, 2005; Hedberg, 2017). Almost all the approaches described involve developing the capacity to gain new perspectives on the matters at hand through collective reflection, questioning, negotiation or the creation of environments in which the relational aspects of collective accomplishment are highlighted.

As Solsø explores in more detail in her chapter, the DMan uses group work to help researchers identify similarities in what happens in the research community to organisational life. Probably the best example is in the use of 'community meetings' in the tradition of the Institute of Group Analysis (IGA), held three times each quarterly residential weekend. That is, the whole research community, faculty and students meet for an hour and a half each time to explore the experience of being together as a temporary academic community dedicated to the individual task of completing theses, and the group task of collaborating together to do so. Known as a median experiential group in IGA terms, the supposition is that very similar patterns of inclusion and exclusion, rivalry and co-operation, dominance and resistance will occur in a research community as in any other work group. The task, then, is to explore what happens in this particular group in terms of conscious and unconscious processes as well as to make links with similar processes in organisational life in which the part-time students make their living. Meaning-making is both theoretical and practical and pays attention to both conscious and unconscious processes.

The practice of this experiential group is consonant with the underpinning intellectual assumptions of the DMan programme that individuals are social through and through: the paradox that the self arises from the interdependence with other selves. The aim is for individuals to understand themselves better, but with the assumption that the best place to make this discovery is in a group. SH Foulkes, the founder of the IGA, put forward the idea that the group is like a hall of mirrors (Foulkes and Anthony, 1984 [1957]), in which participants come to see themselves reflected. In a practice-based academic programme, then, students have an opportunity to discover through the reactions of others how they habitually present. Foulkes also understood this as a kind of ego-training. With practice, participants can become less self-absorbed, less worried by the unpredictability of being in a group, and more group-minded and are able to think about the dynamics of the group as a whole, rather than their more narrow concerns. As Mowles (2017) argues, three to four years of sitting in the group enable graduates of the programme to sit more comfortably with their anxiety, to experience uncertainty directly (because nobody, not even faculty knows what will come up in discussion) and to depathologise conflict. The exploration of difference, which is a necessary condition of maintaining plurality, inevitably leads to conflict of a greater or lesser degree and arguably is the source of novelty emerging in the group.

We have come to think of the community meeting on the DMan programme as another method of research in the sense that it provides a practical and live resource for studying group life, as well as furnishing individual researchers with deeper insight into their own practice and participation in groups.

A note on methodological coherence

The inter-disciplinarity of the complex responsive processes perspective we have been describing can be seen as a challenge to arguing for the methodological coherence of research. For example: in theorising a breakdown in practice, one analysis might draw on Dewey's ideas about perplexity and abductive reasoning; another on Freud's thoughts about intrapsychic conflict and psychological determinism and another on Foucault's concepts of eventalisation and genealogical inquiry into the taken-for-granted. All of these could fall within the scope of research based on a complex responsive processes perspective as all could help to illuminate a practice problem. This offers an initial (if slightly glib) counter-argument to the challenge: if problems in social life are generally unconstrained by concerns about methodological coherence, researchers who are trying to take experience seriously can be similarly open-minded about which traditions they draw on.

Of course, researchers are trying to obtain research admission to an Academy concerned with well-designed research, so how might we argue for the coherence of inquiry methods and the ideas used if the traditions are as diverse as the complexity sciences, pragmatist philosophy, process sociology and psychodynamic theory? As Tracy (2010, p848) notes, the challenge here is perhaps less about trying to subsume multiple theories under one amongst them, but rather to create something through which those multiple theories can be brought together in a theoretically coherent way:

> Meaningfully coherent studies (a) achieve their stated purpose; (b) accomplish what they espouse to be about; (c) use methods and representation practices that partner well with espoused theories and paradigms; and (d) attentively interconnect literature reviewed with research foci, methods, and findings… I do not mean that a study cannot or should not be messy, disturbing, unexpected, or jarring… Furthermore, meaningful coherence does not mean that a study cannot borrow or use concepts from multiple paradigms… Indeed, some studies are creative or groundbreaking precisely because they borrow from various theories or frameworks to create something new.

The complex responsive processes perspective has always had this project in mind as its founders tried to come to a better account of the richness of human experience in relation to the problems they encountered in their practice, to a degree based on their own practice traditions. Its original formulations (e.g. Stacey, 2003) attended closely to bringing theories that help to illuminate organisational life into a coherent relationship with each other, highlighting the centrality of some key concepts (see Table 1.1).

Researching in this inter-disciplinary way means that, while any number of theories may help to illuminate a problem, those theories need to be considered critically and brought into coherence with the principles listed. This avoids the criticism of an 'anything goes' or 'pick and mix' approach to theory while at the same time maintaining an open-mindedness about what may provoke practice insights and development.

In this tradition of problem-based research into breakdowns, graduates and faculty of the DMan continue to try to explore and theorise (e.g. Stacey and Mowles, 2016; Mowles, 2017, 2021; Chauhan et al., 2022; Mowles and Norman, 2022; Sarra et al., 2022) about sociological aporia: how we think,

Table 1.1 *Key* Principles for Establishing Methodological Coherence

Concept	*Researchers' questions*
Processuality – identity and social ordering are ongoing and emergent processes that cannot be predicted in advance or abstracted away from the people, times, places and historical contexts in which and among whom they arise. This requires attending to what people say and do, and an anti-dualistic account of contradictions in experience, including the paradox of self-consciousness and the fractally symmetrical paradox of individual and society	• What is becoming, where and when? • What is the historical context? • What is this event an example of locally, and in wider society?
Interdependence – individuals are bound to each other in often under-articulated ways that reflect what they need from each other; these power relationships have implications for the identities people are invited to take up, and habitually perform.	• With whom? • To what anticipated ends? • Who benefits?
Pluralism – experience constitutes plural perspectives on what is happening, with differences arising from the uniqueness of personal history and interests, in the context of wider social patterns concerning, gender, sexuality, neurodiversity, disability, race, age, class and race.	• What interpretations am I drawn to and why? • Who might disagree and why? • How else might we understand what's happening?
Sociality – individuals are social through and through, with meaning as an emergent property of the confluence of social histories (and therefore intentions, ideologies and values) in the living present.	• What does this change for me? And us?

how we communicate, how we act, how we make ethical judgements, how social norms emerge and evolve and the relationship between individuals and society. The chapters in this volume offer new perspectives in relation to these themes, in the context of researching practice.

Audiences, contributors and a summary of chapters

This book is written for academics who are interested in first-person research methods and managers who are curious about understanding their experience at work more deeply. As mentioned earlier, the contributors are all graduates or faculty of the DMan programme, who have developed aspects of their doctoral research to offer insights for the practice of researching organisations. The book is organised into three sections: the first deals with using subjectivity as an analytical resource; the second considers approaches to exploring organisational life and the third looks at the personal and political implications of concluding research.

Part I: Decentring subjectivities

Research using first-person accounts can attract criticism – for being parochial, or impossible to generalise from. The first part of this volume argues for the utility of subjectivity as a valuable resource for exploring organisational life – our histories provide unique perceptual and interpretive tendencies, which if we can bring into view, offer the possibility of unique and novel insights.

It begins with Chapter 2 and **Kiran Chauhan's** account of how understanding our histories of sociality – that is, how we have come to be able to imagine the perspectives of multiple others in the context of wider society as we interact – is important in enriching the fields of our attention. Drawing mainly on pragmatist philosophy, he argues that bringing more of our own peculiar stratification of the lifeworld into view can complexify our perceptual field, increasing our capacity to notice and act. This is useful not only for the development of research contributions and management innovation but also as a process of moral development.

In Chapter 3, **Sune Bjørn Larsen** takes on the topic of writing about oneself as a means to gaining reflexive distance to our engagement with others. Drawing on his work as an organisational development consultant, Larsen explores how the use of first-person narrative material in reflexive research can illuminate the stories in which we are 'emplotted', and the narratives which we perpetuate and disrupt through our participation in organisational life. As such, he makes a case for autoethnographic writing as an important resource in research and management.

In Chapter 4, **Sophie Wong** describes how personal and cultural histories can be put to work in understanding organisational life. Drawing on her background as a Hong Kong born, mixed Chinese immigrant in Australia, Wong explores how comparing the Chinese concepts of *face* and *guanxi* with key ideas in Western anthropology (Goffman, Bourdieu and Mauss) can shed new light on her experience engaging with high net worth donors as a board member of an Australian Neuroscience Research Institute. In doing so, she offers a perspective on the value of Karad Barad's concept of *diffraction* as an analytical tool.

Reflexivity is a theme throughout this section, and indeed the whole volume, and in Chapter 5, **Chris Mowles** draws together the emerging threads to offer a more systematic view and taxonomy of the concept. He discusses some of its limitations and explores how we may be co-opted into reproducing the very conditions we seek to transform through critical reflexive engagement. While rejecting the idea that it is an unfettered good, Mowles suggests that reflexivity may be one of the best resources we have to find connection with each other and work out the bases of hope.

Part II: Exploring practice and its breakdowns

The second part of the book offers insights into some of the mechanisms of exploring practice and what moments of perplexity can offer our understanding of organisational life.

In Chapter 6, **Karina Solsø** explores what a commitment to John Dewey's principles of anti-dualism and inquiry with a scientific attitude means for experiential learning. Taking the DMan programme as a case, Solsø describes how three pedagogic approaches – the use of learning sets, community meetings modelled on experiential groups in the group analytic tradition and more well-known experiential learning activities – enable researchers and managers to become more aware of the politics of interdependence and what may be at stake in their relationships with others. Experiential learning here is therefore a mode of engagement with experience that provides a richer basis for open-ended abductive reasoning and reflexivity, which is distinctly socially oriented, world-open and pragmatic.

Mikkel Brahm expands our understanding of the world of work by exploring how everyday conduct and norms are understood to involve both human and non-human actors in Chapter 7. Taking the example of enterprise architecture, he considers the power and politics that are revealed by taking materiality seriously, and the moral responsibilities that go alongside designing and deploying material actors. He argues that while non-human actors lack the intention and spontaneity we attribute to human actors, they remain implicated in these processes and, as such, remain important to pay attention to in trying to research or make sense of the working world.

Life for researchers and managers inevitably involves compromising, so argues **Helle Therkelsen Stoltz** in Chapter 8. Using examples from her research degree and her work as an international development consultant, Stoltz explains how compromise can be understood as a social process of mutual adaptation that involves power, values, emotions and ethics. She explores how the feelings of loss associated with giving up some of what we feel attached to might be important for the emergence of novelty and finding ways to stay in generative relation with others, when the alternative seems to be stalemate or breakdown in relationships.

Part III: Good enough endings

One aim of doctoral-level research is to produce contributions to theory and practice that will be of generalisable interest. If social sciences research is understood as being descriptive rather than predictive, generalisability has to be understood in terms of plausibility, resonance and utility. This section explores what kinds of contributions are possible and how the researcher's relationship to their research changes over time.

In Chapter 9, **Jannie Rasmussen** argues that taking a perspective on organisational life that situates knowledge in temporal and social relations invites a different understanding of the basis of contributing to knowledge and practice. Using Bourdieu's concepts of habitus, capital and field, Rasmussen explores what may be at stake in the negotiation of what counts as contributions as good enough endings to research or management projects. This leads to an exploration of the paradigmatic struggle between scientific and practical rationality, and the dilemmas faced by researchers and managers in trying to navigate the power and politics of endings.

The ethics of writing about ourselves and others goes far beyond the protocols of ethics committees designed to manage universities' risk, and so Chapter 10 presents a dialogue between **Tobit Emmens** and the editors on the dilemmas faced by and safeguards available to researchers using first-person methods. The authors interweave theory and accounts of their experiences as a recent student (Tobit), supervisor (Kiran) and programme director (Chris) to illustrate the complexity of privileging uncertainty over risk and of taking the paradox of the individual and group seriously.

Finally in Chapter 11, **Maj Karin Askeland** discusses the affectual qualities of endings, which, like grief in general, are often under-attended to in organisational life as we are encouraged to move on from the things we have cared about. Askeland uses key ideas from grief studies, and in particular the notion of continuing bonds, to illuminate the ambivalences involved in endings and how these may be navigated without trying to tie everything up in a neat bow.

While the contributors have used their experiences of their own research degrees to inform their chapters, they have not limited their analyses just to the academic arena: they have considered how the issues they have encountered are relevant to any inquiry process that relies on first-person accounts. This means that the chapters should be of use to both researchers and managers alike, insofar as either want to take seriously both their experience, and their responsibilities for realising the brighter view of humanity being called for by the Academy itself.

References

Adams, T.E., Holman Jones, S., and Ellis, C. (2022) *Handbook of Autoethnography*, 2nd Edition. New York: Routledge.

Alajoutsijärvi, K., Juusola, K., and Siltaoja, M. (2015) The Legitimacy Paradox of Business Schools: Losing by Gaining? *Academy of Management Learning and Education*, 14, pp277–291.

Alvesson, M., Blom, M., and Sveningsson, S. (2017) *Reflexive Leadership: Organising in an Imperfect World*. London: Sage.

Banerjee, A., and Duflo, E. (2011) *Poor Economics: A Radical Rethinking of the Way to Fight Global Poverty*. New York: Public Affairs Book.

Bennis, W.G., and O'Toole, J. (2005) How Business Schools Lost Their Way. *Harvard Business Review*, *83*, pp96–104.

Bhaskar, R. (1975). *A Realist Theory of Science*. New York: Routledge.

Boje, D. (2001) *Narrative Methods of Organizational and Communication Research*. London: Sage.

Briner, R.B., and Rousseau, D.M. (2011) Evidence-Based I-O Psychology: Not There Yet but Now a Little Nearer? *Industrial and Organizational Psychology: Perspectives on Science and Practice*, 4(1), pp76–82.

Brinkmann, S. (2012) *Qualitative Inquiry in Everyday Life*. London: Sage.

Bruner, J. (1986) *Actual Minds, Possible Worlds*. Cambridge, MA: Harvard University Press.

Cassel, C., and Johnson, P. (2006) Action Research: Explaining the Diversity. *Human Relations*, 59(6), pp783–814.

Chang, H., Ngunjiri, F. and Hernandez, K.A.C., (2016) *Collaborative Autoethnography*. London: Routledge.

Chauhan, K., Crewe, E., and Mowles, C. (2022) *Complexity and Leadership*. London: Routledge.

Ciuk, S., Koning, J., and Kostera, M. (2018) Organisational Ethnographies. In Cassell, C., Cunliffe, A.L., and Grandy, G. (eds.) *The Sage Handbook of Qualitative B and Management Research Methods: History and Traditions*. London: Sage, pp270–285.

Clandinin, D.J. (2022) *Engaging in Narrative Inquiry*, 2nd Edition. London: Routledge.

Clandinin, D.J. and Connelly, F.M. (2000) *Narrative Inquiry: Experience and Story in Qualitative Research*. San Francisco, CA: Jossey-Bass.

Clandinin, D.J., and Rosiek, J. (2007) Mapping a Landscape of Narrative Inquiry: Borderland Spaces and Tensions. In Clandinin, D.J. (ed.) *Handbook of Narrative Inquiry: Mapping a Methodology*. London: Sage, pp35–75.

Cunliffe, A. (2010) Retelling Tales of the Field: In Search of Organisational Ethnography 20 Years on. *Organisational Research Methods*, 13(2), pp224–239.

Cunliffe, A., and Jun, J. (2005) The Need for Reflexivity in Public Administration. *Administration and Society*, 37(2), pp225–242.

Curşeu, P.L., Janssen, S.E., and Meeus, M.T. (2014) Shining Lights and Bad Apples: The Effect of Goal-setting on Group Performance. *Management Learning*, 45(3), pp332–348.

Czarniawska, B. (2004) *Narratives in Social Science Research*. London: Sage.

Dewey, J. (1922) *Human Nature and Conduct: An Introduction to Social Psychology*. New York: Modern Library.

Eikeland, O. (2008) *The Ways of Aristotle: Aristotelian Phronesis, Aristotelian Philosophy of Dialogue and Action Research*. Bern: Peter Lang.

Ellis, C., and Bochner, A. (2000) Autoethnography, Personal Narrative, Reflexivity. In Denzin, N., and Lincoln, Y. (eds.) *Handbook of Qualitative Research*, 2nd Edition. Thousand Oaks, CA: Sage, pp733–768.

Erickson, F. (1992) Ethnographic Microanalysis of Interaction. In LeCompte, D., Millroy, W.L., and Preissle, J. (eds) *The Handbook of Qualitative Research in Education*. Cambridge, MA: Academic Press, pp201–225.

Fleck, L., and Trenn, T. (1992) *Genesis and Development of a Scientific Fact*. Chicago, IL: University of Chicago Press.

Flyvbjerg, B. (2011) Case Study. In Denzin, N.K., and Lincoln, Y.S. (eds.) *The SAGE Handbook of Qualitative Research*, 4th Edition. London: Sage, pp301–316.

Foucault, M. (1970) *The Order of Things*. New York: Random House.

Foulkes, S.H., and Anthony, E.J. (1984 [1957]) *Group Psychotherapy: The Psychoanalytic Approach*. London: Karnac Books.

Friedland, J., and Jain, T. (2022) Reframing the Purpose of Business Education: Crowding-in a Culture of Moral Self-Awareness. *Journal of Management Inquiry*, *31*(1), pp15–29.

Garfinkel, H. (1967) *Studies in Ethnomethodology*. Englewood Cliffs, NJ: Prentice-Hall.

Geertz, C. (1974) From the Native's Point of View: On the Nature of Anthropological Understanding. *Bulletin of the American Academy of Arts and Sciences*, *28*(1), pp26–45.

Ghoshal, S. (2005) Bad Management Theories are Destroying Good Management Practices. *Academy of Management Learning & Education*, *4*, pp75–91.

Hacking, I. (1999) *The Social Construction of What?* Cambridge, MA: Harvard University Press.

Hedberg, P.R. (2017) Guiding Moral Behavior through a Reflective Learning Practice. *Journal of Management Education*, *41*(4), pp514–538.

Holt, R. (2020). Hannah Arendt and the Raising of Conscience in Business Schools. *Academy of Management Learning and Education*, 19, pp584–599.

Honan, E., and Bright, D. (2016). Writing a Thesis Differently. *International Journal of Qualitative Studies in Education*, 29(5), pp731–743.

James, W. (1890) *The Principles of Psychology*. New York: Henry Holt & Co.

Khilji, S.E. (2021) An Approach for Humanizing Leadership Education: Building Learning Community & Stakeholder Engagement. *Journal of Management Education*, *46*(3), pp439–471.

Khurana, R. (2007) *From Higher Aims to Hired Hands: The Social Transformation of American Business Schools and the Unfulfilled Promise of Management as a Profession*. Princeton, NJ: Princeton University Press.

Lancione, M., and Clegg, S.R. (2015) The Lightness of Management Learning. *Management Learning*, *46*(3), pp280–298.

Learmonth, M., and Morrell, K. (2019) *Critical Perspectives on Leadership: The Language of Corporate Power*. London: Routledge.

Lyotard, J.-F. (1979) *The Postmodern Condition: A Report on Knowledge*. Manchester: Manchester University Press.

MacIntyre, A. (1981) *After Virtue*. London: Duckworth.

Moeran, B. (2009) From Participant Observation to Observant Participation. In Ybema, S., Yanow, D., Wells, H., and Kamsteeg F. (eds.) *Organisational Ethnography: Studying the Complexities of Everyday Life*. London: Sage, pp139–155.

Morrell, K., and Learmonth, M. (2015) Against Evidence-Based Management, for Management Learning. *Academy of Management Learning and Education*, *14*, pp520–533.

Mowles, C. (2017) Experiencing Uncertainty – On the Potential of Groups and a Group Analytic Approach for Making Management Education More Critical. *Management Learning*, *48*(5), pp505–519.

Mowles, C. (2021) *Complexity: A Key Idea for Business and Society*. London: Routledge.

Mowles, C., and Norman, K. (2022) *Complexity and the Public Sector*. London: Routledge.

Peirce, C.S. (1877) The Fixation of Belief. *Popular Science Monthly*, *12*, pp1–15.

Pfeffer, J., and Fong, C.T. (2002) The End of Business Schools? Less Success Than Meets the Eye. *Academy of Management Learning & Education*, *1*, pp78–95.

Polkinghorne, D.E. (1987) *Narrative Knowing and the Human Sciences*. New York: SUNY Press.

Rafferty, P.D. (2013) Group Work in the MBA Classroom: Improving Pedagogical Practice and Maximizing Positive Outcomes with Part-Time MBA Students. *Journal of Management Education*, *37*(5), pp623–650.

Reason, P., and Bradbury, H. (2008) *The Sage Handbook of Action Research: Participative Inquiry and Practice*. London: Sage.

Reay, T., Whitney, B., and Kohn, K. (2009) What's the Evidence on Evidence-based Management? *Academy of Management Perspectives*, *23*(4), pp5–18.

Richardson, L. (2009) Tales from the Crypt. *International Review of Qualitative Research*, 2, pp345–350.

Rocha, H., Pirson, M., and Suddaby, R. (2021) Business with Purpose and the Purpose of Business Schools: Re-Imagining Capitalism in a Post Pandemic World: A Conversation with Jay Coen Gilbert, Raymond Miles, Christian Felber, Raj Sisodia, Paul Adler, and Charles Wookey. *Journal of Management Inquiry*, *30*(3), pp354–367.

Rousseau, D. (2006) Is There Such a Thing as 'evidence based management'?, *Academy of Management Review*, *31*(2), pp256–269.

Sarra, N., Solsø, K., and Mowles, C. (2022) *The Complexity of Consulting*. London: Routledge.

Scarlatti, G., Gorli, M., Galuppo, L., and Ripamonti, S. (2018) Action Research: Knowing and Changing (in) Organisational Contexts. In Cassell, C., Cunliffe, A.L., and Grandy, G. (eds.) *The Sage Handbook of Qualitative Business and Management Research Methods: History and Traditions*. London: Sage, pp286–327.

Stacey, R. (2003) *Complexity and Group Processes*. London: Routledge.

Stacey, R. (2012) *Tools and Techniques of Leadership and Management*. London: Routledge.

Stacey, R., and Griffin, D., eds. (2005) *A Complexity Perspective on Researching Organizations: Taking Experience Seriously*. London: Routledge.

Stacey, R.D., and Mowles, C. (2016) *Strategic Management and Organisational Dynamics*, 7th Edition. Harlow: Pearson Education.

Statler, M. (2014) Developing Wisdom in a Business school? Critical Reflections on Pedagogical Practice. *Management Learning*, *45*(4), pp397–417.

Sykes, C., and Treleaven, L. (2009) Critical Action Research and Organisational Ethnography. In Ybema, S., Yanow, D., Wells, H., and Kamsteeg, F. (eds.) *Organisational Ethnography: Studying the Complexities of Everyday Life*. London: Sage, pp215–230.

Thomas, G. (2012) Changing Our Landscape of Inquiry for a New Science of Education. *Harvard Educational Review*, *82*(1), Spring, pp26–51.

Tosey, P., Dhaliwal, S., and Hassinen, J. (2015) The Finnish Team Academy Model: Implications for Management Education. *Management Learning*, *46*(2), pp175–194.

Tracy, S.J. (2010) Qualitative Quality: Eight "Big-Tent" Criteria for Excellent Qualitative Research. *Qualitative Inquiry*, *16*(10), pp837–851.

Van Maanen, J. (2011) Ethnography as Work: Some Rules of Engagement. *Journal of Management Studies*, *48*(1), pp218–234.

White, H. (1973) *Metahistory: The Historical Imagination in Nineteenth-century Europe*. Baltimore, MD: John Hopkins UP.

Ybema, S., Yanow, D., Wells, H., and Kamsteeg, F. (2009) *Organisational Ethnography: Studying the Complexities of Everyday Life*. London: Sage.

Part I

DECENTRING SUBJECTIVITIES

2

HISTORIES OF SOCIALITY

The Challenge of Seeing Our Own Eyes

KIRAN CHAUHAN

Introduction

In *The Prison House of Language*, the philosopher and Marxist critical theorist Fredric Jameson recounts an anecdote from the autobiography of an American journalist, James Thurber (Jameson, 1972, p207). In this passage, Jameson draws attention to the way that structuralism (and indeed much of analytic philosophy) has lacked a theory of its own situation – a sense of being implicated in its own assertions. The anecdote concerns Thurber's experience studying botany at university, where he is unable to adjust his microscope to see the plant cells he is meant to be drawing. Despite his tutor's instructions, all he sees is 'milk' until after much effort something clearer begins to appear. Thurber is excited to have finally seen something which he takes for cells and starts to draw.

> The instructor, noting my activity, came from an adjoining desk, a smile on his lips and his eyebrows high in hope. He looked at my cell

DOI: 10.4324/9781003410522-3

> drawing. "What's that?" he demanded, with a hint of squeal in his voice. "That's what I saw," I said. "You didn't, you didn't, you didn't!" he screamed, losing control of his temper instantly, and he bent over and squinted into the microscope. His head snapped up. "That's your eye!" he shouted. "You've fixed the lens so that it reflects! You've drawn your eye!"
>
> (Thurber, 1933, p66)

For me, Jameson is drawing attention to a key challenge in practice-based research and indeed in management more generally: that of taking sufficient account of one's own subjectivity as a researcher to be able to see how we are implicated in the ways we perceive, interpret and analyse the world.

Qualitative researchers can be in little doubt that their own history and social conditionings are likely to show up in their research. As Denzin and Lincoln note in the most recent edition of their handbook of qualitative research, in light of the postmodernist and poststructuralist turns, it is generally accepted that:

> any gaze is always filtered through the lenses of language, gender, social class, race and ethnicity. There are no objective observations, only observations situated in the worlds of – and between – the observer and the observed.
>
> (Denzin and Lincoln, 2017, p17)

And yet, we have the simultaneous observation that attention to the researcher's biases and intentions is being somewhat neglected in organisational research. For example, the practice theorist Silvia Gherardi (2019, p741) suggests that these inquiries are:

> often accompanied by a sort of innocence that overlooks the crisis of representation that grew out of a literary turn in the 1980s concerning textuality, disciplinary history, critical modes of reflexivity, and the critique of realist practices of representation.

Why should this be? Arguably, it may be due to the long-standing bias for objectivity, detachment and timelessness that goes back to the Greeks (Elias, 1978) and was secured for modernity by Descartes as the Enlightenment's 'grand Either/Or': *either* there is a secure foundation for our knowledge that can objectively ground our existence and moral choices or we are cast into radical relativism and intellectual and moral chaos (Bernstein, 2010). One can imagine that this bias plays out as a reluctance to acknowledge the researcher's role in their research because it weakens claims to generalisability – a kind of 'physics-envy' where experiments need to be assumed to be repeatable in order to be valid. But why do social sciences research at all if we then want to deny responsibility for what we have found (Steier, 1991, p10)? And if one accepts this responsibility, how do we notice when we, like Thurber, might be 'drawing our own eye' and reconfirming the things we already think we know, rather than refocussing our perceptual microscopes to see what else there may be to notice and understand?

In management theory too, there has been a decades-long call to pay attention to what assumptions are made about how work gets done. For example, Gareth Morgan's seminal *Images of Organisation* (Morgan, 1986) set out to describe a range of metaphors that implicitly inform institutional thinking. To name a few of these, organisations that tend to focus on interacting parts that can be designed and controlled through bureaucracy are likely to be operating with a machine metaphor; seeing different forms of organising as being suited to different environments, like species and habitats, might imply an organism metaphor; those that focus on information flows and learning might be operating with a brain metaphor; and so on. Being socialised into organisations often involves managers being invited to take up their roles in particular ways, and an uncritical engagement with these processes can lead to the limitation of possibilities for action. Despite this invitation, how often do we continue to see organisational failure being attributed to poor planning, with a suggested remedy of more and better planning? How often do we continue to see recruitment processes ending up with homogenous teams because recruiting managers haven't considered their own biases? By bringing these institutional habits – and the reasons why we may personally be uncritically drawn to them – perhaps we can gain more opportunities to get along together.

In this chapter, I want to offer a perspective that construes subjectivity as an analytical resource for researchers inquiring into social life, and managers trying to get things done with others in organisations. Taking key ideas from pragmatist philosophy and especially the work of George Herbert Mead, I will argue that while it makes little sense to try to write ourselves out of the picture in terms of our work and research, as though we can occupy a view from nowhere (Dewey, 1929, Nagel, 1986), there are nevertheless important issues to consider when engaging with first-person accounts as a source of empirical data about organisational life. These relate to the extent to which we understand:

- our individual experience as paradoxically social at the same time and therefore holding the potential for generating insights that will be of interest for others in similar contexts.
- the peculiarities of our interpretive and responsive tendencies, so that inquiring into experience can be more than an uncritical or defensive rehearsal of the ways we (and the others with whom we identify) already understand the world.

More than 'just' my experience?

Inquiring into organisational life using first-person accounts as the empirical material upon which to base analysis is sometimes seen as problematic: it can be hard to imagine how the experience of work recounted from the perspective of one individual could ever be similar enough to another's perspective to make contributions arising from that experience useful more generally. Following from this, we might worry that any conclusions someone draws from inquiring into their own practice, while perhaps very useful to them in developing their own professional practice, may *only* be useful to them.

This kind of concern arguably arises from a dualistic understanding of individuals and society, for if society is understood simply as the aggregation of individuals, then it seems very reasonable to be wary of taking one person's experience too seriously. It is surely better in that case to investigate a sufficiently representative range of people's experience and analyse what is common and different between the accounts, and from this try to make some conclusions. However, if we understand individuals as social through and through – that individuals and society are paradoxically forming and being formed by each other – then experience recounted from an individual perspective is necessarily already general. Furthermore, if social life is understood to be fundamentally uncertain, then any idea of the predictive potential (in a strong sense) of social sciences research quickly evaporates. These two ideas are core to pragmatist philosophy and I will briefly explain them here in making a case for needing to account for one's history of sociality when undertaking first-person research; and for making sense of what we are doing in our day-to-day practice as managers or researchers.

Sociality: a paradox of individual and social

The rejection of epistemic dualisms is a central tenet of pragmatist philosophy (Simpson, 2018). Developing the work started by Charles Sanders Peirce (e.g. 1877) and William James (e.g. 1890), and John Dewey, George Herbert Mead, Jane Addams and Mary Parker Follett saw being bound up in the world with others as a continuous, experimental and emergent process; we are continually discovering what we are doing together as we do it rather than being able to know it in advance. Further, meaning in this context cannot be pregiven, rather it emerges and evolves in interaction. This perspective problematises the impulse to classify and control the world because the very terms used in such processes are always on the move and bound up in the politics of relating. One form that this impulse can take is to generate epistemic dualisms that disrupt the flow of experience by separating the experientially inseparable: by claiming that we can engage discretely with, for example, knowledge and practice, thinking and doing or habit and inquiry (see Solsø, this volume) we impose order on the world. Like Morgan's metaphors, these impositions can come to serve purposes we may not understand and, moreover, enable the psychological gains of avoiding facing into the contradictions in and messiness of the world as we find it.

In the concept of *sociality* – 'the capacity of being several things at once' (Mead, 1932, p49), Mead provides an anti-dualistic formulation of individuals and society, which has been framed in the complex responsive processes theoretical canon as a paradox (e.g. Stacey, 2012, Mowles, 2015). This means that the notions of 'individual' and 'society' are both mutually constitutive and conceptually opposite. To understand this, we need some background on Mead's perspective of human development.

Mead on human development

Mead describes the emergence of the individual as a social process that involves responding to an imagined and evolving sense of oneself held in the positions of multiple others all at the same time (Mead, 1925). From the moment we are born, we are in a group; cultural traditions will no doubt determine the size of this group, but there is likely to be at least one primary caregiver upon whom a baby will be entirely dependent for a time, and whose attitude the baby will learn to anticipate in order to have its needs met (Stern, 1985). Human development then involves the widening of the range of perspectives we can simultaneously take as we act, which in Mead's terms occurs through encounters with increasingly diverse other people and situations (Mead, 1925, 1934). For example, at a young age, we move from being able to participate in relatively simple social acts of play where we are required to respond as one of dyadic social configurations (for example, 'cops and robbers' or 'doctors and nurses'), to team games where we are required to respond as one of a more complex group based on our expectations of the likely conduct of several actors.

These are examples of the process of assimilation into the world of social objects that both characterise communities and differentiate them from one another. As I have described elsewhere (Chauhan, 2022), social objects for Mead are the objects of social acts 'that answer to all parts of the complex act, though these parts are found in the conduct of different individuals' (Mead, 1925, p264). They are the expectations shared by at least two social actors as to the completion of a common endeavour, so that the expected differential conduct of each actor is contained within the conduct of the other actors at the same time. These expectations can come to be shared between large numbers of people so that modes of responding to particular stimuli become habitual for community members in relation to specific complex social acts – they become institutionalised (Mead, 1934, p261). Take teaching as an example: we think of the roles of (at least) teacher and student who through different but interdependent activities complete the social act of (hopefully!) stimulating learning. The habitual practice of teaching can therefore be denoted as a social object.

The range and complexity of the social objects we participate in perpetuating increases as we become involved in wider social figurations and encounter more kinds of difference. Eventually, we are able to take the attitudes of not just those in our immediate vicinity, but all those who feature in our experience – be they our relevant social groups, or society at large – in relation to particular social objects. Mead argues that these attitudes of others are organised in individual thinking as an ever-evolving sense of a *generalised other* (Mead, 1934, p261) that provides both an interlocuter as we interact with ourselves in private conversations (the process of *mind*), and an interpretive framing for the gestures of particular others as interact with others to go on together (the process of *society*). The sense of the generalised other also informs how we experience ourselves as social beings, constrained by norms and habits of social conduct in the groups in which we participate and to which we find ourselves responding.

Experiencing social constraint...

Groups of interdependent individuals perhaps inevitably rely on cooperation in some form. This is clearly evident in late modern societies: since the industrial revolution, access to goods and services has become mediated in ways that are hugely more complex than in pre-modern societies, where, for example, we might have known all the members of our community (Giddens, 1990). Chris Mowles' chapter on reflexivity in his volume describes Norbert Elias's take on the civilising process which takes us up to the 20th century; with global intercommunications now the norm for a large proportion of the world's population, contemporary societies are more complex still.

That we continue to find ways to stay in generative relation with each other might suggest that the desire to stay in relation with others – and conform with social norms as a means to that – is an innate human characteristic. A less essentialist perspective is offered by the evolutionary anthropologist Christopher Boehm who speculates in his book, *Moral Origins* (2012), that as soon as our primate ancestors began hunting in the Late Pleistocene age a million years ago, compliance with certain rules of conduct in communities became evolutionarily selected for. With cooperative large game hunting and meat bartering needing to be organised for group members to survive, an understanding of the roles that different community members needed to play so that all members of the community could survive provided a check on any individual's selfish impulses to, for example, more completely satisfy their hunger or to take more than their share. Boehm also describes how these emerging rules of conduct were enforced by the group punishment of bullying, freeloading, cheating and theft that reduced the fitness of non-egalitarian deviants in the evolutionary game – the anticipation of such punishments also helped community members regulate their behaviours. So, from these primitive societies, Boehm describes the evolution of an *opportunistic conscience* that 'enables us to predict the social reactions of our peers and to calculate what we can get away with socially and still keep up a moral reputation' (Boehm, 2012, p175).

While the threat of censure through physical violence may have become the preserve of nation states in the Western world (Elias, 2000), the feeling of social control is arguably a manifestation of the same tendencies to yearn to belong, to fear exclusion from the group or to be unable to have individual and group needs met. The complexity of contemporary societies probably means that more imagination is needed to stay in generative relation with each other, especially as the mechanisms of intentional socialisation processes have become more sophisticated. The American psychiatrist and scholar of thought reform, Robert Jay Lifton, describes increasingly complex modes of persuading others to submit to the norms of a milieu: *coercion* is an instruction to change accompanied by an explicit or implicit threat of exclusion, ostracisation or even death; *exhortation* is an invitation to become good ('change to be more moral, like us'); *therapy* is an invitation to become well ('change to be healthier, like us'); and *realisation* is an invitation to achieve your potential ('you can change to be your best if you think like us') (Lifton, 1967, p438). Being obedient, morally good, healthy or your best in these terms are all aspirations that we might identify as features of a particular group's ideology – the 'magical systems of explanation' that arise unconsciously and function to stabilise communities (Mannheim, 1936, p89) and perpetuate prevailing patterns of power relating.

While they evolve over time, the assumptions and values involved in ideology enable and constrain what it is possible to be in a group. For example, Stacey (2006) draws on Charles Taylor's broad sweep of the evolution of the understanding of human subjects in Western society as a movement through:

- *medieval scholasticism* – the subject was defined in relation to the cosmic order, or God. Subjects aspire to be holy.
- *the Enlightenment* – after Descartes' assertion that the only thing that cannot be doubted was that subjects were thinking things, and Leibniz's monadism, the subject was understood as to define itself in isolation from others. Subjects aspire to be rational and free.

- *humanism and contemporary systems theory* – both draw on Kant's model of systems determined by formative causality, though Kant's exemption of human rationality from this model (as to incorporate it would deny humans free will) is often ignored. Subjects aspire to become what they are able or meant to be.

These patterns of meaning making may be largely underarticulated and understood in an embodied way that may well be good enough for getting by day to day. Indeed, in the absorbed coping of everyday life, we likely couldn't question everything all of the time (Sandberg and Tsoukas, 2011, Dreyfus and Taylor, 2015): if we walk along a mountain path, we won't typically be thinking about each individual step we take unless the path becomes, for example, suddenly unsteady. Similarly, in the day-to-day work of managers, we are unlikely to consider every action we take, unless material mismatches between what we expect to happen and what actually happens start to become apparent.

In those cases, we may experience a breakdown that might be resolvable within our existing resources – walking along the path, we might for example try adjusting our posture or weight distribution as ways of coping that continue our movement along the path. However, if the path is impassable by the usual route, we may need to find another way around that requires mounting a bank or crossing a river – how able we are to see these possibilities as available to us will likely rely on the extent we feel capable of climbing or swimming. I suggest that we are more likely to be able to weigh up these possibilities if we have our current mountain-walking experience more fully in view. So by analogy, in the context of organisational research or finding more helpful ways of working, until our habits of meaning making are brought into view, our perception of what is happening and therefore what it is possible to think about and do remains limited.

...and agential freedom at the same time

And yet, at the same time as a sense of constraint, we also experience a sense of spontaneity, freedom and choice which seems at odds with what we have been saying so far about social control. Mead says that social control 'will depend upon the degree to which the individual does assume the attitudes of those in the group who are involved with him in his social activities' (Mead, 1925, p274). This could easily be taken to imply that we are free to choose the extent to which we comply; however, this makes sense *only* if agential freedom and social constraint are understood as a dualism. Mead, rather, is pointing to the contradictory quality of these phases of experience and asks us to understand them as dialectical phases of the self. Here, 'I' is a way of talking about the unpredictable, spontaneous and responding phase of the self, which is unknowable in advance and recognisable only in retrospect. It is this phase of the self that means we can never really know in advance what will happen as we interact with others or ourselves: from the analogies of non-linearity and the butterfly effect in the complexity sciences – where small gestures can eventuate in big changes and grand gestures may come to nothing based on small difference in 'starting conditions' – we also can have no idea of the longer term consequences of our actions. This makes any attempt to attribute social sciences any predictive potential, or to equate them with physical sciences problematic, not least because physical sciences can also be very political (see Brahm, this volume and Rasmussen, this volume). For Mead, 'me' by contrast is a way of talking about the experience of ourselves as historical phenomena – the patterning of our responsive tendencies, embedded in and constrained by temporal and social relations that provide interpretive frames for the new situations in which we find ourselves (see also Larsen, this volume).

While conceptually opposite, these phases are mutually constitutive because when we respond in our interactions with others and ourselves, we can't stop ourselves from taking the attitudes of others to make sense of the situation at hand. Consequently, we are never independently deciding on an action and then carrying it out apart from the social processes through which we are constituted; rather, our actions are formed by our expectations of how others may respond to us, and our actions go to form expectations of further responses. In this way, society at large is already involved in our agential responding. So, because we participate in communities, individual experience is at the same time general.

However, someone's particular bundle of interpretive tendencies arises from their peculiar history, which also means that no two individuals are exactly alike. It is in this sense that we can understand individuals are thoroughly social, at the same time as having:

> a world that differs in some degree from that of any other member of the same community... each individual stratifies the common life in a different manner, and the life of the community is the sum of all these stratifications.
>
> (Mead, 1925, p259)

Illustration: a peculiar stratification of the common life

Reflecting on my own history, I was born in the late 1970s to parents who had immigrated to the UK from East Africa as African-Indian tensions increased as British colonial rule ended in 1963. My childhood in North London in the 1980s and 1990s was spent at home, at school and at the homes of the various relatives whom we visited nearly every weekend. My experience was perfused with conversational preoccupations with fitting in with British society at the same time as retaining the conventions of our Indian heritage; of tactically code switching between English and Gujarati both to be understood (or not); to show respect to community elders and the many Hindu gods; and of carefully negotiating hetero-normative conversations about my future plans, when I was increasingly recognising my queerness.

Some of my early childhood was also spent in my local hospital – I was quite unwell as a child and, for three or four years, was admitted every few months to recover from the latest exacerbation of my illness. My parents did their best to protect me from the things that made me ill, restricted what I was allowed to eat and drink to things that wouldn't aggravate my condition and made sure that I was taking my prescribed medications. All of this made me feel really abnormal when I just wanted to be free like I imagined everyone else to be. I have come to see how these aspects of my early life sensitised me, in an embodied as well as cognitive ways, to notice and respond to particular aspects of social life over others. First, to conversational patterns and cues that might signal potential exclusion, an ally or a judge; second, to respond to feeling anxious through intellectual creativity; and finally to resist help because I interpret it as an attempt to control.

Sociologically, I find myself arguably rather well-suited to Western society and to working as an organisational consultant to a public sector that privileges logic, autonomy and the suppression of emotion. However, being aware of these habits enriches my unique take on experience, drawing attention both to what I am inclined to notice and what I might be inclined to miss. Working through the three habits I have described: my tendency to look for conversational patterns when group life gets tense is rather helpful in my work as a consultant who mainly works with groups; but perhaps I am less able to notice my own involvement in creating the situations in which I find myself and miss chances to act into what's happening. Next, responding to anxiety through intellectualising gives me access to flights of creativity which can be really helpful in thinking about how to get through tricky situations, but perhaps I take off too quickly to escape my discomfort when sitting in the fire for longer would be important for me and others in making sense of what's going on between us. Lastly, being used to being self-reliant means I can feel confident in handling most of the situations that I find myself in, especially when I don't really know what I'm doing; but perhaps I don't hear the offers of help as signals that I might need help; and perhaps I miss the same cues in others who are asking for help.

These are just some of the ways in which I might reflect on my history to understand my subjectivity as an analytical resource: as well as making the most of my particular bundle of well-practiced perceptual habits, the aspects of experience that I might be less open to noticing might be those that turn out to provide better explanations of group life.

I have tried to illustrate how, for inquiries based on first-person accounts of experience, examining how we have come to interpret the world as we do helps us to understand what we are used to seeing, and also what we might be missing. Identifying the latter and noticing what difference the expansion of our perceptual sensitivities makes to our appreciation of the world as we encounter it (rather than staying with the more familiar aspects of it) is a process of development in Mead's terms as described above: that this change in awareness also may change what we do makes this kind of inquiry also a reflexive process. As Mowles says (2015, p60):

> In reflecting we will be thinking and feeling deeply about something, possibly our own experience, whilst in becoming reflexive we are bringing that reflection back to ourselves and may be changed by it.

More than this, however, if we are interested in producing new academic contributions, or finding new ways of dealing with challenges at work, relying on the things we already know may limit the scope for novel insights in our inquiries.

To give an account of oneself

With the ideas outlined above in mind, giving an account of one's history of sociality – how, through our interaction with groups over time, we have come to be able to imagine being in the positions of multiple others or in multiple points in time at once – is a way of describing how we have come to interpret the world as we do. It is therefore a way of facing head on into Gherardi's critique of innocence by taking seriously our embedding in social and temporal relations. This is both so that we can appreciate the unique account we are able to provide of experience, and to recognise when we are rehearsing the ways in which we already understand the world, rather than being open to other possibilities. In these ways, a researcher or manager's subjectivity can be understood as a valuable analytical resource for examining the common life of a community. However, accounting for who we are in this way is not necessarily a straightforward task.

Brown (2022, p1206) suggests that in organisation and management studies:

> Most often … subjectively construed identities are conceived as 'the meanings that individuals attach reflexively to themselves' (Brown, 2015: 23), and may be understood as individuals' answers to fundamental existential questions such as 'who am I?', 'who do I want to become?' and 'how should I act?'

The quotation alludes to a continuity in experience which gives us a sense of *ontological security* – a term coined by the British psychiatrist R.D. Laing to describe one's 'sense of presence in the world as a real, alive, whole and in a temporal sense, continuous person' (Laing, 1969, p40). The sense of continuity is therefore arguably an aspect of our absorbed coping, reliant on the embodied and pre-reflective understanding of the world we have gained through our development to navigate it. If uncertainty brings anxiety that we learn to prefer to avoid (Marris, 1991, 1996), then we can start to imagine the attachment we may feel to the stories we hold about ourselves and why it might be quite difficult or disturbing to recast those stories in ways that open up our fields of attention. This means our past experience may be informing our understanding of the present in anticipation of the future in ways that we may never have had to consider or acknowledge.

Going back to my earlier comments about ideology, our ability to acknowledge and articulate how we have come to think the way we think is itself enabled and constrained by the ideologies of the groups we have valued and continue to value – by our desire or need to belong – and what risks there may be in making our accounts public.

In the context of research, naturally, those to whom we are giving an account may seem relatively clear: on the one hand, it's the readers of academic writing – journal editors and readers, or those examining a doctoral thesis – who will likely be judging the quality of academic contributions according to norms of the academy. In a similar vein, in using first-person accounts, we may also be anticipating colleagues or future employers as potential audiences; the latter raises ethical issues considered in Chapter 10 of this volume. In a work context, our accounts may be to our bosses or colleagues, or those whom we need to persuade to try a course of action, who are likely to have their own ideas (informed by the habitus of the sector and their own personal histories) about what kinds of arguments are persuasive. Having all these audiences looking over our shoulders (the generalised other with whom we are in dialogue) no doubt moderates what we are prepared or able to say to others.

In using first-person accounts, however, there is another aspect to consider in exploring what it may be possible to say. On the one hand, writing autobiographically 'one is seeing a "self" narrated much more in that 'self's own terms than in any other imaginable type of account' (Watson, 2009, p432). In that sense, there is the potential for a more direct exposition of thoughts, feelings, fantasies and intentions than one could ever elicit from another, for example through qualitative interviews or observation. On the other, there may be aspects of our history that we have simply never thought about and indeed giving an account of oneself may be *necessarily* partial. As Judith Butler argues taking up Freud's major insight, we can only ever be partially known to ourselves (Butler, 2005, p39) because there are periods of our experience – our earliest years, for example, or periods of trauma – that may be very material to how we have come to understand the world but are hard to bring to mind or acknowledge; these periods may have informed the development of heightened sensitivities or lacunae in our perceptual or interpretive tendencies which if we are trying to inquire into experience as part of research or work more generally may lead us down some paths rather than others. For these reasons, giving an account of oneself may involve ontological disturbance which we may or may not be willing or able to tolerate.

To give one example in my own case, noticing my tendency (mentioned above) to downplay my own involvement in the creation of the situations in which I find myself has sometimes impaired my ability to make sense of my working world. In one role, I seemed unable to get anywhere with a project I was responsible for and felt rather bored by it all. I started to get interested in boredom as a theme in my life more generally and looked into the work of the Austrian psychoanalyst, Otto Fenichel. Fenichel, following Freud, suggested that boredom could be characterised as a state of someone 'searching for an object [to discharge a drive], not in order to act on it with his drive-impulses, but rather to be helped by it to find a drive-aim which he is missing' (Fenichel, 1954, p351). Translating that into terms consistent with an understanding of human interaction as complex responsive processes, I considered how I might be neglecting a sense of meaning or purpose, which I was perhaps unprepared yet to acknowledge. It was at this point that I became able – and not without some consternation – to start to appreciate my own self-interested political manoeuvrings in relation to the piece of work – it happened to be for the director who was responsible for a restructuring process in which I was implicated – and so the consequences could be significant for me if I made a bad impression through a poor piece of work. I had been quite oblivious to my own part in the game to date and certainly didn't like to think of myself as someone who 'played politics' in organisations. As a result, the acknowledgement felt a bitter pill to swallow. At the same time, it opened up a whole new aspect of my work that I could attend to and consider in relation to the current piece of work and in the future.

Accounting for oneself as a process of moral development

The purpose of reflecting on one's history of sociality in these contexts of course has a utility, but I see it as more than an academic exercise: it has the potential to increase the richness of the world as we experience it and our understanding of what we have learnt to value through our history. The pragmatists' focus on experience and emergence naturally led to a dissatisfaction with understandings of ethics that rely on abstract norms or duties. Their alternative was strongly situational: each situation calls out a novel combination of competing goods which need to be weighed without the outcome of any act being knowable in advance.

If ethical judgement, then, is about the rational weighing of competing goods (e.g. Mead, 1934, p388) then attending to the matters discussed in this chapter can enrich our deliberative processes and therefore our ethical potential. The movement of our tendencies is therefore a process of moral development. I'll continue with the example I was just giving of becoming more aware of my own political manoeuvrings. Noticing this previously underacknowledged capacity for self-interest brought more competing goods into view. In addition to considering the goods involved in trying to do the work to a high standard (e.g. rigour, timeliness and various stakeholder interests), I was able to think about how my self-interest might be influencing how I was going about the work: I noticed I was probably trying particularly hard to show my creativity and tenacity to an extent not warranted by the work itself. Being aware of potential impact of wanting to come across well to my director meant I was able to consider the relative importance of this 'good' in relation to the others. In the event, I was able to put aside this concern in the project work (which made it easier and more interesting) and consider my future in the organisation more directly. This more rational weighing of goods led me to consider what I wanted to achieve in the world through my work, and, in the end, I decided that I wasn't that interested in staying during the restructure. I left the role a few months later with a better understanding of what was important to me and what I was and wasn't prepared to do as a result.

I hope I am convincing you that by sticking only to paths we are used to, we may well deepen our understanding of our existing habits and also reaffirm and further sediment our current understandings of how to get by in the world. This could serve us well enough if we feel relatively capable and effective in our day-to-day lives. If, however, we are confronted with problematic situations, ones that perplex us or initiate doubt, or that require a deliberate creativity, then our existing habits may be insufficient to guide our action. For practice-based research where there is a requirement to produce new academic or professional insights based in the researcher's own professional practice, or in dealing with intractable or novel problems at work, we may need to try out other paths: by doing so, we have the opportunity to make our existing habits available for critical and reflexive engagement and to consider other possibilities for understanding our interactions – both with ourselves and with each other.

In these ways, we can start to use our subjectivity – our own peculiar histories of sociality – as an analytical resource: once we've started to see the ways we are already going about navigating the world, we can become more detached about our involvement. We can become more adept at noticing when we are 'seeing our own eye' and the concomitant opportunity to consider what more there may be to explore and understand. In doing so, we further enrich our interpretive and responsive sensitivities, and therefore our capacities act.

Conclusion

The introduction to this volume sets out the case for approaches organisational research and management education that are geared towards developing group-mindedness, thoughtfulness, wisdom and an attention to the pro-social goals of long-term welfare, global citizenship and sustainability. In this chapter, I have tried to describe how developing a greater understanding of our histories of sociality as researchers or managers helps us to see more of the richness of experience – a richness that we may be ideologically or defensively constrained from acknowledging. If we accept that we can never really know what will happen when we act, this enrichment at least gives us the ability to notice more about others and ourselves when we interact, and our histories bump up against each other. As well as providing new capacities to act, and greater possibilities for research contributions, complexifying our perceptual field and bringing more of our interpretive and responsive tendencies into view can also be a process of moral development.

References

Bernstein, R.J. (2010) *The Pragmatic Turn*. Cambridge: Polity Press.
Boehm, C. (2012) *Moral Origins*. New York: Basic Books.

Brown, A.D. (2015) Identities and Identity Work in Organizations. *International Journal of Management Reviews*, 17(1), pp20–40.

Brown, A.D. (2022) Identities in and around Organizations: Towards an Identity Work Perspective. *Human Relations*, 75(7), pp1205–1237.

Butler, J. (2005) *Giving an Account of Oneself.* New York: Fordham.

Chauhan, K. (2022) Moving beyond Neutrality: Recognising the Moral Agency of the Consultant through Reflexive Inquiries into Shame. In Sarra, N., Solsø, K., and Mowles, C. (eds.), *The Complexity of Consultancy.* London: Routledge, pp16–37.

Denzin, N.K. and Lincoln, Y.S. (2017) *The SAGE Handbook of Qualitative Research*, 5th ed. London: SAGE.

Dewey, J. (1929) The Quest for Certainty. In Boydston, J.A. (ed.), *John Dewey: Later Works, 1925–1953* (vol. 4). Carbondale: Southern Illinois University Press.

Dreyfus, H. and Taylor, C. (2015) *Retrieving Realism.* Cambridge, MA: Harvard University Press.

Elias, N. (1978) *What Is Sociology?* Oxford: Blackwell.

Elias, N. (2000) *The Civilizing Process*, revised ed. Oxford: Blackwell.

Fenichel, O. (1954) On the Psychology of Boredom. In Fenichel, H. and Rapaport, D. (eds.), *The Collected Papers of Otto Fenichel.* London: Routledge & Kegan Paul, pp349–361.

Gherardi, S. (2019). Theorizing Affective Ethnography for Organization Studies. *Organization*, 26(6), pp741–760.

Giddens, A. (1990) *The Consequences of Modernity.* Cambridge: Polity Press.

James, W. (1890) *The Principles of Psychology.* Cambridge, MA: Harvard University Press.

Jameson, F. (1972) *The Prison-House of Language – A Critical Account of Structuralism and Russian Formalism.* Princeton, NJ: Princeton University Press.

Laing, R.D. (1969) *The Divided Self.* New York: Pantheon Books.

Lifton, R.J. (1967) *Thought Reform and the Psychology of Totalism.* Harmondsworth: Penguin.

Mannheim, K. (1936) *Ideology and Utopia.* London: Routledge, 1960.

Marris, P. (1991) The Social Construction of Uncertainty. In Parkes, C.M., Stevenson-Hinde, J., and Marris, P. (eds.), *Attachment across the Life Cycle.* London: Routledge, pp77–90.

Marris, P. (1996) *The Politics of Uncertainty: Attachment in Private and Public Life*. London: Routledge.

Mead, G.H. (1925) The Genesis of the Self and Social Control. *International Journal of Ethics*, *35*, pp251–277.

Mead, G.H. (1932) *The Philosophy of the Present*. La Salle, IL: Open Court

Mead, G.H. (1934) *Mind, Self and Society: from the Standpoint of a Social Behaviorist*. Chicago, IL: The University of Chicago Press, 2015.

Morgan, G. (1986) *Images of Organization*. Newbury Park, CA: Sage.

Mowles, C. (2015) *Managing in Uncertainty – Complexity and the Paradoxes of Everyday Organizational Life*. London: Routledge.

Nagel, T. (1986) *The View from Nowhere*. Oxford: Oxford University Press.

Peirce, C.S. (1877) The Fixation of Belief. *Popular Science Monthly*, *12*, pp1–15.

Sandberg, J. and Tsoukas, H. (2011) Grasping the Logic of Practice: Theorizing through Practical Rationality. *Academy of Management Review*, *36(2)*, pp338–360.

Simpson, B. (2018). Pragmatism: A Philosophy of Practice. In C. Cassell, A. Cunliffe, and G. Grandy (eds.), *SAGE Handbook of Qualitative Business and Management Research Methods: History and Traditions*. London: SAGE, pp54–68.

Stacey, R.D. (2006) Theories of Change in Therapeutic Work. *Clinical Child Psychology and Psychiatry*, *11*(2), pp191–203.

Stacey, R.D. (2012) *Tools and Techniques of Leadership and Management: Meeting the Challenge of Complexity*. London: Routledge.

Steier, F. (1991) *Research and Reflexivity*. Thousand Oaks, CA: SAGE.

Thurber, J. (1933) *My Life and Hard Times*. New York and London: Harper and Brothers Publishers.

Stern, D. (1985) *The Interpersonal World of the Infant*. London: Routledge.

Watson, T.J. (2009) Narrative, Life Story and Manager Identity: A Case Study in Autobiographical Identity Work. *Human Relations*, *62*(3), pp425–452.

3

NARRATING ONESELF AS ANOTHER

Reflexive Autoethnographic Inquiry

SUNE BJØRN LARSEN

Introduction

> Anna told me that they had decided to hire another consultant. I was disappointed and ashamed, and I tried to hide these feelings from Anna and myself. The moment after, she encouraged me to apply for a job as their manager, and I felt happy and proud. This was an emotional rollercoaster, and I did not experience events as if I were controlling them but rather that they were controlling me.
>
> (Larsen, 2020, p146)

I wrote this about an experience I had with a client in my work as an organisational consultant. It was a part of a narrative of being interviewed for a job, and an example of the starting point of an autoethnographic inquiry.

DOI: 10.4324/9781003410522-4

I had been contacted by Anna (an employee in a family treatment centre) and asked to meet monthly to reflect with her and her colleagues about their job challenges. She said I had been recommended, and although I initially declined because of a busy calendar, I was talked into meeting with her and her colleagues about the job. Because I had been recommended, I had expected a supportive atmosphere but found out that the group had diverging preferences regarding the choice of a supervisor – I was in competition with others. I suddenly found myself trying to convince *them* to work with *me*. Facing their rejection, I was disappointed and ashamed, and I tried to hide these feelings from Anna, and from myself. This episode from my practice was surprisingly emotional for me and in researching it, I became curious to understand why I reacted the way I did. What was my disappointment about when I hadn't even wanted the work? Why did that bring about shame, rather than anger or irritation? Why did I hide the feelings from Anna rather than express them? One can imagine these questions being of interest to me personally as they might help me make sense of what happened; one may also think their exploration would be best suited to a conversation with a coach or therapist. But in what ways can inquiring into them reveal something about organisational life? How can such a personal account have any wider generalisability? Isn't it just anecdotal and, besides, an awful lot about me?

In this chapter, I will argue that the use of first-person narrative material can serve as a starting point for reflexive inquiry into one's own practice that also illuminates wider organisational phenomena of interest to other practitioners in similar fields. My curiosity towards everyday experiences, such as in the quote above, is the starting point for a reflexive exploration with others where I move on to explore the broader context of this experience enabling me to draw conclusions, if only temporarily, about organisational development processes. I draw on the French philosopher Paul Ricœur to argue that we discover and reveal ourselves through encounters with others. Ricœur claims that we are emplotted. In a research context, I interpret this to mean that we can understand how and why we act – the implicit plot of our lives – through writing about our practice and discussing this with others. Autoethnography is a research method that is suited for this purpose. As we write about our experiences, we encounter them and ourselves anew.

An example of reflexive autoethnographic inquiry

As my initial questions indicate, what stood out in the job interview was how emotional the event was. I was puzzled by the interaction and my interest was aroused because I found my emotional reactions 'strange, but interesting' (Brinkmann, 2012, p12). According to Brinkmann's view on qualitative research, these strange incidents can direct the focus of our research in everyday life. Through an ongoing process of writing, discussing, reflecting, and re-writing for about a year I found that my emotional reactions in the detailed interactions revealed a complexity that I hadn't appreciated before (Larsen, 2020): it was not only a struggle for control to influence or direct other people's behaviour or the course of events but also a struggle to maintain a certain view of myself in my interaction with others. I found that I was revealing myself in my research.

Staying with this curiosity about my disappointment and shame, I started exploring emotions in the organisational studies literature (e.g. Burkitt, 1999, Clancy et al., 2012, Wetherell, 2012, Gherardi, 2017). This turned out to be a door opener to understanding the relational character of emotions, and discussions with my research colleagues about this helped me become aware of and more detached about a pattern I noticed in my behaviour: that making a good impression is highly important to me. This 'default' eagerness to impress offered an explanation for why I had been so preoccupied by the group's rejection of me and, for example, why I hadn't noticed how a fraction of the group in the job interview was dependent on me to change the power relations in the larger group, while others were opposed to this. I realised that I had not paid attention to the nuances of these relational interdependencies and the politics of the situation, which led me to consider power and ethics in consulting work. I started to see how consultants are often asked to act into the competing politics in the specific situation with groups of clients having diverging intentions and – importantly – that consultants have intentions of their own: professionally, ethically, and financially. This is different from pervasive ideas about consultancy where consultants are expected to be neutral in their facilitation of change for the clients.

Anthropological and sociological research approaches allowed me to 'think relationally' (Bourdieu and Wacquant, 1992, p224) and gain detachment from my experienced need to impress. I started to see that consultants more generally experience a need to impress their clients due to a relational, rather than merely individual, pressure to perform. Inquiring into the narrative led me to think about how emotions point to societal trends that I hadn't previously been aware of. For example, what society values, what counts as success or failure, and how impression management is part of the politics of everyday organisational life. I concluded that impressing clients in particular ways is an inevitable part of the politics of consultancy within organisational development (Larsen, 2020).

This inquiry led me to take others seriously in ways where I am sharing my reactions, emotions, reflections, and convictions to a higher degree than before. This is a marked departure from the way I had previously practiced consultancy and what would have been possible for me before I conducted this research. I now experience consultancy as a space to engage and explore differences. Several clients have expressed that it feels comfortable to explore disagreements with me as a consultant. Ironically, they are often more impressed with my interventions when I am trying less hard to impress. Although my research never had a therapeutic aim, my understanding of how I am dependent on my research and work colleagues as well as family and friends and how they depend on me – as interdependent beings – has entailed similarly profound change to how I live my private life with others.

This example shows how first-person narrative material can help us to understand what we are doing in our practice as researchers or managers. As we write and read about ourselves, we can take ourselves as an object to ourselves. One becomes other to oneself. We realise how we are not only a subject, nor solely an object to ourselves, but we might find how we are discovering and revealing ourselves with and through others. The essence of the chapter is that writing about our own practice allows us the potential to attain a reflexive distance from ourselves (see also Mowles on reflexivity, this volume).

However, writing and reading about ourselves is only the starting point. Ongoing discussions about the narrative with others are necessary to be challenged in this process. The turning back on ourselves can create a movement in our practice and in our sense of self. In my case, working with others to think about the experience helped me to notice my tendency to impress, which I probably would have shied away from thinking about. So, others can help us to engage more critically with our experience.

Indeed, this critical engagement from others is arguably *needed* to challenge and thereby establish the narrator as reliable. Writing and discussing is part of a systematic chain of steps to deal with how a local experience can claim some generalisability and broader usefulness in the understanding of processes of organisational development. Writing about oneself in an autoethnographical-inspired narrative approach provides a method for this.

Writing about oneself has a general use beyond research in general and impression management as a specific theme. I've been working with a group of pedagogues working with children with special needs, encouraging them to write about and inquire into their experience together, with me as a guide. Using first-person narratives has been useful for them to develop their practice. They wrote about their own practice, allowing them to discuss what they were doing and why they were doing it. This illustrates how an autoethnography-inspired narrative approach can develop organisational practice and thinking about the ethics involved. But before I describe this further, I will describe how autoethnography is helpful to see oneself as another.

Writing about oneself

This chapter's title is an extension of the French philosopher Paul Ricœur's title on his seminal book *Oneself as Another* (1992). He writes within the Hegelian tradition and argues 'that the selfhood of oneself implies otherness to such an intimate degree that one cannot be thought of without the other' (Ricœur, 1992, p3). His philosophical writings are dedicated to describing the self as relational. We discover and are revealed to ourselves through the encounter with the other. Bringing his views to research into organisational life means to take account of how one can only *be with oneself in another* (Hegel quoted in Honneth, 2000, p29).

The kind of research I am describing requires methods that allow researchers to reflexively engage in experiences that animate us to explore how this might reveal broader patterns of relating. Autoethnography based on breakdowns in practice sits within a problem-driven approach to research (Alvesson and Skoldberg, 2018, p4), with abductive reasoning as its central logical principle (see Rasmussen, this volume). Autoethnography simply means to describe (graphy) the researcher's personal experiences (auto) to examine the broader context of that experience (ethno) (Brinkmann,

2012, p79). Autoethnography is a first-person approach with the aim of showing rather than telling. The narrator describes the experience of the vulnerable self in its relation to the world and explores what this experience might say about the broader context of the situation (Ellis, 2007, p14). As the autoethnographic scholars Bochner and Ellis write about this strand of research method: 'We simply were acknowledging that researchers live in the world, too' (2016, p50). Our entanglement with the world and our response to this entanglement are important to understand the field we research or work within. So, disentangling is not possible nor desirable. 'Rather than subscribing to an illusion of independent research … we as organizational ethnographers get entangled with the fields that we study' and explores the 'implications this might have for our practices and representations of these fields' (Gosovic, 2019, p66).

A common concern, as I alluded to in the introduction, is about the generalisability of first-person research; many worry that autoethnography can succumb to the pitfall of self-absorbed descriptions of personal experience that lack analytic outcome (Delamont, 2007). Indeed, the quote I presented in the introduction relied primarily on my reactions, and since that narrative was written by me and I was drawing the conclusions subsequently there is reason to question its utility. Further, narrators are specific individuals with histories, intentions, and ideological positions. They have a variety of incentives to present themselves in certain ways in their narratives. They might wish to come across as competent and attractive; there is a little acting in any action, as Scott reminds us (1990, p1). We all put an effort into managing the impression we leave in others which is what the sociologist Goffman coined impression management (1959).

Since narrators are somewhat unreliable on that account, the entanglement of the narrator and the narrated might seem undesirable in a pursuit of generalisable conclusions. Although this is particularly relevant to the study of an experienced need to perform, as I have studied, it is relevant to research and practice of organisational development in general. Impression management is per definition entangled in human relating in general. Wanting to create a good impression is inherent in most human interaction. Managers, employees, and consultants as well as researchers are all under pressure to perform and project an image of themselves as competent and credible as they are submerged in processes of organisational development. So, how can we safeguard reliability and the analytical utility of autoethnography?

Writing in support of analytic autoethnography, Anderson (2006) argues that these kinds of concerns can be mitigated by the researcher being (1) a full member in the research group or setting, (2) visible as such a member in published texts, and (3) committed to developing theoretical understandings of broader social phenomena (Anderson, 2006, p373). The third item on this list points to the importance of reflexivity – of paying attention to how our presence and thinking affects what happens as we engage with the world.

Communities of inquiry

The first item on Anderson's list of safeguards (being a full member in the research group or setting) points to the importance of working with others: autoethnography requires collaboration with others to find resonance, to discuss the ethics of writing about others involved in the events being recounted, and to point to blind spots. Such collaboration can take the form of a community of inquiry (Shields, 2003). A 'community of inquirers' is a pragmatist notion where colleagues contest and resonate with individually experienced local interactions to make links to similar phenomena more broadly in organisations. Knowledge emerges in the back and forth of discussions with colleagues. The resonance from others may be indicative of the generalisability in the work (Shields, 2003, Pardales and Girod, 2006, Martela, 2015).

So, as a community of inquirers interested in exploring rather than solving problems, we contest and resonate with interpretations of the interactions described in narrative accounts. We can explore the broader context of our individual experience, employing the narrative material as empirical data to be explored in dialogue with others and relevant scholarly literature. Inquiry 'never starts from a neutral *tabula rasa* position, but it takes place through the actions of the inquirer that are shaped by his or her particular world-view' (Martela, 2015, p549, italics in original; see also Chauhan on sociality, this volume). To make the most of this community, researchers must be willing to listen to others to take a plurality of views into account and sit in the discomfort of differences of perspective, and movements in self-perception. Through these processes, researchers can produce abductive theories about organisational life that are as good as they can be, if only temporarily: any explanation is provisional and potentially fallible which means that it may be challenged in the future.

Reflexivity

A distinction between reflection and reflexivity is often made, where reflection is 'based on the idea that there is an original reality we can think about and separate ourselves from' (Cunliffe and Jun, 2005, p226). In contrast reflexivity 'calls into question how we know what we know and how we have come to know it … We "bend back" (*re-flectere*) our thinking on itself and on ourselves to call into question our own role in understanding what it is we are trying to understand' (Mowles, 2015, pp60–61, italics in original). Reflexive inquiry allows us to understand our interaction with the world differently, to see and transform organisations and the public discourse and undergo change ourselves in the process. This reflexivity requires detachment as formulated in another book in this series '…reflexivity, which we understand in Elias's terms (1956) as becoming more detached about our daily involvement in the work' (Mowles and Norman, 2022, p198). As we become detached from our own involvement, our possibilities to interpret and understand what we are doing with others increase. This might sound easy. Why wouldn't anyone want to be reflexive and discover new ways to think and act? Particularly as Cunliffe argues that we have an ethical obligation to understand how our words and thinking affect the policies, social realities, and identity of others (2005).

There are several reasons why reflexive inquiry isn't as easy as it might sound. For one, we cannot see what we cannot see. Although we can detach ourselves and take ourselves as an object there is never a completely detached position. We only have our own thinking to do the thinking about ourselves, and this is never in isolation from others. It is always affected by, in relation to, or directed towards others. Therefore, reflexivity is never solely an individual endeavour. Second, it is often destabilising to discover one's habits and patterns of relating. It is often felt as mental unrest and can even be somewhat painful, as Dewey put it (1910, p12). This requires that we dare to look critically at what we and others do. Then we can become ashamed, disappointed, offended, and angry with ourselves and each other. This has existential consequences since we come to examine our own habits, taken-for-granted assumptions, and values (Cunliffe and Jun, 2005, p229). At times, realising the consequences of how our ways of acting might have oppressed or hurt others can be too difficult to deal with identity-wise. The pressure to relieve this frustration can lead us to close further exploration.

> ... conversational processes having transformative potential, by their very nature threaten the continuity of identity... conversations with transformative potential inevitably arouse anxiety at a deep existential level. Such anxiety provokes defenses such as denial ... conversation with transformative potential inevitably threatens current power relations, which are also an important aspect of identity.
>
> (Stacey, 2003, p80)

The last sentence in the quote addresses how reflexive inquiry might have critical and political implications since we explore and engage in surfacing techniques of discipline, power, and norms in organisations (Alvesson and Willmott, 2003, p3). This leads to the third point about how power and privilege are at stake in any reflexive inquiry. Bringing patterns of relating and how they are reproduced into view often challenges power relations; this can have profound effects on people's sense of themselves and might lead to identity struggles.

The quote in the introduction is illustrative here. First-person experiences of mental unrest as mentioned in the quote *can* be self-absorbed, anecdotal, and without broader relevance. However, they can also show relevance beyond the individual experience leading to an understanding of the broader context with a community of inquirers. This requires a careful attention to the experience of emotions because they reflect broader patterns of relating.

Emotional reflexivity

The thoughts and feelings we experience are not solely our own. They are also a reflection of patterns of relating and interacting that social life has left in us as tattoos on our bodies. Individuals are created in and create the social world at the same time. Bourdieu argues that the individual reflects social norms and values and how the social forms our habits and ways of orienting, thinking, feeling, and moving. Habitus reflects the social world we live in. We are entangled in social norms and values, and we can't see them. But we can be reflexive about how and why we act, react, think, and feel as we do. 'It is because subjects do not, strictly speaking, know what they are doing, that what they do has more meaning than they know' (Bourdieu, 1977, p79).

My experience of being rejected for a task as a consultant after a job interview was indicative of a broader pattern of relating involving ideals of success, and an eagerness to perform and impress in certain ways. It also illuminated an intuitive unwillingness to explore why the events unfolded as they did because I felt defeated, weak, and ashamed. It felt like a blow to my sense of what kind of person I was, and I only managed to stay with the uneasiness of the situation and reflexively engage because I was in a researching position where my supervisor and colleagues pushed me to try and understand what happened.

Narrators as emplotted

The description of the felt experience from a first-person perspective is important in understanding what we are doing in organisational life. It is indicative of the norms and expectations towards us, but it also tells us about our own incentives because the narrator is a central part of the narrative and are plots themselves (Ricœur, 1992, p143) – or *emplotted* as Ricœur has coined it (Ricœur, 2005, p100).

> A character is someone who *carries out* the action in the narrative. The category of character is therefore also a narrative category, and its role in the story stems from the same narrative understanding as does the plot itself. The character, we can say, is him- or herself emplotted.
>
> (Ricœur, 2005, p100, italics in original)

Ricœur claims that the character is not distinct from his or her experiences. 'The narrative constructs the identity of the character … It is the identity of the story that makes the identity of the character' (1992, pp147–148). So, every narrative about practice is also a narrative about identity, and it is relevant to elaborate on questions such as: how does the story reflect our identity?; what is important for us as narrators?; and why are we writing what we are writing? This implies a critical reflexive attention not only to what we write as narrators but also to how and why we write the way we do. In fact, the latter questions are key to understanding the politics of organisational life. By continuously writing, discussing, and re-writing, we might develop our thinking about a particular situation. We can become other to ourselves, and the development this creates is of importance to understand the field of study or practice. Since we are emplotted, we must pay careful attention to what we write, how and why we write it, how we react towards our own writing, how others react to what we have written, and how we react to others' reactions. These reactions and experiences might tell us about the broader context of the situation.

We can become aware of this by exploring our reactions and feelings. Emotions are felt in the individual body, but always arise in relationships, where they also express cultural norms and values (Burkitt, 1999, p122). Emotions are at the heart of narratives and the exploration of them. They might be individually felt but our emotional responses are key to paying attention to what we are influenced by and what has value to us and other people. It is relevant and valuable to pay attention to emotions as 'data' or 'information' because they might reveal broader patterns of relating. This is not to suggest that our emotions have an objective character or that they are observable from a detached perspective but only as an offer to allow us to discuss how and why we act and react as we do (Larsen, 2020, p183, Mowles and Norman, 2022, p194).

Again, this is easier said than done because we are emotionally invested in what we do. In my case, presenting myself as competent is at the core of the politics of consultancy because it influences whether one gets jobs or not (Alvesson, 2009, p166). Consultants may wish to appear knowledgeable, trustworthy, ethically aware, or relaxed because it has an impact on the relation, the task, and their sense of self. We have feelings as pride, vanity, disappointment, and shame and experience these as both conscious and unconscious incentives to repress our reactions and move on. In the quote from the introduction where I was rejected for a consultancy task, I felt incompetent, disappointed, and ashamed and my first incentive was to forget the whole matter and move on to the next assignment – not to stay and explore what was going on.

Obviously, I didn't leap from one local experience of mental unrest to these broader arguments. According to Ricœur's *hermeneutics of suspicion*, we need to be curious or even suspicious towards our own and others' motives (Josselson, 2004). We need to be suspicious to allow for alternative interpretations about what is happening. Understanding ourselves 'is inseparable from an exercise of *suspicion*' (Ricœur, 1992, p341, italics in original). Suspicion is not to be understood as judgemental pejorative doubt but as 'attempts to decode meanings that are disguised' (Josselson, 2004, p1). Writing narratives and discussing them with each other can help us to understand how we are emplotted and help us to explore the patterns we engage in. Reflexivity is vital to understand responsibility in one's relation to others 'and helps an individual to move beyond the routine and habitual act, to see how to act with intention, will, and moral responsibility' (Cunliffe and Jun, 2005, p239). This means that reflexively engaging with our own practice allows us to develop a critical attention to what we do, why we do it, and how this attention might change who we are. Since we are emplotted in what we write we must be curious about our motives to *what*, *how*, and *why* we write.

Narrative identity

This brings a strong focus on the identity of the narrator as central to research and practice. Ricœur offers the term 'narrative identity' to understand identity as the dialectic between sameness and otherness (1992, p140, 2005, p91). *Sameness* is about character and keeping one's word as the permanence in time in one's sense of self (Ricœur, 2005, pp117–118). 'Character, I would say today, designates the set of lasting dispositions by which a person is recognized' (Ricœur, 2005, p121). Further, to be responsible as an individual means to account for oneself as the same self over time.

> Self-constancy is for each person that manner of conducting himself or herself so that others can *count on* that person. Because someone is counting on me, I am *accountable for* my actions before another. The term "responsibility" unites both meanings: "counting on" and "being accountable for".
>
> (Ricœur, 1992, p165, italics in original)

We are responsible to be the same so that others can count on us (Ricœur, 1992, p165). But we are also, paradoxically, responsible to change at the same time. This relates to *otherness*. Because when we recognise others and take them seriously as individuals, we will inevitably change. In other words, other people interrupt our sense of sameness, which might lead to a loss of identity (Ricœur, 1992, p149–150). However, otherness does not only concern other people; it also concerns our own body (Ricœur, 1992, p319). By this Ricœur means that our body is not our possession. We are thrown into the world that was already there, and we are only gradually 'being delivered over to oneself' (Ricœur, 1992, p327). We are obliged to recognise ourselves as another and reflexively investigate what we are subjected to and thereby who we are (Ricœur, 2005, pp91–92).

We should allow ourselves to be surprised about what we find ourselves doing and rather than denying our experience we should explore why we are doing what we do. Identity is paradoxical because it is something we are and yet, at the same time, we continuously change and are thereby other to ourselves. The self is an ongoing narrative formation with others involving obligations to others as well as to ourselves. Ideally, autoethnographical narrative accounts should both create and reveal this movement. Narrating oneself as another is not simply an instrumental exercise where we take ourselves as an object. It is discovering and revealing ourselves with and through others. Like anthropology: 'It changes the lives of everyone involved' (Ingold, 2018 in Crewe and Walker, 2020, p199).

Implications to organisational development research and practice

As a practical example about method, curiosity made me return with my account of events, to people who have appeared in my narratives, to hear what sense they have made of events and my account. It relates to my theme of affirmation and impressing others because a reflexive approach to impression management requires an attempt to explore rather than seeking affirmation. I hadn't intended to share my thoughts with participants as a research design, but it developed as a method in my doctoral thesis which has influenced my practice as a consultant where I also share my convictions and experiences to a larger degree than earlier. In my own experience, I sat with my feet in the fire and faced up to what I found difficult to face up to. Having noticed that I may not have done everything right in my first interactions, I came back to it again and again until I had made better sense of it for myself and for my clients, and for my researching colleagues. Autoethnography as well as consulting in processes of organisational development is about sticking with the experience, coming back to it, practicing again, reading, writing, reflecting, and practicing again to understand what is going on together.

I have taken these ideas seriously in my practice as a consultant with development of institutions for children with special needs. Because to develop one's practice as a pedagogue also requires a critical reflexive attention to what one does, why one is doing it, and an openness towards how this might change one's thinking about oneself in processes of organisational development.

Narrating oneself as another in pedagogical work with children

I have taken ideas from my autoethnographical research to my work as a consultant in the public sector where I work to develop pedagogy with children with special needs. I have let the autoethnographically inspired narrative approach bleed into my work by inviting both management and employees to write their everyday practice down whereafter we read, discuss, re-write, and publish their experiences for a broader audience of practitioners.

In the specific development process, the participants' initial incentive was to write glossy narratives about how they successfully overcame difficult situations. However, as we grew to know each other they got into writing more nuanced narratives about their experiences to understand the emotional entanglement in their everyday work life. We have not tried to paint idyllic pictures of our practice or of ourselves. We have striven to create a book with greater honesty than usual, because we believe that it can break down taboos that prevent difficult but necessary reflections on special education practice. This vulnerability allows for important discussions about the field's challenges rather than idealised theoretical and methodological points that involuntarily can make practitioners in the field feel incompetent, because reality is far more complex and difficult. It is important to understand how the incentive to write and present successful stories for each other reflects a typical pattern in the field which is a significant hindrance for a reflexive practice in the work with children with special needs.

In the specific work in a home for children with special needs, I have practiced this approach in meetings with staff for more than a year to reflexively inquire into their work with them. Their practice as staff consists of providing a home and a childhood for children with attachment disorders to develop as human beings (Larsen, 2022). It is emotionally charged work because the children's difficulties are often transferred or mirrored within the staff, leading staff to contain and handle feelings of incompetence, powerlessness, disappointment, and shame.

In one example, a group of pedagogues shamefully admitted how no-one intuitively liked a particular boy. However, writing about this experience of shame led them to explore their antipathy for the child and work to change this. In another example, a pedagogue voiced his shameful feelings of aggression towards a child whom he had saved from a conflict and who in return had spat on and hit him. The development process involved that they wrote narratives, discussed, and rewrote them while making new sense of their work and themselves in the process. As their consultant, I was a critical supervisor rather than an expert on pedagogy. Their experiences are included in a book containing their endeavours and new insights to the field (Larsen, 2022). The book is a compilation of what we have done and developed during the process. Writing and publishing these narratives led to conversations about feelings of powerlessness, and an ability to use their reactions, thoughts, and feelings to understand what was going on relationally. It allowed them to understand and help themselves and their colleagues to understand the feelings they had and feel empathy for both children. The narratives legitimised reflections and conversations about 'forbidden' feelings in their field which in turn led them to help the children in better ways. However, acknowledging these feelings called for intense identity-work. Because the ideal pedagogue is often characterised as an autonomous stoic character absorbing whatever is thrown at them with calmness and understanding.

The process resulted in conversations about powerlessness, despair, feelings of incompetence, and their reactions of cynicism and self-blame to cope with these feelings. It created a space to deal with these experiences as a group rather than as individuals, which was a relief for the staff. Further, pedagogues in other institutions have read the narratives, which has started important conversations in the field more broadly.[1] This illustrates how sharing personal accounts as narratives offers ways to reflexively engage in the emotional dimensions of the experience. '… the art of storytelling is the art of exchanging *experiences*' (Ricœur, 1992, p164, italics in original).

Working in this way requires continual relational work where managers and groups of employees have regular meetings with the consultant to build trust as they engage with difficult issues and the inevitable identity-work in processes of organisational development processes. This can involve several years of work with organisations, dealing with emotionally difficult issues without providing easy answers. The negotiations that enable this kind of work in organisations are not always easy.

Concluding remarks

I have described how we can become more detached from our habitual 'plot' through processes of writing about experience, paying attention to emotions, thinking about how these are aspects of wider patterns, thinking about how they reveal us to ourselves, and testing our emerging insights through collaboration. These are all aspects of writing autoethnographically using narrative accounts of breakdowns, through which we can start to see ourselves as another. I hope that this will help researchers and practitioners to move away from decontextualised approaches to theory based on abstract ideas about what one should do, and on to a more engaged practice-based discussion of values recognising organisational members as reflexive humans as they make ethical choices in their practice. Writing about oneself as another has the potential to engage others emotionally, reflexively, and ethically. When we manage to explore situations through the lens of norms, values, and pedagogy, we are getting less caught up in impressing each other and more concerned about ethics.

> Self-reflexivity is about becoming a self-conscious and self-questioning being … this means questioning our own assumptions and writing from the first person rather than the objective (reflective) third person. It means complexifying rather than simplifying, questioning rather than answering or accepting, looking for paradoxes and contradictions rather than order and patterns, recognizing multiple perspectives rather than

imposing our worldview, thinking about what lies unsaid as well as what is said.

(Cunliffe and Jun, 2005, p237)

I have claimed that writing about one's practice – narrating oneself as another – allows for a reflexive engagement with who we are. Therefore, it is obvious to take a reflexive turn and ask whether and how my writing of this chapter has led to reflexive changes. Have I changed from writing this chapter? My answer is both yes and no, as the spirit of Ricœur would describe. I have certainly enjoyed re-engaging with previous thinking about autoethnography and reflexivity. I have even met and discussed the work with old colleagues from the university where I encountered this approach to research, and I have thought about the period and my insights with joy. It has been a useful reminder and has revived my insistence on creating spaces to think about power and identity in organisations and to bring these ideas into conversations in my work. Further, writing about my work with the development for children with special needs has led me to sharpen my arguments about what I am actually doing in my everyday work. It might look well-ordered and neatly planned as it is presented here. But this is, as it goes for all narrative accounts, only due to the work and re-work I have done prior to this version.

First-person narratives are an analytical resource allowing us to draw more general conclusions about what goes on relationally as well as sociologically. So, when we want to perform, when we work too much, when we feel stressed, disappointed, ashamed, or incompetent, we are also encountering cultural norms. We can feel insignificant and very small when it dawns on us how we are also simply carriers of the cultural patterns that we happen to find ourselves in. At the same time, it can be a relief if we can accept that, although we have a moral responsibility to act, we are also carriers and not the only source of the patterns we experience. If we can find ways to reflect together on our experiences and identify the stories we participate in, we increase the possibilities from which we can choose our next steps.

Note

1 For example, in a podcast where I and two pedagogues were interviewed by a pedagogical union as a contribution to a broader debate about pedagogy.

References

Alvesson, M. (2009). At-Home Ethnography: Struggling with Closeness and Closure. In S. Ybema, D. Yanow, H. Wels, F. Kamsteeg, and M. Alvesson (Eds.), *Organizational Ethnography: Studying the Complexities of Everyday Life*. London: SAGE Publications Ltd, pp. 156–174.

Alvesson, M., and Skoldberg, K. (2018). *Reflexive Methodolcgy*, 3rd ed. London: SAGE Publications Ltd.

Alvesson, M., and Willmott, H. (2003). *Studying Management Critically. Studying Management Critically*. London: Sage Publications Ltd.

Anderson, L. (2006). Analytic Autoethnography. *Journal of Contemporary Ethnography*, *35*(4), 373–395.

Bochner, A., and Ellis, C. (2016). *Evocative Autoethnography*. New York: Routledge.

Bourdieu, P. (1977). *Outline of a Theory of Practice*. Cambridge: Cambridge University Press.

Bourdieu, P., and Wacquant, L. J. D. (1992). *An Invitation to Reflexive Sociology*. Cambridge: Polity.

Brinkmann, S. (2012). *Qualitative Inquiry in Everyday Life – Working with Everyday Life Materials*. London: Sage Publications Ltd.

Burkitt, I. (1999). *Bodies of Thought*. London: Sage publications.

Clancy, A., Vince, R., and Gabriel, Y. (2012). That Unwanted Feeling: A Psychodynamic Study of Disappointment in Organizations. *British Journal of Management*, *23*(4), 518–531.

Crewe, E., and Walker, A. (2020). *An Extraordinary Scandal: The Westminster Expenses Crisis and Why It Still Matters*. London: Haus Publishing.

Cunliffe, A. L., and Jun, J. S. (2005). The Need for Reflexivity in Public Administration. *Administration & Society*, *37*(2), 225–242.

Delamont, S. (2007). Arguments against Auto-Ethnography. *Qualitative Researcher*, *4*(1), 2–4.

Dewey, J. (1910). *How We Think*. Boston, MA: D.C.Heath & Co.

Elias, N. (1956). Problems of involvement and detachment, *British Journal of Sociology*, *7*, 226–252. (*Involvement and Detachment*. Dublin: UCD Press, 2007 [Collected Works, vol. 8], pp. 68–104).

Ellis, C. (2007). Telling Secrets, Revealing Lives: Relational Ethics in Research with Intimate Others. *Qualitative Inquiry*, *13*(1), 3–29.

Gherardi, S. (2017). Unplugged – "Carte blanche." *Management (France)*, *20*(2), 208–220.

Goffman, E. (1959). *The Presentation of Self in Everyday Life*. New York: Anchor Books.

Gosovic, A. K. J. (2019). Gifts, Reciprocity and Ethically Sound Ethnographic Research: A Reflexive Framework. *Journal of Organizational Ethnography*, 9(1), 66–79.

Honneth, A. (2000). *Suffering from Indeterminacy. An Attempt at a Reactualization of Hegel's Philosophy of Right*. Assen: Van Gorcum & Comp.

Josselson, R. (2004). The Hermeneutics of Faith and the Hermeneutics of Suspicion. *Narrative Inquiry*, 14(1), 1–28.

Larsen, S. (2020). *Are you impressed? An exploration of the pressure to perform and impress from the perspective of an organisational development consultant*. Doctoral Thesis University of Hertfordshire.

Larsen, S. (2022). *Low Arousal og veje ud af afmagt*. København: Self-published. http://www.raison.dk/wp-content/uploads/2023/02/Magnoliegaarden-Laeringsbog-Final.pdf

Martela, F. (2015). Fallible Inquiry with Ethical Ends-in-View: A Pragmatist Philosophy of Science for Organizational Research. *Organization Studies*, 36(4), 537–563.

Mowles, C. (2015). *Managing in Uncertainty: Complexity and the Paradoxes of Everyday Organizational Life*. London: Routledge.

Mowles, C., and Norman, K. (2022). *Complexity and the Public Sector*. London: Taylor & Francis.

Pardales, M. J., and Girod, M. (2006). Community of Inquiry: Its Past and Present Future. *Educational Philosophy and Theory*, 38(3), 299–309.

Ricœur, P. (1992). *Oneself as Another*. Chicago, IL: The University of Chicago Press.

Ricœur, P. (2005). *The Course of Recognition*. Cambridge, MA: Harvard University Press.

Scott, J. C. (1990). *Domination and the Arts of Resistance: Hidden Transcripts*. London: Yale University Press.

Shields, P. M. (2003). The Community of Inquiry: Classical Pragmatism and Public Administration. *Administration and Society*, 35(5), 510–538.

Stacey, R. D. (2003). *Complexity and Group Processes: A Radically Social Understanding of Individuals*. Oxfordshire: Routledge.

Wetherell, M. (2012). *Affect and Emotion*. London: Sage publications.

4

DIFFRACTION AND THE MOBILISATION OF CROSS-CULTURAL IDENTITIES IN PRACTICE RESEARCH

SOPHIE WONG

Introduction

Habitus – culture and identity

I have been involved with non-governmental organisations (NGOs) in the mental health/social welfare sector as a volunteer counsellor and fund raiser for some decades now. I am drawn to NGOs within these sectors in part because I have a personal connection with mental illness and displacement, but it was also my wish to give back to the community of my adopted country. I immigrated from Hong Kong to Australia in my early teens.

I had been recruited to join the board of a Neuroscience Research Institute in order to help with fund-raising. It was the institute's poor relationships with their donors which led my research into reciprocity. In fact, reciprocity and gift-giving have always been subjects of interest since being exposed to the western Australian culture, I find it very different to

DOI: 10.4324/9781003410522-5

east Asian culture. As a child growing up in Hong Kong, I had learnt the importance of gratitude in giving and receiving. As a young adult, I was living in Japan as an exchange student and subsequently doing business in mainland China. I became acutely aware of the etiquette of the gift-giving culture. It is in part about staying in relation, but I have also come to find that the sense of reciprocity is far more complex, particularly in the business/social network arena. Here, it is frequently disguised as a power play to gain dominance/accumulate capital through the accruals of *renqing*: a Chinese term to depict the etiquette of reciprocity through the exchange of gifts and favours. Another subject matter closely linked to reciprocity is the Chinese notion of *face*. In its simplest terms, it is about identity, a presentation and preservation of an image of ourselves we choose to identify with, and how we want to be perceived. The notion of *face* and reciprocity seem less important in Australian/western culture.

I was prompted into thinking about this just the other night when something happened which might seem quite trivial: my daughter coming home from a first date with a man whom she had met on Hinge, the latest online dating app. I dared to ask her how her date went. 'What a complete waste of time that was'. She went on, describing the evening, I was sympathetic; I was also quietly amused. Fortunately for me, the timing of her sharing was perfect. Her reaction to this event captured precisely the collision of cultures I wish to explore in this chapter. Before I share my daughter's date night so publicly (with her blessing!), I wish to explain my reasons why I chose this particular event to introduce my chapter.

My daughter's instant dislike of someone prompted the following questions for me: How do culture and identity influence what's going on? What function might culture be serving? What is at play? How do we, as social researchers, sharpen our investigation by attending to the relational nature of difference: neither dismissing the kind of difference as inconsequential nor accepting it in an absolute sense?

Another reason for including my daughter is to provide a perspective on who I am – my *habitus*. You may ask why it is important to know about me and what knowing me has to do with the research method this book is about. My assumption is that the self is thoroughly social. We are who we are because of the groups we belong to, for reasons of survival. We learn and we accept, we inhale the culture/habitus of the groups we join.

Our socially acquired dispositions and prejudices serve a particular function: to preserve the history and figurations of power relationships of our group/s. As an example, French philosopher/historian Foucault researched into how mental health patients are dealt with and silenced. He shed light on the disciplining effects of power through processes of normalisation, containment and control. In an interview, Foucault stated: 'in a society like our own – the games are numerous, and desire to control the conduct of others is all the greater – as we see in family relationships, for example, emotions and sexual relationships' (1994 edited by Rabinow, p300).

Both Bourdieu and Elias refer to the power relations of our group as *habitus*. This means our habitual ways of responding to each other have the quality of a pattern. We form this pattern, and we are formed by it, both at the same time. The culture or habitus of the groups we belong to also determines to a degree the way we are perceived and treated by others. Culture is influential in shaping our sense of identity: 'it is the source of our emotional response to the values that belong to us as a member of that community' (Mead, 1934, p199). Through these values, we gain our deepest sense of identity within a given culture. When we find ourselves a member of one culture, co-present with another more dominant culture, we are likely to find ourselves adjusting to the community to which we want to belong. As a mixed Chinese living in Australia, I noticed my desire for inclusion as a first-time board member of the Neuroscience Institute was not too different from my younger years trying to belong in an Australian school. I was eager to perform, contribute and assimilate. In the former case, fitting in required my ability to raise funds, with the latter, performing well academically would have the opposite effect: I would have been at risk for being further marginalised socially because being good at school wasn't valued by my peers.

We may think of cultures as coherent wholes, each with its distinctive integrity that distinguishes it from other cultures. But cultures are complex, changing and dynamic rather than deterministic (Bernstein, 2016, p63). I argue that we need to pay attention to this dynamic intersection of cultures. Doing this can be helpful in researching what's going on in organisations and society at large. Using diffractive methodology, in Barad's (2007) term, is about being actively engaged with the material, taking accountability 'to marks on bodies' and responsibility for the entanglement of which we are a part which I explore further in this chapter. Before continuing, I would like briefly to define what diffraction is and what it means in a social context.

Diffraction

Diffractive methodology is founded in the scholarship of the contemporary feminist science scholar Donna Haraway. In classical physics, diffraction is a pattern unique to waves' behaviour – be it water, sound or light – in the way they bend and spread out when they encounter an obstruction. A good example of wave patterns occurs when stones are thrown into a pond and the ripples overlap. Haraway employed diffraction figuratively to denote a practice of consciousness-raising to the relationality of differences. Her large body of work traverses disciplines as she examines the boundaries of science, technology, nature, culture, and human/non-human being; she describes diffraction as a mapping of interference. For Haraway, 'a diffraction pattern does not map where difference appears, but rather maps where the effects of difference appear' (Haraway, 1992, p70). In her view: 'the first invites the illusion of essential, fixed position, while the second trains us for more subtle vision'. Diffraction here is contrasted to her critique of reflection or reflexivity: such a practice 'only displaces the same elsewhere' and creates oppositional distinctions. In her view, diffraction is about making a difference in the world by making visible the patterns of interference in our everyday lives. This brings us to a central aspect of Karen Barad's work on entanglement.

Barad, a theoretical physicist who took inspiration from Haraway, was particularly interested in calling into question notions of identity, agency, objectivity, embodiment and causality. Barad (2007) uses the term diffraction with a particular emphasis from quantum theory in thinking about entanglements and differences that matter. Diffraction, understood from this perspective, is not just a matter of interference but of entanglement. This underlines her position that 'knowing' is a direct material engagement: that there is no separating of subject and object but rather entanglement of subject and object.

In the context of social inquiry, diffractive analysis is 'a practice of reading insights through one another, paying attention to the relational nature and specificities of difference and how they matter' (Barad, 2007, p71). Barad also took inspiration from physicist Niels Bohr who saw philosophy as inseparable from and an integral part of physics, specifically the relation to quantum physics and the nature of knowledge and reality. In Bohr's view, the practice of science without philosophical understanding is meaningless (Barad, 2007, p68). Barad parallels his proposition by adding 'Ethics is about mattering, about taking account of the entangled materializations of which we are a part, including new configurations, new subjectivities, new possibilities' (Barad, 2007, p394). Barad's idea of entanglements has urged me to become more vigilant in the role I play in research and in my practice.

Intersections of cultures

With my daughter's permission, I now share her account of the event. I am paying particular attention to her struggle with *face* (how she wants to be perceived) and power (not wanting to walk away owing). I noticed my daughter was not only clashing cultures with her Anglo-Saxon date but was also conflicted by her own mixed Chinese and Australian identity.

> (Met up at a restaurant bar after work)
>
> When I sat down, he offered to buy the first drink. We started talking about what we do for work. In fact, he didn't stop talking about his job. My glass had been empty for about twenty minutes, but he didn't notice or chose not to. I was tempted to leave but didn't want to be rude. I felt obliged to wait until he had finished his drink. I also thought I needed to shout him one: I didn't want to owe him.
>
> When I did finally get a word in, I asked if he'd like another beer, and if he would like to share some chips. I was feeling hungry: I didn't want to have two drinks on an empty stomach.
>
> 'That would be lovely,' he said. (*She mimicked with a mock sneer*).
>
> He made himself appear superior while he was eating my chips! I don't get it, Mum. Why would anyone insist on meeting in the evening with no intention of having dinner. Every table around us had food

My daughter became very animated when she shared her adventures, and at that point I couldn't help but laugh. My daughter is Australian born Chinese. Growing up in Australia means negotiating between her western values and the Chinese identity of her parents. To put things in broad terms, the Australian way of life values individuality: Chinese customs value the institution/group/family before personal freedom. Raising my family in Australia has meant an opportunity, particularly for my daughter, to break away from the values and standards imposed upon me in my upbringing as a woman of Chinese descent.

My daughter is not the typical Chinese girl of my generation. She can be feisty and outspoken. Instead of continuing with her violin lessons to please her grandparents, she became a surfer. She plays touch football. I imagine my daughter's strong Australian accent is another way of over-compensating for her migrant family identity. Just like I did in choosing to be more Chinese being a 'mixed breed' – a term I grew up with in Hong Kong. At the same time, people such as my husband who is pure Chinese have clung on to 'Britishness' of the frozen colonial kind more fiercely and rigidly. My daughter's competitiveness with boys, with her brother and her father, is a breaking away from the tradition of a patriarchal culture.

Another intersection of cultures is between my daughter and me. In my generation, introductions from trusted friends and relatives were common. They were a safe way to meet prospective partners. While it still came down to the individual to see if there was an attraction to someone, the evaluation of individuals and of their character and background was often shared and known. These days, dating apps make it difficult to know what to expect. Eva Illouz's (2012) scholarly work involves exploring the changes that modernity has made to our intimate relationships, and how they have become individualised: 'Attractiveness is based on rapid judgements of strangers in short interactions' (Illouz, 2012, p50). The need to impress or to compete for identity, love and power seems a far more brutal process in modern times and across cultural differences.

My intention, however, is not to examine a young couple's romantic involvement but to relate my daughter's narrative to my research on gift-giving theories and philanthropy. What interests me in my daughter's exchanges with a potential partner is the introductory engagement. Introductions still play a major role in the business/social networking arena with which I am most familiar. Wealthy individual donors (HNWIs – *high-net-worth individuals*) are often introduced by board members who are fund-raising for the institutions. Much like the matchmakers in Jane Austen's novels, the task of introducing is to enable the development of intimate relationships over time, striving to mitigate any party's potential loss of face and concealing the truths of rejections or of a mismatch.

The second insight I gained from my daughter's narrative is the struggle over power in the way she agonised over reciprocation. It made me think about HNWI donors and the power position they hold in giving gifts. The choice of timing to reciprocate can have particular meanings. In my daughter's case, it was her struggle, or her competing, for a power position. Bourdieu points out in his theory of gift-giving after observing the Kabyle people in Algeria that manipulating the pace of action can also be an instrument of power (Bourdieu, 1990, p106).

In the case study I provide below, I let you be the judge: what meaning did it hold for the institution, in its choice of timing, to reciprocate to my Chinese donor?

The Case

I draw on my experience of joining an Anglo-Saxon board of a Neuroscience Research Institute in Australia. The experience of becoming a new trustee, being the only Chinese female on a male-dominated board, had particular qualities for me as a settled immigrant to Australia. I was eager to perform well. My specific responsibility was to attract HNWI donors. During this process, I noticed how instrumentally donors were treated. I also noticed what this provoked in HNWI donors themselves. Themes of identity and power become more amplified in a charitable organisation as the needs of the individual being drawn to 'give' are put front and centre. The withdrawal of attention/love/recognition after a gift has been solicited does not necessarily discourage someone from donating more. At the same time, the opportunity to assert one's power position can also become transparent. I found myself in the role of a translator: not only mediating *face* between the institute and Chinese donors but also mediating the insecurity which such exchanges inevitably provoke.

A Chinese donor, through my introduction, made a substantial donation at an event held at the research institute. The institute's CEO expressed the opinion that, whatever it might be, the initial gift donation reveals an individual's capacity to donate by tenfold. It was not surprising, based on that assumption, and in their eagerness to pursue her, that they presented my donor with a further research proposal of A$3M[1] – it was a surprise, however, that they did so without my knowledge. They then assumed that a way of reciprocating her generosity was to propose to her that they would acknowledge her gift donation publicly at the next annual gala event. It was also anticipated that the announcement of her gift donation on the evening would rally other potential donors to follow suit. But I discovered that the proposal they made to her had caused great offence. I was asked by the fundraising team of the institute to intervene as she had not been returning their calls.

I was baffled by their approach in soliciting donations. I had wondered what kind of game they thought they were playing. I imagine the CEO and his team were equally frustrated with my donor and me for not sharing the same enthusiasm about what they were proposing. To try to make sense of it, I began looking into gift-giving and reciprocity in various traditions.

Below are my findings from diffracting Chinese texts with western sociological/critical thinkers. Reading and thinking diffractively is essentially about engaging in a conversation with theorists; being attentive without uncritically or unconditionally accepting of one disciplinary approach over another, but holding the various texts simultaneously to see what comes to light.

Gift theory

In trying to understand why there was a mismatch in expectations between the research institute and my Chinese donor, I begin with the work of Marcel Mauss, and his most influential work on reciprocity. *The Gift* (1922/1990) begins by describing the native North American potlatch (in essence: to feed and to consume) as an extreme form of a total system of giving that is found in every region of the world. He describes the rendering of 'total services', how gift exchanges are not merely material obligations but carry an emotional component added to the motives of reciprocity. Mauss' observations capture the commonality I share with my Chinese donor who is also a long-term friend of the family.

The emotional aspect Mauss draws attention to is very much imbued in children as a part of Chinese cultural upbringing. The positive emotions induced by reciprocity through *renqing* (informal social obligation) are one way of cultivating *ganqing* (sentiment or feelings of emotional attachment). Chen and Chen (2004, p314) explain the difference: *Renqing* is built up through the exchange of gifts for events such as marriages, birthdays and funerals. It emphasises the sense of obligation owed to each other. *Ganqing* literally means 'feel affection' and is an important concept in social relations rooted in Confucianism. The two concepts put against each other denote a complicated social relationship in the Chinese culture and often convey how deeply people are affected by reciprocity as a moral process.

Mauss captures the many facets of the gift exchange that also depicts the nature of Chinese cultural practices. He writes:

> ... such exchanges are acts of politeness: banquets, rituals, military services, women, children, dances, festivals, and fairs, in which economic transaction is only one element, in which the passing on of wealth is only one feature of a much more general and enduring contract. Finally, these total services and counter-services are committed to in a somewhat voluntary form by presents and gifts; although in the final analysis they are strictly compulsory, on pain of private and public warfare.
>
> (1990, p7)

In this description, Mauss is referring to the cultural etiquette of belonging to a particular group, clan or tribe. It inevitably entails adherence to the 'norm' as the pain of violating would succumb to some form of private or public humiliation. These culturally compulsory practices of reciprocity disguised as voluntary are, in fact, heavily laden with moral judgement.

Through his exposition of the forms of potlatch across that region, Mauss identified the three major themes which he claims are universal: the obligation to give, to receive and to reciprocate. He also identified the temporal aspect as an important element in the art of gift-giving where immediate reciprocity can be interpreted as a rejection of the gift-giver. In his *Outline of a Theory of Practice* (1977), and in response to Mauss, Bourdieu's treatment of the gift theory also emphasised the separation in time of successive gift-giving, so that each individual gift appears to be an isolated act of generosity.

When my colleagues at the institute offered to acknowledge her donation publicly on the evening, they made an assumption that it would be an incentive to entice my Chinese donor to give more. This act of immediate reciprocity caused great offence because something that was meant to remain hidden was made visible. The operation of gift exchange, Bourdieu writes, 'presupposes (individual and collective) misrecognition of the reality of the objective 'mechanism', of the exchange, a reality that an immediate response brutally exposes'. But he goes on:

> If the system is to work, the agents must not be entirely unaware of the truth of their exchanges, which is made explicit.... while at the same time they must refuse to know and above all to recognize it. In short, everything takes place as if agents' practice, and in particular manipulation of time, were organized exclusively with a view to concealing from themselves and from others the truth of their practice....
>
> (Bourdieu, 1977, p6)

The implicit aspect of the social game Bourdieu elucidates here in the unspoken rules of concealing the truth is precisely how Chinese relationships are sustained. Personal wishes and desires are never to be expressed or exposed even if it is blindingly obvious. This brings me to the concept of *face* – the most important intangible gift exchange in the Chinese culture.

Face-work

Through inquiring into Mauss' work, I discovered *face* as fundamentally important not only in Chinese culture but also in North America and other regions of the world. I began examining my own cultural practice drawing on the work of Goffman.

In *On Face-Work* (1967), Goffman, drawing on Smith[2] (1894), accords the Chinese *face* as a mask that they wear and refers to a 'line' as something that someone 'tends to act out', the role he is assumed to have taken on for himself, delineated in terms of approved social attributes (Goffman, 1967, p11). I think there are similarities between Goffman's idea of face-work and George Herbert Mead's (1934) theory of the self, concerning the paradox of the 'I' and the 'me'. It is by taking the generalised attitudes of others to ourselves that we find ourselves adjusting to social expectations. We mutually adapt in this co-operative process within the community to which we belong.

Goffman's consideration of 'micro-sociology' proposed that every member within a social circle would have some knowledge of face-work and some experience in its use. In an Anglo-American society, this kind of capacity is more commonly understood as tact, *savoir-faire*, diplomacy or social skill. Tacit cooperation, as coined by Goffman, arises naturally when each participant in an undertaking is concerned with saving his own face and the face of others. I was convinced at the time that my Anglo colleagues at the research institute would have had very little understanding of this complex game of *face* in which my Chinese donors and I were engaged.

Holcombe (1895, cited in Goffman, 1967, p29) summarises Chinese culture quite neatly. He writes in *The Real Chinaman*:

> Much of the falsehood to which the Chinese as a nation are said to be addicted is a result of the demands of etiquette. A plain, frank 'no' is at the height of discourtesy. Refusal or denial of any sort must be softened and toned down into an expression of regretted inability.

Similarly in *The Chinese* (1836, cited in Andre, 2013), Davis discussed the manners and customs of Chinese people. Analogous to the ethnographic work of Mauss, Davis recounted the niceties of gift-giving; the courtesies involved in 'excessive' politeness at Chinese banquets. He described how the Chinese would consider it rude to refuse a request directly and would, therefore, lie. Perhaps a point worth noting is that Chinese culture was popularised by western commentators written during a time the Chinese (Hong Kong and Macau) were channelling trade between other western British colonial territories in the 1800s. Although I find Davis's depiction of Chinese as liars somewhat condescending,[3] his comment has evoked in me the ineffable aspect of *face* as I think about my own agonising discomfort in rejecting someone. I appreciated the shocked surprise my donor would have felt when she received the A$3M proposal from the institute. Reflecting on the imposition placed upon my donor at the time, my presence constrained (and enabled) her in the way she behaved towards them. She could have rejected them outright but instead, she avoided their calls, she might have had concerns as to how it would affect our relationship or how I would interpret or judge her – I discuss this further below.

Meanwhile, in encounters with people whom we will not have dealings with again, where we have no intention of staying in relations, Goffman (1967, p7) claims that we have more freedom to act 'cut of line' without the fear of being judged. For example, my donor would have more freedom to turn them down as they would have had little importance for her. But Goffman (1967, p12) went on to describe something about power relations 'She may also be preserving an image of herself, be it of pride or honour, or of the power her presumed status allows her to exert over them' (Goffman, 1967, p12). I believe this might be what was going on for my daughter (as well as my donor): trying to preserve an image of herself – an identity she identifies with – overrules the freedom to act out of line even though she may not have any intention to remain in relationship.

Interim summary

I have explored the Chinese concept of reciprocity through Mauss' anthropological examination of gift-giving, and Bourdieu's treatment of reciprocity. I have used Goffman's facework to illuminate the implicit aspects of communication my donor and I shared as a result of our culture, gender and disposition. The reading of Goffman and Bourdieu provided further insight into how we were all caught up in and by the game of power and status recognition. By diffracting the Chinese concept of *face* and reciprocity through various traditions, one can better appreciate the universal nature of gift-giving, not only as ways to stay in relations but also showing the entangled nature of power relations of which we all participate in our cultural practice/habitus (to be further discussed). It demonstrates all cultures may share similar struggles of interdependent processes of competition and cooperation.

This brings me to another complex relational concept of *guanxi* – the motivations behind the gift culture. Before introducing it, I would like to offer a brief overview of the social matrix of relationships and connections that dominate Chinese culture by shedding light on the type of relationship I share with my donor as a generalisable phenomenon and not one unique to this narrative. I turn to Chinese texts as a contrast from western thinkers.

Entanglement of Chinese relationships

Chinese has a phrase: *li shang wanglai*. It is taken from the *Analects* of Confucius: 'for the sake of propriety/etiquette (*li or li yi*), people must engage in social intercourse (*wanglai*)- or giving and repaying is the thing to be attended to'. Although it relates to etiquette and propriety, in The *Book of Rites* (Li Yi, a book by Confucius), this teaching applies to every aspect of social life (Chang, 2016, p106). Chinese society is defined by relations and obligations to our primary relationships because our obligations extend from family to society (Bian, 2006). To this day children in Chinese families are taught to address friends/acquaintances of parents as Uncle and Aunt. The Chinese underline the importance of this interrelatedness by extending their relations beyond their families, constructing pseudo families with outsiders.

If I were to interpret the above Chinese phrase, *li shang wanglai*, and add to it other similar injunctions, my translation would be this: in order for one to be included and accepted in the community upon which one is dependent, one must learn a correct way of being, that is, to attend to relationships with a sense of duty, obligations, humility and generosity. This is achieved by giving and repaying with abundance and, most of all, by showing gratitude and respect for position (knowing one's place). Furthermore, having a firm grasp of li (propriety and etiquette) brings prestige and honour, or what Bourdieu (1986) might refer to as a form of cultural capital, to one's own family, which can then be refined and cultivated amongst one's community. This mirrors the solidarity and social order that Mauss advocates.

By making the character of Chinese culture more explicit, I am drawing attention to the compulsory practices of what it takes to be part of a group. The norms of interpersonal behaviour/etiquette of reciprocity are necessary to ensure one's survival (Mauss, 1990) in Chinese culture. But I am also making a parallel with the negotiation I have been going through in order to become a member of the institute board. In my interactions with the board and my dealings with the CEO and his team, I have been trying to understand what is required of me to belong and how I might contribute.

Guanxi – manufactured reciprocal obligation

With this understanding of ritual propriety which dominates Chinese culture in the history of time, I now contrast the modernised version of reciprocity – *guanxi* with Bourdieu's notion of capital and fields. I would like to unravel another layer of structure in examining the game in which my donor and I were caught up.

In recent times, *li shang wanlai* (for the sake of propriety, giving and repaying is the thing to be attended to), the phrase previously described, and which is grounded in moral conduct, is rarely heard; it has been replaced by *guanxi*, specifically, a Chinese idiom for social networks. It often relates to the reproduction of power and the everyday practice of Chinese social relationships (Zhai, 2005). Chinese philosopher, Liang (1893–1988, cited in King, 1985, p63) argued that Chinese society is neither an individually based nor group-based, but relation-based. The focus is not fixed on any individual, but on the particular nature of the relations:

> Chinese guanxi building can be characterised as ego-centred social engineering of relational building ...based on shared "attributes" such as kinship, locality, surname, and so on, which are the building blocks the individual employs to establish "pluralistic" identifications with multiple individuals and groups.
>
> (King, 1991, p79)

This reliance on social relations, the embeddedness and the notion that Chinese people have a natural tendency to manufacture reciprocal obligation is fundamental to Chinese culture (Bian, 1994). The art and etiquette of *guanxi* rests implicitly (rather than explicitly) on mutual interest and benefit. Once *guanxi* is recognised between two people, each can ask or offer a favour with the obligation or expectation of a return of the favour sometime in the future. This mirrors the idea (less the emotional aspect) of Social Exchange Theory, a cognitive theory which assumes that individuals make a cost/benefit calculation about the advantages of giving or not. Mathur (1996) used cost/benefit analysis as one of the mechanisms in exchange theory. The proposition is that donors want to maximise the rewards they receive from giving: rewards should exceed costs. *Guanxi* can, therefore, be understood as the means to exchange or to increase one's capital.

Accruing favour – capital conversion

For me the Chinese concept of *guanxi* is a very close approximation of Bourdieu's notion of accumulating capital. Bourdieu understood social positions to be organised predominantly by two types of capital: economic and cultural (Wacquant, 2007). The dominant class has the potential to possess a large volume of either capital in contrast to the dominated class deprived of both. Amongst the dominant class, those who possess more economic capital are business owners or people in high executive positions vis-à-vis those who possess more cultural assets such as intellectuals and artists. Maintaining or improving one's position in the social space is achieved not only by increasing what one already has in abundance but also by pursuing strategies of conversion of one form of capital into the other. The objective is to be even more distinguished amongst one's own class and, furthermore, to impose the hierarchy of capital most favourable to one's own endowment (Wacquant, 2007). My research on gift-giving has helped me to better understand how charitable giving can be used as a means for people to find, maintain or manipulate 'their sense of place' (Goffman, 1956, 1967) or image of one's position in the field/social space (Bourdieu, 1998).

I have provided some background to understand the complex concept of *guanxi*. This aspect of my connection with my Chinese donor, tightly held as it is by our culture, means an implicit understanding of the game in which we were engaged. Rather than being about economic gains, our exchange of gifts, favours and obligations is about recognition: symbolic capital. In essence, symbolic capital means the capital of recognition (Bourdieu, 1977). We were engaged in the mutual exchange of recognition.

By contrast, I find myself temporarily wrong-footed in my relationships with my Anglo colleagues, which seem to rest on a different set of understandings about what is important in our exchanges. Reflecting on how the institution had presented my donor with an A$3M proposal provided more insight into the organisational culture. In my view, the staff and the CEO had a very instrumental, perhaps transactional way of understanding and working with people, particularly their key donors. I was beginning to wonder if the clinical approach employed in scientific research – abstracting human experience as mere functions of the brain – was being taken up unconsciously in the way people related to one another in this organisation. I also wondered if the temporal aspect of reciprocity is different in western culture where they are more familiar with the practice of 'immediate' reciprocity as distinct from the 'time-delay' reciprocity the Chinese or some of the ancient cultures are accustomed.

Face gifting in the struggle for status and identity

As I mentioned previously, the most important intangible gift exchange in the Chinese culture is in the form of *face*. Continuation of reciprocity leading to uncertainty is avoided as the parties involved are taking turns at being in debt, and the relationship grows along with the exchange of gifts and favour (Yang, 1994). In saying that, one also has to anticipate losing out on an investment. My daughter and her date were clearly incapable or unwilling to tolerate any uncertainty of losing out or to owing.

As Bourdieu points out, it is all a question of style, the choice of timing and occasion, so that the same act can have a particular meaning and unfolding. In this instance, the institute's attempt at 'immediate reciprocity', the making explicit of instrumental goals, crudely violates the art and etiquette of gift-giving where eagerness, normally a sign of submission, is here a sign of impatience with dependence, and therefore virtually an ingratitude (Bourdieu, 1998, p94). In the end, even though my Chinese donor rejected the proposal, she surprised everyone by making a substantial donation the day after the gala dinner.

With my account of *face* and recognition, I have only scratched the surface. I still haven't accounted for the complexity of what was going on. But I do have a greater clarity regarding donor relationships, more specifically, my own entanglement/involvement in the reproduction of power/social hierarchy as an active participant. In the field[4] of philanthropy amongst HNWIs, the potential and willingness to donate can 'buy' power/status and recognition through social networking/*guanxi*. Bourdieu's idea of field and capital is one way of understanding this particular aspect of HNWI donors. It marks a further opportunity to impose a hierarchy of capital and/or strategies for conversion of one form of capital to another. Another major concern is the influence major donors have in driving scientific research. The demand for research is dependent on funding. Educational institutions and government in particular have a high degree of power in favouring one type of research over another. At any given time, cultural practices determine what will count as an object for serious investigations (Foucault, 1962, p116). This is at the heart of Haraway's and Barad's work in pointing us to the effects of interference pattern, paying particular attention to what is excluded from mattering.

I have also gained greater clarity in recognising my colleagues at the institute. While I can't agree to the way they have gone about it, I do have more understanding and sympathy with the choice of timing to reciprocate as their own struggle for power and mutual recognition, perhaps not too dissimilar to the way my daughter did.

Reflections

I am aware that my choice to use a particular frame of the exchange to explore excluded other historical facts or what was happening between acting agents. As Bourdieu pointed out, the same act can have different meanings as the act unfolds. Barad (2007, p361) made this parallel proposition: 'It matters which cuts are enacted: different cuts enact different materialised becomings'. There are important far-reaching consequences as we grasp and attend to what we choose either to see or to exclude and where the story begins and ends (see also Brahm in this volume, on *punctuation*).

In her critique of Canadian philosopher Ian Hacking's emphasis that intervention is the key in experimental practice in *Representing and Intervening* (Hacking, 1982), Barad (2007) argued that 'theorizing and experimenting are not *intervening* (from the outside) but about *intra-acting* from within and as part of, the phenomena produced' (p56). She continued to explain: '…we are already materially entangled across space and time with the diffractive apparatuses that iteratively rework the "objects" that "we" study' (p384). What I take from this in thinking about how I am trying to understand the events I have described is this: I play an intimate part as the 'measuring apparatus'[5] in the ongoing articulation of the world as to what comes to matter. What we choose to pay attention to and what we exclude are therefore critical. The theorists with whom I have chosen to engage and the events I have chosen to spotlight mean that I am an active agent intra-acting across space and time reproducing phenomena. I am reminded by Barad that causality is an entangled affair. As I have discussed earlier my concern in regard to the influence donors (corporations or major institutions) have in driving research, and as a board member of an Australian Neuroscience Research Institute we are not exempt from the dominant ways of organising[6]. My choosing to explore and interpret a particular frame of event carries consequences. My choice of cuts to the narrative is not only capable of doing violence but also holds the potential to open up and rework what Barad defined as the agential conditions of new possibility.

New understanding from diffraction

Reading diffractively has helped me to reflect on the idea of culture and on how cultural values emerge and become habituated. Locating what I knew culturally in a discourse on anthropology and power relations led me to a new appreciation of the subtleties involved in relation to reciprocity, to gift-giving and to relationships which depend on power and status. In broad terms, the concept of *guanxi* describes relationship building. Being Chinese, and, in particular, being a woman, gives me an implicit understanding of obligations and pseudo relations involved in the concept of *guanxi*/reciprocity. Drawing from Bourdieu, Goffman and others has provided the language I have needed to articulate these embodied knowings. Reading them through, one after another, allowed me to remove the layers of my emotional attachment to these values.

In any group culture, the process of inclusion and exclusion marks how group members experience power. Power is, therefore, enacted in dynamics of enabling and constraining in relation to needs: money, status, love, knowledge, recognition or other elements (Elias, 1987). This dynamic can encourage an individual to perform certain functions for the group to which they wish to belong in order to form or to maintain membership, and a sense of place and of identity. My own experience represents the various groupings to which I have belonged: they provide useful insights. In saying that, I recognise that our acquired social dispositions are inherently biased. Haraway claims that our ability to see ourselves with 'self-satiated eyes' is not always possible, as there are 'no innocent positions to see from' (Haraway, 1988, p594).

As an older Chinese immigrant, typically known to keep her head down and to work hard, I am practiced at accumulating capital/wealth. I have a justification: 'It's for a rainy day'. As a parent, I would not hesitate to seek or to repay a favour to someone in exchange for opportunities that could open doors for my children. These positions are far from innocent. They are neither neutral nor objective: there are no positions exempt from critical examination. Translation is always interpretative, critical and partial (Haraway, 1988, p599). The ground for objectivity is to be more attuned to power-sensitive conversations. An example I noted previously in my footnote is that the earliest theorising about *face* originated from the perspective of western employers accusing their Chinese servants of stealing. These insights add values to our understanding of history and context.

Although she was referring to a community rather than to an individual, Haraway coined a useful term: *situated knowledges*.[7] The term defines a view from a given perspective, it is a view constituted by a social relationality[8];

here, Haraway is arguing for a practice of objectivity that privileges contestation and deconstruction of webbed connections. Haraway also gives us the term *passionate detachment* to define an embodied practice of objectivity which requires more than acknowledged and self-critical partiality. She is referring to the ability to hold onto tension[9] and contradictions.[10] She refers to:

> One who can interrogate positionings and be accountable, and one who can join rational conversations and fantastic imaginings that change history.
>
> (Haraway, 1988, p586)

This implies a self-accountable, critical and responsible engagement with the world by bringing out more interference patterns in our everyday lives. It is by holding onto these tensions, by thinking with and through others in productive dialogues, that we learn a new way of working with each other.

> Productive dialogue involves different theoretical positions, themes, and categories from one approach (or author) to reread and reconsider another perspective (or author). The interlocutor stimulates the search for a new meaning and new distinctions enabling the other party to "find thoughts which I had no idea I possessed.
>
> (Tsoukas, 2009, p4)

The aims are threefold: to produce something new, to generate new research opportunities and to trigger novel conceptual combinations, extensions and framing (Tsoukas, 2009, cited in Nicolini et al., 2022, p42[11]).

Implications for researchers and managers

This chapter has been an exploration of culture, specifically of the node of intersection that actively intertwines day-to-day relationships, both of a personal and of a professional kind. My daughter was confronted by cultural differences on her date; meanwhile, I found myself interweaving culturally between an HNWI Chinese donor/friend and the research institute. It was not until my daughter's event which prompted me to think more deeply about my involvement. When I thought I was merely translating one culture for another, I too became caught up in my role as a director competing for status and identity. Parallel to my daughter's date night, I have not ever felt more Chinese than as when I was dealing with an Anglo culture. At the same time, I could appreciate why Anglo culture might find baffling the Chinese sense of reciprocity. Recognising my own entanglement provided an in-depth view of the game. It was a view on what's going on in my organisation, and the impact my organisation and their donors was having on the board of directors, their staff, their research and, more broadly, on the mental health community that we were there to serve. I came to understand myself and my situation in a more nuanced way.

To understand better the process of culture, I have drawn in this chapter on the idea of diffraction, explored by both Haraway and Barad, which takes an interest in interference patterns. Both scholars are anti-determinist in their writings: they are opposed to the idea that we are determined by culture or gender. They are interested, instead, in understanding how things work, who is in the action and what might be possible. Although we cannot escape them, categories are necessary, but they are, after all, a socially agreed-upon system of distinctions and insufficient for understanding what perplexes us. Experience always bursts out of the labels and categories that we impose on it. It obliges us to take history, context and specificity seriously and be sensitive to the ripples that we form when we interact. In Judith Butler's (1993) terms there are no pre-constituted subjects and objects, there are only 'contingent foundations'; bodies that matter are the results of a particular culture at a particular time.

Recognising the enculturated selves that we bring to work may prompt in us a better insight into material-social dynamics which privilege a culture that governs exclusions and selections as to who and what comes to matter. Diffracting one set of attitudes through another, and attending to their various entanglements, allow us better to understand the ripple effects of how we intra-act, what this allows and what it inhibits. This recognition provides possibilities and hope for a much larger space for change.

Notes

1 At the time of writing, AUD $3m is about GBP£1.57m.

2 Smith (1894) has lived in China for over five decades argued that face is based on a love of theatricality describing '*face* is a mask that the Chinese wear'.

3 The negative attributes (e.g. the masks they wear, theatrical lies or deception) associated with *face* came from domestic tales as a marking of inferiority by western masters who suspects their Chinese servants of their theft (for example: of a coolie who steals a tennis ball or a servant who steals a penknife). Hence, *face* from western perspectives were limited to consist of a desire to avoid shame/owning up to some bad deed (Andre, 2013).

4 Fields presuppose that actors have unequal resources to compete on a given social space.

5 'Apparatuses are not to be understood as mere laboratory instruments, static instrumental embodiments of human concepts, but as open-ended and dynamic material-discursive practices, through which specific "concepts" and "things" are articulated' (Barad, 2007, p334).

6 At the time of writing, I had retired from my role as a foundation member for over a year after five years of service.

7 'The world must always be articulated, through people's point of view, through situated knowledges' (Haraway, 1988, 1992).

8 Haraway contrasts this view against those who make representations on behalf of the represented without seeking local knowledges. This is a view from everywhere and, therefore, from nowhere (p590). Haraway speaks of seeking knowledges particularly from those ruled by partial sight and by limited voice. This is not for the sake of partiality but for the sake of the connections and unexpected openings brought by these local knowledges.

9 Haraway defines tension as a splitting of senses, a confusion of voice and sight, rather than of clear and distinct ideas. She defines objectivity as positioned rationality which is both contestable and contested.

10 See also Mowles (2015), *Managing in Uncertainty.*

11 For a masterclass in state-of-the-art diffractive approach to research, please read Nicolini et al. (2022).

References

Andre, J. (2013) How the Chinese Lost 'face'. *Journal of Pragmatics*, 55, 68–85.

Barad, K. (2007) *Meeting the Universe Halfway*. Durham, NC: Duke University Press.

Bernstein, R. (2016) *Pragmatic Encounters*. London: Routledge.

Bian, Y. (1994) *Guanxi* and the Allocation of Urbans Jobs in China. *China Quarterly*, 140, 971–999.

Bian, Y. (2006) Guanxi. In J. Beckert and M. Zafirovski (Eds.), *International Encyclopedia of Economic Sociology*. New York: Routledge, 312–314.

Bourdieu, P. (1977) *Outline of a Theory of Practice*. Cambridge: Cambridge University Press.

Bourdieu, P. (1986) The Forms of Capital. In J. Richardson (Ed.) *Handbook of Theory and Research for the Sociology of Education*. New York: Greenwood, 241–258.

Bourdieu, P. (1990) *The Logic of Practice*. Stanford: Stanford University Press.

Bourdieu, P. (1998) *Practical Reason*. Stanford, CA: Stanford University Press.

Butler, J. (1993) *Bodies That Matter: On the Discursive Limits of "Sex."* New York: Routledge.

Chang, X. (2016) Recipropriety (lishang-wanglai): A Chinese Model of Social Relationships and Reciprocity – State and Villagers' Interaction 1936–2014. *Journal of Sociology*, 52(1), 103–117.

Chen, X.P. and Chen, C.C. (2004) On the Intricacies of the Chinese *guanxi*: A Process Model of *guanxi* Development. *Asia Pacific Journal of Management*, 21, 305–324.

Davis, J. (1836) *The Chinese: A General Description of the Empire of China and Its Inhabitants*, 2 vol., New York: Harpers & Brothers.

Elias, N. (1987) *Involvement and Detachment*. Oxford: Blackwell.

Foucault, M. (1962/2006) *Madness and Civilisation: A History of Insanity in the Age of Reason*. London: Vintage Books.

Foucault, M. (1994/1997) *Ethics: Subjectivity and Truth*. P. Rabinow (Ed.). New York: The New Press.

Goffman, E. (1956) *The Presentation of Self in Everyday Life*. Edinburgh: University of Edinburgh Press.

Goffman, E. (1967) *Interaction Ritual: Essays on Face to Face Behavior*. New York: Doubleday.

Hacking, I. (1982) Experimentation and Scientific Realism. *Philosophical Topics*, 13, 71–87.

Haraway, D. (1988) Situated Knowledges: The Science Question in Feminism as a Site of Discourse on the Privilege of Partial Perspective. *Feminist Studies*, 14(3), 575–599.

Haraway, D. (1992) The Promises of Monsters: A Regenerative Politics for Inappropriate/d Others. In C. N. L. Grossberg (Ed.) *Cultural Studies*. New York: Routledge, 295–337.

Illouz, E. (2012) *Why Love Hurts*. Cambridge: Polity Press.

King, A. (1985) The Individual and Group in Confucianism: A Relational Perspective. In D. J. Munro (Ed.), *Individualism and Holism: Studies in Confucian and Taoist Values*. Ann Arbor: Center for Chinese Studies, The University of Michigan Press, 57–70.

King, A. (1991) The Living Tree: The changing Means of Being Chinese Today. *Journal of the American of Arts and Science*, 120(2), 63–84.

Mathur, A. (1996) Materialism and Charitable Giving: Can They Coexist? *Journal of Consumer Behaviour*, 12, 149–158.

Mauss, M. (1990) *The Gift: The Form and Reason for Exchange in Archaic Societies*. W. D. Halls (trans.). New York: W.W. Norton Press.

Mead, G. (1934/2015) *Mind, Self and Society:from the Standpoint of a Social Behaviorist*. Chicago, IL: University of Chicago Press, 2015.

Mowles, C. (2015) *Managing in Uncertainty – Complexity and the Paradoxes of Everyday Organizational Life*. London: Routledge.

Nicolini, D., Pyrko, I., Omidvar, O. and Spanellis, A. (2022) Understanding Communities of Practice: Taking Stock and Moving Forward. *Academy of Management Annals*, 16(2), 680–718. doi:10.5465/annals.2020.0330 ISSN 1941-6520.

Smith, A. (1894) *Chinese Characteristics*. New York: Fleming H. Revell Company.

Wacquant, L. (2007) Pierre Bourdieu. In R. Stones (ed.) *Key Sociological Thinkers*, 2nd edition. London and New York: Macmillan

Yang, M. M. (1994) *Gifts, Favors, and Banquets: The Art of Social Relationships in China*. Ithaca, NY & London: Cornell University Press.

Zhai, X. (2005) *Mianzi, Renqing and Reproduction of Power*. Beijing: Peking University Press.

5

REFLEXIVITY AND ITS LIMITATIONS

CHRIS MOWLES

Introduction

In this chapter, I intend to become a bit more reflexive about reflexivity, to explore how it arises, what functions it serves, how it figures prominently in a number of social science disciplines including organisational research, and how some scholars problematise it as an unalloyed good. By reflexivity I mean a third-order activity which enables the capacity to think about how we are thinking and potentially problematise our assumptions, thought styles and value orientations.[1] The research community from which the chapters in this book emerge is dedicated to developing critical and collaborative reflexivity using a variety of methods, from the discussion of texts, scholarly and the researchers' own, through to group work informed by the group analytic tradition. If the doctoral theses produced by the research community have one thing in common, it is that they are all extended demonstrations of reflexivity. The first task students are given is to reflect back on the traditions of thinking they have been immersed in and to become reflexive about

DOI: 10.4324/9781003410522-6

them (see Chauhan on histories of sociality, Chapter 2). Thereafter every step of the research process is an encouragement to reflect and become reflexive further. All of this is undertaken in a group context. This degree of reflexivity is of a different order to requirements for most doctoral research and differs from the way that many organisational theorists write about reflexivity, which I explore later. With such a commitment to a particular orientation in our research and dealings with each other, it is worth thinking about what exactly we are doing and the merits and demerits of doing so. How does the capacity for reflexivity arise, what does it enable, and what are its limitations?

At the risk of using the same tools which helped build this reflexive edifice in the first place, to start the inquiry into our capacity for reflexivity and how it is taken up in this particular research community, I turn to the philosophical canon which informs it. I hope to gain some critical distance on methods and intention nonetheless, and in doing so to demonstrate that although reflexivity is valorised in qualitative research, it is at the same time an ordinary characteristic of being human.[2]

I account for reflexivity firstly from within the discourse that informs this particular research community, rather than beginning with a review of the broader organisational literature. Locating our perspective may come across as a kind of theoretical nativism. That is not my intention. Instead, and in relation to key ideas of complex responsive processes of relating which I explain in the preface to this volume, I want to demonstrate how appealing to these particular traditions of thinking is an attempt to work out consistently how to respond to and study the flux and change of experience, the stable-instability modelled by the complexity sciences. This has involved drawing on pragmatism, process sociology and group analytic theory, which all have something interesting to say about the interpenetration of mind, self and society, demonstrating how human, social animals relate to each other corporeally and psychologically. Arguably this frames a broader discussion about the nature and qualities of reflexivity than does the critical management scholarship on reflexivity as research method, which, for obvious reasons, is principally concerned with action in organisations.

Reflexivity and the social self – a pragmatic view

The research community is informed by pragmatic philosophy because of the latter's preoccupation with the engagement with experience. The students take the experience of trying to get things done with others as their subject and object of study. Although there is great diversity in the tradition of thought to which one might apply the term pragmatism, one aspect that pragmatists would probably all agree on is that we don't understand the world as detached, cognising subjects, but through our everyday, practical engagement with it, with each other, and with ourselves. We are always already in relation. For pragmatists, it is through our engagement with each other that we become selves, which develops an insight from Hegel. Knower and known are entangled, caught in a loop of mutual, and mutually defining influence. From a pragmatic perspective, we create the world and are created by it both at the same time, and this process of reciprocal forming is an important process to pay attention to, to better understand reflexivity.[3] Mead understands this dynamic as follows:

> Rational conduct always involves a reflexive reference to self, that is, an indication to the individual of the significances which his actions or gestures have to other individuals.
>
> (Mead, 1934, p122)

He developed a suite of ideas about mind, self and society, ethics and values, communication, time and action fundamentally informing the perspective of complex responsive processes of relating, which are predicated on this reflexive loop described in the quotation. Becoming ourselves is a constantly recursive process of relationality, and it allows us to proceed in the world in a way which allows us to adapt and respond, to express our individuality and to integrate into society both at the same time (see Chauhan Chapter 2 in this volume for a treatment of sociality).

Mead's theories relating to human consciousness and interaction are both material and paradoxical all the way down. By material I mean his ideas are rooted in his interpretation of the way that human biology and psychology works, as much as abstract thinking about the nature of the self. Although pragmatic philosophy nods to idealism, that the world of ideas is primary, I think there are clear differences between pragmatic epistemology and, say, social constructionism, which I don't have time to go into here, but are to do with the pragmatists' assumption that reality acts back, what original pragmatist CS Peirce referred to as brute constraint (Bernstein, 2010, p50). We cannot create the world exactly as we would like it to be because it has an independent reality, but one which we can only come to know through our engagement with it. Mead and Dewey's exploration of experience in particular dwells in the object, and the experience of the object both at the same time. It is this doubleness which I think is key to understanding reflexivity and is both an ordinary and extraordinary aspect of being human.

Mead's major work treats the inseparability of mind, self and society 'from the perspective of a social behaviorist' (1934) informed equally by his studies with the German philosopher and physiologist Wundt, the first scholar to call himself a psychologist, and his reading of Darwin, as it is from his reading of Hegel. Meaning making, co-operation, ethics all arise in the material world of nature, of which humans are part, and are explained using the same application of systematic einquiry that one would apply to exploring objects in nature. The most important guiding principle is to inquire with ways of thinking which are relevant to the subject of inquiry, rather than assuming, say, that there is an inverted hierarchy of importance between subjective and objective, society and nature, qualitative and quantitative research.

So Mead roots the origins of mind and self in the body and in the paradoxical, mutual self-referencing dynamic alluded to previously. Because of the way the human central nervous system has evolved, he argues, we can be both subject and object to ourselves; we experience spontaneous responses to the world which we can never get on top of, and at the same time, as we express our unique response we can come to see ourselves as others might see us. This is how the self emerges as unique but equally explains the basis for self-regulation and social integration. It is a paradox, or perhaps double paradox. Mead gives some small examples (1934, pp202–204) of what he means by this double paradox. In certain situations, we will sometimes surprise ourselves by what we say or how we act. This is the first paradox of the spontaneous 'I' emerging in all its uniqueness in ways that we cannot anticipate and only realise retrospectively. The surprise then is the consequence of having said or done something different from what might have been expected in the social situation, an emergent 'I' sparking novelty in the face of the organised attitudes of others, which we take to ourselves, the 'me'. Meanwhile, other people can say things to us which surprise us about ourselves and about them, so as unique and interdependent I/me's we are constantly wrong footed by the otherness of others. This is the second paradox.

We come to see ourselves as others see us. The self/object to self which we term self-consciousness and self/other participation of the individual in the group are paradoxes. For Mead, they arise from a gesture-response cycle involving what he terms significant symbols.

Significant symbols are mutually understood vocalisations and bodily gestures which call out a similar response in ourselves, the relation to self, as in those towards whom we direct our gestures. These can be non-verbal, like a shrug, or spoken language, or even bodily dispositions, like the 'body language' of defeat displayed by a football team losing 5-0. They are the basis for understanding ourselves and anticipating each other and substantiate Mead's claim that we are social through and through. As we gesture and respond, our bodies resonate with each other. In this double loop of gesture-response spontaneous, adaptive and anticipatory movements of meaning are possible. As I outlined in the examples in the previous paragraph, communication is predictably unpredictable and not deterministic in the sense that we cannot fully predict exactly what we are going to say until we hear ourselves saying it, because we respond to what we say just as others do. Equally, we cannot fully predict how our conversation partners will respond, although over time we may have internalised a general idea about how they might. So Mead argues that mind arises as the activity of a body directed towards itself, just as the sense of self arises from our ability to take ourselves as an object to ourselves, and thus see ourselves as others might see us. Mead describes the me, which is inseparable from our spontaneous I, as the generalised other, a general sense of how we think others experience us. We acquire a sense of the generalised other through interaction and encounters with difference and me is our history of I-ing imagined/understood/evaluated from that perspective. The activity of mind is a private, embodied rehearsal of the gesture we make towards others, a process which is also occurring in them. Thinking and talking are the same social act, with the former being directed privately towards ourselves.

The very fact that we are born into a world in a particular place, at a particular time, and where there is already a play going on conducted in particular significant symbols means that we are formed primarily outside-in. That is to say, in the sociological debate about whether the self or society is preeminent, for Mead the answer is that is both at the same time, but society is prior. Internalising our *habitus*, the complex language, accepted ways of behaving, value-orientations, what we might refer to as 'culture', is the process that makes us the individuals we are through our unique responses to our environment and to specific and general others. The general patterns of a society we refer to as culture show up in particular form in everyday conversations of gesture and response as people negotiate how to go on together.

What I find interesting in Mead's formulation of the process of mind and self is that it is both unremarkable and extraordinary. It is unremarkable in the sense that the reflexive, paradoxical loops involving the self and other selves are an everyday part of being human. At the same time, our capacity to notice the social process while engaging with it affords us an increased opportunity for making sense of experience, and for changing ourselves and society. Mead argues that we can only imagine how we would like things to be different through our ability to take the organised attitudes of the wider group to ourselves. Additionally, he takes a radical view that the self is not already there but arises in this reflexive process he terms the I/me dialectic. The fluid self emerges in the process of social interaction: if you are looking for a self 'inside', one which is a kernel of 'who you really are', then for Mead you are looking in the wrong place.

So, we become socialised over time widening our understanding of the social games we are obliged to play (elsewhere described by Mead as social objects, Mead, 1938) as we grow up. Our socialisation involves an expanding sense of the attitudes of many others involved in the complex activities of highly developed societies to which we have the potential to respond spontaneously. And in our widening repertoire of responses, we become ourselves. Without this capacity for spontaneity and individuality, there would be nothing novel in experience, he argues. But integration with society involves accommodating our conduct within the broader expectations of the society of which we are part, and our understanding of these expectations might also galvanise us to try and change them. Everyday reflexivity allows us to become ourselves and to become part of society, and to try and change it and ourselves, both at the same time.

Paradox and reflexivity contributing to social and psychological development

So far, I have drawn on the pragmatic canon, particularly GH Mead to explore the everyday paradoxical materiality of reflexivity. But the dualisms

I refer to, self and other, I and me, are mobilised by another contributor to the research community, the process sociologist Norbert Elias.

Elias sketches out a social evolutionary view of how the capacity for reflexivity emerged. Where Mead locates reflexivity in the body, Elias develops the insight that the emergence of highly integrated societies over time, which he refers to as the civilising process (2000), has also created our personality structure. As more and more people become more dependent on more others, more of the time, so social advantage accrues to those who can pay attention to the complex game of social life and notice how they and others are playing it in the moment. In the process, those who can better regulate their emotions are in a stronger position, as they are in a better position to consider dispassionately what's going on. So the drama of the public negotiation of felt emotions moves internally: Elias argues that the civilising process has been accompanied privately by rising tides of guilt and shame. Although there is no predicting outcomes of the game of games which is social life, those who are able to regulate themselves and anticipate the potentialities of the patterning the game affords one or two moves ahead are likely to be able to play more skilfully. There are big benefits in reflexive acuity.

In two complementary essays *Problems of Involvement and Detachment* and *The Fisherman and the Maelstrom* (1987), Elias attempts a developmental sociology of knowledge and explores the question of which research methods best uncover social processes of which we are part. By illustration, the second essay highlights an episode in a short story by Edgar Allen Poe which depicts three brothers facing their wrecked fishing boat sinking into a whirlpool. One brother was lost to the waves; the second, paralyzed by fear, found himself cowering and helpless in the sinking boat. Meanwhile the youngest brother, despite the pandemonium, noticed that small, cylindrical objects circulated round and round the mouth of the whirlpool without sinking. He grabbed a barrel and jumped into the water, perhaps a counter-intuitive thing to do, encouraging his brother to do the same. While the younger brother was saved, the elder brother sank with the boat.

Elias doesn't recommend this cool detachment in all circumstances but notices how, as the title of the first essay suggests, the younger brother was able to become more detached about his involvement, a paradox. Elias offers this formulation, involvement and detachment, as a more helpful alternative to subjective or objective. It's more helpful in the sense that it recasts the sometimes sterile competition of the value of subjective/objective positions, where greater value can be attributed to the 'objective' position, even though what is taken to be objective may be under-explored. Given that he takes a highly social view of individuals, that we can never be fully objective about the social conditions of our own becoming, Elias argues that we are always working with an amalgam of involved detachment, or detached involvement. Greater detachment from our involvement in the sometimes unhelpful and even destructive dynamics of interdependent group life might enable us to become just as competent at controlling our social affairs as we are about objects in nature, he argues. Elias notes with regret that the former ability has lagged far behind the latter but is nonetheless optimistic that a greater detached-involvement, or what we term reflexivity in this chapter, will bring about greater harmony in human affairs.

The methodological point that Elias makes, on the unavoidability of dualisms – detached-involvement as he expresses it here, or elsewhere as taking the perspective of the airman and the swimmer (1991) – is widely taken up in sociology and is explored by scholars involved in other disciplines such as social anthropology, political philosophy and organisational studies, which I explore briefly later on.

Reflexivity as method – group analysis

Norbert Elias and the founder of the group analytic tradition, SH Foulkes, both attended seminars at the Institute for Social Research (IfS) in Frankfurt after it was founded in 1923. In their subsequent work as sociologist and group psychotherapist respectively, both scholars adopted an interdisciplinary perspective that was current in the ISS, and which developed insights from Hegel, Freud and Darwin. Subsequently both fled to the UK as Jewish refugees from Nazi Germany, and they had a long and troubled friendship, with Elias at one time sitting on the board of the Institute for Group Analysis (founded by Foulkes).

We have briefly explored Elias' insights into how psychological and social development occurred hand in hand because of our interdependence and our relationships in groups and between groups, and Foulkes developed a radical method of group therapy which is predicated on the idea that the best place better to understand the thoroughly social self is in a social setting such as a group (Foulkes and Anthony, 1984). His insights and methods were a significant departure from dyadic psychotherapy and the Tavistock school of group consultancy based on the ideas of Freud, Bion and Klein (Mowles, 2017).

The primary working method is for people to sit together in a group in a circle of chairs, face to face, without an agenda with the only task of talking about what matters to them. In the process of doing so, the group leader, known as the conductor, and group members make sense of what is going on through their interpretations. These, in turn, are reinterpreted by others, so there is a constantly emerging sense of what is happening which is plural and polyvocal. The focus is on both manifest and the unconscious content. In the process, everyone in the group has the potential for gaining deeper insight into how they come across to others and are obliged to act and react to one another as particular and general others. As I mentioned in the passages on Mead, this might arise by our saying or doing something which surprises us, or being surprised by the insights of others, or may result from the 'rising tides of guilt and shame' which Elias attributed to the civilising process.

As the group continues and members learn to orient themselves more to taking the attitude of particular others, and the group as a whole to themselves, they are likely to become less attached to their particular neuroses and anxieties. Visible and active engagement with others touches them in a more profound way than just appealing to intellect but arises because of the intense feelings provoked by staying in relation, and with the possibility that emerges of re-narrating their own perspective and making different sense of it.

The format of the experiential group is adopted on the DMan programme but not primarily as a therapeutic intervention. Rather it is a live experiment in working improvisationally and an encouragement to pay attention to group dynamics and one's own practice. Researchers may not start out self-aware but are able to develop a greater reflexive ability over time: they become more practised at noticing their habitual ways of being in relation to others because they notice themselves and/or they have their habitual patterns pointed out to them by other members of the group. Some organisations adopt action learning sets or reflective groups to bring about similar outcomes.

An experiential group is considered to be working well when a large proportion of its members are capable of identifying and addressing themes of importance to the group and of giving expression to them, while at the same time becoming wiser about their own particularities, perhaps eccentricities. This is a method of encouraging individual reflexivity by amplifying group-mindedness.

Linking reflexivity to organisational theory

The research community involved in contributing to this book has been immersed in a pragmatic project of uniting thinking, talking, acting and responding. Researchers draw on traditions of thought which privilege the social self and interdependence and work in a way in which these interdependences are explored and made more public. The process involves paying attention to the full range of human conduct in order to think about what it means to be in ethical relation with others, and how we might think about the production of knowledge of our social conditions. Researchers draw upon scholars not confined to the pragmatists, or to Elias, but also include post-structuralists such as Bourdieu as well as a range of philosophers in the European critical tradition and social anthropology. The aim is, as Cunliffe encapsulates it:

> ...acknowledging the constitutive nature of our research conversations; constructing "emerging practical theories" rather than objective truths; exposing the situated nature of accounts through narrative circularity; focusing on life and research as a process of becoming rather than already established truth.
>
> (Cunliffe, 2003, p991)

More realist and representationalist research aims to reduce the human influence in the research process to consider social conditions 'as they really are', unmediated by subjectivity. This makes a clear separation between subjective and objective. In contrast, the traditions of thought underpinning the DMan are interested in the subjectivising process and assume a dialectical relationship between the two poles of subjective and objective. As Bourdieu expressed it, 'the body is in the social world, but the social world is also in the body' (1982, p38).

According to these assumptions, radical changes in the social world bring about significant shifts in the way that subjects become subjects and reveal something important about the relationship between structure and agency.[4] For example, Lash (2003) argues that major sociologists writing in the 1990s and 2000s, such as Jurgen Habermas, Ulrick Beck and Anthony Giddens (Beck et al., 1994), make a distinction between our current phase of informational modernity and the industrial modernity which preceded it. Where *modernity 1* comprises strong nation states, industrialisation, careers for life, strong social institutions, grand narratives, *modernity 2* comprises globalisation through networks, flows, fragmentation and decentring, which results in a more radical individualism. In *modernity 1*, linearity and equilibrium are assumed to prevail, so reflection is privileged. *Modernity 2* is characterised by non-linearity when reflexive, self-making subjects cannot depend on following the rules of an established and stable world but need constantly to adapt to a changing world no longer governed by identifiable universals; reflexivity, then, is understood as a response to more uncertain times, when self-authoring subjects are much more dependent on themselves to make their own rules. Adams (2006) refers to this shift in the focus of sociology as the extended reflexivity thesis and goes on to argue that it places too much emphasis on agency at the expense of structure. In placing the reflexive subject front and centre, it is important not to lose sight of the structuring influence of the *habitus*.

In my argument to date, drawing on the traditions of thinking which inform complex responsive processes of relating, I have made the case that a reflexive ability is an innate capacity of interdependent human beings; indeed, it has become more pronounced as a result of our increasing interdependence. In effect, I have agreed to an extent with Bruno Latour (1993) that 'we have never been modern' – reflexivity is not just a condition of the times we find ourselves living in with their unique demands but is a process arising from our evolutionary capacity to take ourselves as objects to ourselves. However, I concur with the sociological argument that reflexivity can be a helpful response to the state of frenetic standstill (Rosa, 2015) that we find ourselves confronting:

> in the frenetic standstill that we experience in contemporary society: self- projects which are oriented toward stability appear to be anachronistic and condemned to failure in a highly dynamic environment,

> while forms of identity based on flexibility and readiness to change are systematically favoured.
>
> (2015, p243)

Uncertain times demand an enhanced adaptive ability, and this involves a more pronounced reflexive ability; this may have its advantages of making us more aware of how we are caught up, but, as I explore later in the chapter, it also brings its own disadvantages.

Reflexivity is very widely explored in organisational literature, particularly in the social constructionist, critical and process philosophical traditions, which take seriously the idea that organisations are sites of complex and non-linear activity, as much formed by creative, meaning-making actors as being formed by them. Scholars are concerned with making management education more critical, bringing to the fore ethical considerations involved in research, and producing knowledge which is less abstract, rarefied and remote from the concerns of everyday managers working in organisations. This often involves linking reflexivity to practical judgement, or *phronesis*. For example, Antonacopoulou (2010) argues that reflexivity needs to be critical, i.e., provoke *krisis* or judgement, particularly in those moments of practical activity which require sifting competing priorities. Reflexivity enriches experience by problematising it, and making it more complex, with the intention of rendering the choices we make more convergent with the complexity of the dilemmas we face. Meanwhile, Shotter and Tsoukas (2014a, 2014b) hold that reflexive practical judgement is necessary to make sense of confusing situations where we can only feel our way into new situations based on our moral sensibilities. The kind of insight required can never rely solely on rationalisation but involves taking into account a whole bodily response: taking ourselves as an object to ourselves. Or reflexivity may mean making many positions and many voices more explicit, as Alvesson et al. (2008) explain, including, and perhaps especially, that of the person wishing to provoke critical reflexivity in others. From the education sector, Thomas (2010, 2012) argues that phronesis has a self-referencing reflexive quality, is knowledge from practice for practice and in this sense has a different kind of generalisability to what might be expected in more respresentationalist forms of knowledge.

As a way into exploring reflexivity in more detail and understanding its limitations, I draw on a paper by Hibbert et al. (2010) which sets out four modes of reflexivity ranging from weak to strong forms. The four modes demonstrate a gradual movement away from the individual cognising researcher towards one more affected by the otherness of others. The authors do not present these as a hierarchy, and they suggest that it is possible to engage in more than one mode, but they do consider the later modes to be more radically open to otherness. Equally, they understand reflexivity to be both an active and a passive process, initiated by the researcher or imposed on them through the circumstances they find themselves in and the groups of which they are members. They argue that reflexivity involves reflection, standing back from something, and also recursivity where there is a return to self to contemplate what the implications of the reflection might be for the research and the researcher.

Mode 1 they term *repetition* is a rather narrow, self-directed process which is intended to correct for 'bias'. This is a mode of reflexivity which I encounter frequently as an examiner of doctoral theses, in which candidates acknowledge the subjective nature of research, and perhaps are slightly embarrassed about it, then add a coda of reflexivity towards the end of their theses to account for the ways in which they may, or may not, have accounted for their assumptions and prejudices. This may involve little discussion of the texts and the ideologies of the discourses which they have borrowed to theorise about their subject of inquiry. In everyday organisational life, I have encountered an ambivalence on the one hand of taking metrics at face value, given that they may be proxy values and/or generated on the basis of a number of assumptions. And on the other hand, and when confronted by the assumed objectivity numbers, managers may be self-conscious about giving their opinion about how the work is working. The inability to completely trust in numbers (Porter, 1995) when everyone present is aware of how the numbers were put together can result in a queasy negotiation about how much we can exclude human judgement from the area of work under discussion.

Mode 2 Hibbert et al. think of as *extension* usually provoked by the experience of being stuck in the research and being struck by something which requires further explanations than the one ready to hand for the researcher, a process Alvesson and Kärreman have termed 'mystery as method' (2011). The researcher is arrested by something which prevents them from proceeding in terms of explanations they have to hand. Alternatively and in more radical form, extension might be provoked by some kind of failure, or breakdown of experience (see Chapter 6, by Solsø on breakdown and abductive inquiry), which might involve shame (Garrety et al., 2003). This more powerful form of disruption is more likely to provoke the researcher into finding other explanations for their experience. Extension may involve seeking out different research communities, perhaps where there is a vigorous debate going on, in order to find alternative theories to the ones which have proved helpful up to the point of mystery.

And in this more emphatic form, extension shades into the third mode of reflexivity which Hibbert et al. (op. cit.) term *disruption*, what one might think of as the deliberate attempt to combine the individual and personal, and the collective and general. Although the search for alternatives may be actively sought, the disruption may be inflicted externally on the researcher provoking them into abandoning identity-containing ideas, a process which is likely to be painful and disorienting. In his seminal work *The Sociological Imagination*, C Wright-Mills (1959/2000, p195) argues for the importance of just such a combining of the personal and the general in the cause of producing imaginative and impactful research, which he expresses in the appendix: 'the most admirable thinkers within the scholarly community you have chosen to join do not split their work from their lives'. Imaginative sociology, for Wright-Mills, involves bringing sociological analysis back to the self and making it relevant for other selves. Similarly, in a famous essay, *Thinking as a Moral Act*, the social anthropologist Clifford Geertz (1968) encourages social researchers to develop the ability to look at people, and events, and he adds, oneself, with an eye which is both 'cold and concerned'; in Elias' terms, detached and involved. Geertz poses a number of paradoxes which are at the heart of carrying out social research: the particular and the general, the personal and the social in order to point to what he considers the moral obligation of maintaining the paradoxical position. To do otherwise is to fall into subjectivism, being unproductively and narcissistically involved, or scientism, treating other human beings as though they are objects in nature towards whom we have no commitments or obligations.

The last mode of reflexivity described by Hibbert et al., they term *participation*, which they define as a: 'situation in which one comes to choose to engage with a particular community and be transformed by it' (2010, p56). I imagine this to be a description of the process I have described previously in the passage on Foulkes and group analytic methods. What is significant about the participation mode of reflexivity for Hibbert et al. is that it shares, at least partially, the orientation and sense-making of the research project with the group of which the researcher is part. It is much less researcher-directed and may be experienced in groups such as religious communities, which 'speak to the researcher's condition'. In extreme form, and in my experience of working in the DMan research community, the process of researcher decentring may lead to feeling entirely taken over, or negated, which may then lead to a sense of feeling lost, or equally, to a form of conversion experience where the researcher is convinced that the ways of seeing inherent in group membership are the 'truth'. In these circumstances, it is only with time and experience can researchers come back to a more stable sense of self.

Many researchers will have experienced modes 2 and 3 of reflexivity described by Hibbert et al., which will have involved them in being struck (Shotter, 2006), engaging in a variety of texts and different thought collectives, possibly experiencing breakdown and shame. To become familiar with mode 4 of reflexivity will have involved being part of a group of researchers similar to the research community like the DMan, or being moved by the group they are researching into, where their inquiry and interpretations are guided by the encounter with the otherness of others. Where I disagree with Hibbert et al. about the last mode of reflexivity, participation is that I don't regard it as in any sense passive as they describe it, partly because I understand participation in a group to turn on a paradox. Without active participation, i.e., taking the risk of speaking out and showing up in the group, there can be no encounter with the otherness of others. With mature participation, in no sense is direction handed over to the group: rather the self comes into being through the active negotiation of inclusion and exclusion in group life. A more successful negotiation of the paradoxical dynamics of inclusion and exclusion, individuality and membership of the group enables the researcher more fully to find their own voice amongst the voices of others. Two factors may be important in this settling of the sense of the negation of identity, so that the negation is itself negated. The first is time to reflect upon the repeated experience of negation, which one can come to see as the inevitable process of being part of a group. Next is the mobilisation of critical judgement that Antonacopoulou (2010) points to as a result of the reflexive episode and consideration of what the experience might mean.

Reflexivity and its limitations

Lastly in this chapter, I want to describe some critiques of reflexivity in its various modes and to think about its limitations, while making note of responses and ways of working which might mitigate these.

In a provocative article entitled 'Against reflexivity as a virtue and source of privileged knowledge', Lynch (2000) argues as I have at the beginning of this chapter, that being reflexive is a necessary and ordinary part of being human. When researchers are self-consciously trying to be reflexive, they may end up sounding trivial or silly. There is nothing inherent to being reflexive that necessarily produces profound insights about the human condition. In my view, researchers working in the first mode of reflexivity, a narrow and self-directed attempt to 'correct for biases', betray a misunderstanding of the nature of qualitative research. To assume a thoroughly social self orients the researcher better to understand how selves become selves in the more objective social processes: this is not a process to be corrected for, but to be inquired in to, since asking how we come to believe what we believe offers up interesting insights.

Next Lynch challenges the idea that reflexivity can be relativising, destabilising and can lead to infinite regress, some of the phenomena identified in modes 2 and 3 of reflexivity. Infinite regress traps the researcher in an endless inquiry into origins and causality of the type: if God made the world, then who made God? This for Lynch credits reflexivity with too much power, although there is plenty of testimony from reflexive researchers of the destabilising experience of becoming reflexive. The political philosopher Hannah Arendt (1971) also noted the destabilising tendencies of a dialogue with oneself. Thinking, which she termed a conversation between me and myself, has a tendency to unravel things, just as Penelope unravelled her tapestry every night to put off her suitors while she waited for Odysseus' return. So the deconstructive tendency of reflexive critique of the foundations of one's thinking may also require a reconstructive phase of putting together a response to the disorientation, as Alvesson et al. have argued (2008). C.S. Peirce, the original pragmatist philosopher, argued that we cannot doubt everything all of the time but must start with concerns that prevent, or cover over our practical engagement with life (in Bernstein, 2010: 33). Reflexivity becomes a directed activity into identified and practical questions, in recognition of the fact that mostly we engage unreflectively in making our way through the world. One could go further and make a case for a kind of anti-reflexivity, as Alvesson and Spicer (2012) do, only partially tongue in cheek, referring to the ubiquitous phenomenon of not thinking too hard in organisations as 'functional stupidity'. In other words, not being reflective and becoming reflexive, being functionally 'stupid', also has a role in stabilising the world and works against the unsettling process that we have spent most of this chapter exploring.

Next comes the critique that the doubling process, recursively thinking about how one is thinking to which I have alluded, simply replicates the status quo. If we are all products of our particular time and culture, then there is a limit to what we can imagine as different. Modes 1 and 2 reflexivity which still largely preserve the impermeability of the self-directing researcher also leave intact the structures which might prevent radical insight. I understand this to be the basis of Karen Barad's critique of reflexivity. In *Meeting the Universe Half Way* (2007), Barad argues that reflexivity still contains representationalism, because it involves a double mirroring, thinking about how one is thinking:

> Mirrors upon mirrors, reflexivity entails the same old geometrical optics of reflections.
>
> (2007, p88)

Barad describes reflexivity as 'nothing more than iterative mimesis', and although she was writing long before the recent emergence of artificial intelligence, it is possible to see a parallel argument that large language models are mostly adroit at giving back to us what we already know. Wong (Chapter 4 this volume) explores the concept of diffraction, which she offers as an alternative, where the agents in the dialectic do not simply reflect each other but are changed by the encounter. Hibbert et al. also grant the more amplified mode 3 of reflexivity and mode 4, participation, with this potential to alter the self which is recursively referred to.

The degree to which reflexivity has emancipatory potential that it allows us to stand back from and challenge existing power structures and ways of thinking (Hibbert and Cunliffe, 2015) is contested by some scholars (Vince et al., 2018). If we assume that we are thoroughly immersed in our habitus, as Bourdieu and Elias argue, and that cultural dominance is produced and reproduced in our interactions with each other (Bourdieu and Wacquant,

1992), then the potential for reflexive criticality to reimagine alternative futures is limited by the very ways of thinking which are currently available to us and create the status quo. There are limits to the extent that the reflexive self can remake themselves, and the world. The fallacy of the idea of blue skies thinking is that you can only see the sky from where you are standing.

Further, there is an argument to be made that reflexivity is not simply incapable of challenging the status quo because it is naturally delimited by the language and concepts that are available to us, but that it has been coopted by the socio-political order it seeks to undermine. In Chapter 4 of my last book (Mowles, 2021), I note how the processes of individualisation identified by Elias as having taken place over many centuries have reached something of a nadir in the late 20th and early 21st centuries. We are more likely to consider ourselves to be *homo clausus*, individuals cut off from one another, rational and autonomous, rather than interdependent rationally irrational social beings, as I have alluded to in this chapter. Additionally, we live in a highly marketised, financialised world where one of the principal dynamics is competition. It is a world where we are encouraged to think of ourselves as a brand, as a human resource, as an imperfect and ongoing project which needs to be objectified and optimised as a digital self, as a life-long learner, as a product. Here, we are invited to collude through reflexively and constantly monitoring the self to make us better organisational performers, to be more attractive to others, to lead a full life. We are no longer a surveillance society, argues German-Burmese philosopher Byung-Chul Han (2015), but an achievement society where we are at war with ourselves better to participate in a neoliberal society which at the same time hollows us out. We enlist our own reflexive resources in making ourselves obedient corporate citizens and consumers.

The social and cultural theorist Eva Illouz points to a similar phenomenon about our emotional lives. In a body of work which treats the larger social, economic and political forces which shape our emotions, particularly romantic relationships (2007, 2012), Illouz considers the ways in which modernity has depleted our rich cultural resources to experience love by trying to render it more predictable and controllable. Emotions have become individualised, abstract, and through insights from the psych sciences and feminism, proceduralised. Illouz considers herself to be a feminist and is critical of the way in which modernity has been of greater benefit to men, particularly if they are caught up in choosing without commitment. But at the same time, she points to the ways in which the feminist response to this inequality, subsuming erotic relations under rules of fairness and equivalence, contributes to demystifying love and transforming desire. Technology in the form of dating apps has afforded much more choice in the 'love market'. There is a greater availability of possible partners, thus greater competition, which has in turn resulted in the development of highly cognised forms of introspection and self-scrutiny, which help treat the subject as object. The consequences are that the process of constant reflexivity demanded in today's market of love transforms the nature of desire by curtailing the ability to experience each other spontaneously and in an unmediated way:

> The demystification of love by political ideals of equality and fairness, by science and by technology, has made sexual relationships into a self-reflexive object of scrutiny and control through formal and predictable procedures.
>
> (2012, p177)

Illouz argues that we participate in creating the conditions of our own impoverishment: through reflexive monitoring, we rationalise and abstract from a structure of relations which used to be more overtly ambiguous, uncertain, spontaneous and contextual. Perhaps ironically she makes a reflexive invitation to consider the mess that reflexivity may have led us into.

I think two points are important here. One is that reflexivity can be the antithesis of what Rosa (2019) refers to as resonant experience, where we are lost in mystery, beauty and perhaps a sense of the sacred; experience can be ineffable. Reflexivity may help make sense of resonant phenomena after the event, but sometimes there is no substitute for being absorbed, of being enchanted. For Illouz, this is particularly the case for romantic relationships, but her thesis extends more widely than this in her other work (Cabanas and Illouz, 2019) that modernity shapes the experience of being human. Something is lost while something is gained: while reflexivity can reveal implicit power relationships, for example, what gets lost is ambiguity and the aesthetic of multiple meanings of human relating. Secondly, when reflexivity becomes unmoored from time to consider its effects critically, then, rather than unsettling and problematising social trends of which one is part, it may be end up by reinforcing them. We might end up internalising and becoming proficient at adapting to the demands of liquid modernity so that we lose ourselves and the qualities of our bonds of interdependence with others.

Conclusions

In this chapter, I have explored the concepts and practices which inform the research community, the graduates from which have contributed to this volume. This has involved rehearsing some of the key insights of pragmatic philosophy, process sociology and group analytic theory and practice. I have argued that our reflexive ability is an everyday and ordinary phenomenon rooted in our biological, psychological and social evolution. In traditions of research which privilege human beings and what they are saying and doing to co-construct their social reality, reflexivity may help us discern the process of our own forming. Additionally, one of the insights from the complexity sciences, which also informs the body of thought our approach draws upon is that complexity models are not useful for making predictions, but they do demonstrate qualitative changes over time. Reflexivity is one skill which we can draw on as human beings to notice, and be struck by qualitative changes to our own sense of belonging and identity, our inclusion and exclusion, as well as that of others. Reflexivity is a practice which we can become more skilful at exercising.

But it has its limitations, and we need to continue to be reflexive about reflexivity. First, it exists in weak and strong forms, which involve the otherness of others more or less. While Hannah Arendt extolled the virtues of thinking, the conversation between me and myself, it requires an exceptional mind not to get caught up in some kind of solipsistic loop. She was able to 'think without a banister' as she described it, by which she meant to be able to imagine alternatives to the taken-for-granted discourses which govern the herd, and which might save us when the chips are down (1971, p446). But are we a resource enough to ourselves to be able to do this? Equally, we need to be mindful that by engaging with modernity, we are automatically caught up, encouraged even, to use our reflexive resources to produce and reproduce the very conditions that we might be trying to resist. The emancipatory intent of some social constructionist thought can sometimes feel a little naïve, if we assume that there is no place to stand outside the situations we may have ambitions to transform. Equally, we need to be conscious that reflexivity can be the antithesis of spontaneity and resonant human experience, which may become lifeless when subject to our reasoned attempts to examine and deconstruct.

However, perhaps there is some comfort in the experience of practical solidarity which we may experience in what Hibbert et al. term the fourth mode of reflexivity, participation. Particularly in the experiential group which is at the heart of the research community contributing to this volume, there are moments of insight and connection, a rediscovery of the self in and through others, that no other human capacity can produce, and which may form the basis for hope in complex times. It is no substitute for the spontaneous enjoyment of human interaction, but it can help us make sense of it after the fact.

Notes

1 The first order is primary experience itself, what another pragmatic philosopher William James referred to as a 'blooming buzzing confusion', James, W. (1890/2007) *Principles of Psychology*, Vol. 1, New York: Cosimo Classics, p488. Second order I think of as reflection, standing back and thinking about experience. Third order reflects on how we are reflecting.

2 There are a handful of other mammals, bonobos, dolphins, elephants, which are thought to have a similar capacity of taking themselves as an object to themselves, of having a sense of self, as are the corvid family of birds. See de Waal (2011) *The Age of Empathy; Nature's Lessons for a Kinder Society*, London: Souvenir Press.

3 This is also a central insight from evolutionary complex adaptive systems, which is another influence on the research community.

4 As I have discussed elsewhere (Mowles, 2022), the dynamic between the actions of individuals and the societies they form is one of the central concerns of sociology.

References

Adams, M. (2006) Hybridizing Habitus and Reflexivity: Towards an Understanding of Contemporary Identity?, *Sociology*, 40(3), pp511–528.

Alvesson, M., Hardy, C. and Harley, W. (2008) Reflecting on Reflexivity: Reflexive Textual Practices in Organization and Management Theory, *Journal of Management Studies*, 45(3), pp480–501.

Alvesson, M. and Kärreman, D. (2011) *Qualitative Research and Theory Development: Mystery as Method*, London: Sage Publications.

Alvesson, M. and Spicer, A. (2012) A Stupidity-Based Theory of Organizations, *Journal of Management Studies*, 49(7), pp1194–1220.

Antonacopoulou, E. (2010) Making the Business School More 'Critical': Reflexive Critique Based on Phronesis as a Foundation for Impact, *British Journal of Management*, 21, ppS6–S25.

Arendt, H. (1971) Thinking and Moral Considerations, *Social Research*, 38(3), pp417–446.

Barad, K. (2007) *Meeting the Universe Half Way: Quantum Physics and the Entanglement of Matter and Meaning*, Durham, NC: Duke University Press.

Beck, U., Giddens, A. and Lash, S. (1994) *Reflexive Modernization*, Cambridge: Polity.

Bernstein, R. (2010) *The Pragmatic Turn*, Cambridge: Polity Press.

Bourdieu, P. (1982) *Leçon sur la Leçon*, Paris: Editions de Minuit.

Bourdieu, P. and Wacquant, L. (1992) *An Invitation to Reflexive Sociology*, Chicago, IL: University of Chicago Press.

Cabanas, E. and Illouz, E. (2019) *Manufacturing Happy Citizens*, Cambridge: Polity Press.

Cunliffe, A. (2003) Reflexive Inquiry in Organizational Research: Questions and Possibilities, *Human Relations*, 56(8), pp983–1003.

Elias, N. (1987) *Involvement and Detachment*, Oxford: Blackwell.

Elias, N. (1991) *The Society of Individuals*, Oxford: Blackwell.

Elias, N. (2000) *The Civilizing Process: Sociogenetic and Psychogenetic Investigations*, Oxford: Blackwell.

Foulkes, S.H. and Anthony, E.J. (1984 [1957]) *Group Psychotherapy: The Psychoanalytic Approach*, London: Karnac Books.

Garrety, K., Badham, R., Morrigan, V., Rifkin, W. and Zanko, M. (2003) The Use of Personality Typing in Organizational Change, *Human Relations*, 56, pp211–235.

Geertz, C. (1968) Thinking as a Moral Act: Ethical Dimensions of Anthropological Fieldwork in the New States Author(s), *The Antioch Review*, Summer, 28(2), pp139–158.

Han, B. (2015) *The Burnout Society*, Stanford, CA: Stanford University Press.

Hibbert, P., Coupland, C. and MacIntosh, R. (2010) Reflexivity: Recursion and Relationality in Organizational Research Processes, *Qualitative Research in Organizations and Management*, 5(1), pp47–62.

Hibbert, P. and Cunliffe, A. (2015) Responsible Management: Engaging Moral Reflexive Practice through Threshold Concepts, *Journal of Business Ethics*, 127(1), pp177–188.

Illouz, E. (2007) *Cold Intimacies: The Making of Emotional Capitalism*, Cambridge: Polity Press.

Illouz, E. (2012) *Why Love Hurts*, Cambridge: Polity Press.

Lash, S. (2003) Reflexivity as Non-linearity, *Theory, Culture & Society*, 20(2), pp49–57.

Latour, B. (1993) *We Have Never Been Modern*, London: Longman.

Lynch, M. (2000) Against Reflexivity as a Virtue and Source of Privileged Knowledge, *Theory, Culture & Society*, 17(3), pp26–54.

Mead, G.H. (1934) *Mind, Self and Society: from the Perspective of a Social Behaviorist*, Chicago, IL: University of Chicago Press, 2015.

Mead, G.H. (1938) *The Philosophy of the Act*, Chicago, IL: University of Chicago Press.

Mills, C.W. (1959/2000) *The Social Imagination*. Oxford: Oxford University Press.

Mowles, C. (2017) Experiencing Uncertainty – On the Potential of Groups and a Group Analytic Approach for Making Management Education More Critical, *Management Learning*, 48(5), pp505–519.

Mowles, C. (2021) *Complexity: A Key Idea for Business and Society*, London: Routledge.

Porter, T.M. (1995) *Trust in Numbers: The Pursuit of Objectivity in Science and Public Life*, Princeton, NJ: Princeton University Press.

Rosa, H. (2015) *Social Acceleration: A New Theory of Modernity*, New York: Columbia University Press.

Rosa, H. (2019) *Resonance: A Sociology of Our Relationship to the World*, Cambridge: Polity Press.

Shotter, J. (2006) Understanding Process from Within: An Argument for 'withness' Thinking, *Organization Studies*, 27(4), pp585–604.

Shotter, J. and Tsoukas, H. (2014a) In Search of Phronesis: Leadership and the Art of Judgement, *Management Learning and Education*, 1(2), pp224–243.

Shotter, J. and Tsoukas, H. (2014b) Performing Phronesis: On the Way to Engaged Judgment, *Management Learning*, 45(4), pp377–396.

Thomas, G. (2010) Doing Case Study: Abduction Not Induction, Phronesis Not Theory, *Qualitative Inquiry*, 16(7), pp575–582.

Thomas, G. (2012) Changing Our Landscape of Inquiry for a New Science of Education, *Harvard Educational Review*, 82(1), pp26–51.

Vince, R., Abbey, G., Langenhan, M. and Bell, D. (2018) Finding Critical Action Learning through Paradox: The Role of Action Learning in the Suppression and Stimulation of Critical Reflection, *Management Learning*, 49(1), pp86–106.

Part II

EXPLORING PRACTICE AND ITS BREAKDOWNS

6

EXPERIENTIAL LEARNING, REFLEXIVITY AND THE PRODUCTIVE USE OF DOUBT

KARINA SOLSØ

Introduction

At a time when the world feels particularly unstable and uncertain, it seems pressing to question some of the assumptions that permeate the dominant style of thinking both in society and in the domain of organisation and management. Most scholars within organisation and management studies (OMS) probably share a longing to stabilise the world. The question is: through what methods? Resting on what assumptions about the world and our being with each other? This book about research methods aims to complexify our thinking about everyday experience in organisations. As such it is a response to widespread and dominant patterns of simplification that characterise theories about organisational phenomena as noted by Cunliffe (2022), Mowles (2021), Tsoukas (2019), Stacey (2012) and Nicolini (2012).

These simplifications manifest themselves in how assumptions from the natural sciences continue to dominate research in the social sciences

DOI: 10.4324/9781003410522-8

(Flyvbjerg, 2001). Within OMS, this leads to theories that underestimate the complexity of everyday life for managers, which is then reflected in the pedagogy of many management development programs. Such programmes tend to present a simplified view of the practice of management, for example, through idealised descriptions of the organisation as an orderly hierarchy with clear strategic targets, rules and tools that secure movement in the direction of strategic ambitions (Larsson et al., 2020).

Interestingly, in their award-winning research project into a management development programme, Larsson et al. (2020) conclude that the managers who had been 'bad students' – meaning that they questioned the simplistic notion of management – were better at acting into the complexity within their everyday work after the end of the programme. In contrast, the 'good students', who more or less uncritically took the simplistic, hierarchical image of management into their daily practice, often ended up in conflicts with their staff, having a difficult time engaging them in strategic conversations. The study concluded that the 'bad manager students' knew very well that staff didn't necessarily see the formal organisation as a source of managerial authority, and hence they also realised that authority arises through engagement with knowledge that emerges through everyday work.

So if becoming a good manager requires more than familiarity with simplified models and categories, how can managers increase their capacity to engage reflexively with experience? This chapter will argue that this can be developed through experiential methods.

Simplifications within organisation and management studies

Taking the results of the study by Larsson et al. seriously leads to a questioning of the assumption that the natural sciences offer a sufficient parallel for the social world, including organisations. In OMS, management is often described in individualised, instrumentalised and idealised ways, all of which simplify the complexity of the everyday experience of social engagement with others in organisational settings (Solsø, 2024):

- *individualised* in the sense that management is typically seen an enterprise that is carried out by single individuals. Leaders and managers are portrayed as independent and autonomous people who are more or less free to make choices about what they want to do, when and how – as if decisions are not enabled and constrained by the actions and attitudes of those around them (Griffin, 2002, Mowles, 2015, 2021, Stacey and Mowles, 2016).

- *instrumentalised* in the sense that abstract typologies, models and 2×2 grids play a key role in the construction of proceduralised descriptions of how managers can respond to particular kinds of problems and tasks (Cunliffe, 2022, Mowles, 2021). Theorising often rests on preestablished categories, which are causally connected to each other in ways that make sense in a cognitive or rational way, but which often fail to fulfil their promises in practice as soon as humans enter the picture (Larsson et al., 2022, Stacey, 2012).
- *idealised* in the sense that there is an implicit tendency to portray the phenomena of interest in a way that ignores the practical issues and conflicts that arise in their functionalisation. The focus of attention is often on descriptions of best practice or categories of action required to gain success or to reach the targets or goals, as though these aren't ideological. Whether it is around recent innovations like, for example, 'psychological safety' (Edmondson, 2018) and 'Daring to Lead' (Brown, 2018) or more historic innovations like eight steps of change (Kotter, 1996), theories tend to describe management in an ideal (and simplified) form focused on best practice rather than drawing attention to the complexity, uncertainty and messiness of actual lived experience (Stacey and Mowles, 2016).

In times of great uncertainty and instability and in times where hierarchies and practices of the past are called into question (Cunliffe, 2022), it is pertinent to ask what more managers may need in order to respond to the dynamic and ever-changing nature of the complex everyday experience of being with others at work. This chapter argues that, while the human capacity to simplify is necessary and important when being blown about by the messy nature of experience, the simplifications are insufficient on their own; managers also need to be able to acknowledge and take seriously the social complexity of human relating rather than oversimplifying it (Cunliffe, 2022, Mowles, 2021, Tsoukas, 2019).

This requires a different kind of engagement with the world, and an appetite for 'inquiry with a scientific attitude' (Dewey, 1922) to illuminate the relational and temporal complexity of experience; through the deepened understanding of complexity that can arise from such inquiry lies a potential to engage with plurality in ways where conflict and difference are not ignored or neglected but dealt with through a focus on developing habits where difference and competing values are progressively integrated (Follett, 2013). This is what Richard Bernstein (1991) calls engaged fallibilistic pluralism, which means taking one's own fallibilism seriously, resolving that "*however much we are committed to our own styles of thinking, we are willing to listen to others without denying or suppressing the otherness of the other*" (Bernstein, 1991, p336).

Finding good enough ground in pragmatism

The impulse to simplify described above is not a new phenomenon. More than 100 years ago, the American pragmatist John Dewey was grappling with this very issue. Being a psychologist and a philosopher, he noticed how simplistic and dualistic notions within psychology and pedagogy left people poorly equipped to go about their lives (Dewey, 1922). Even if simplifications can be helpful at times, Dewey dedicated his professional life to developing theories that complexified thinking and practice. This was done through a consistent rejection of dualisms and through a commitment to developing ideas and methods through which people can respond reflectively to the moral situations they encounter. He insisted on the idea that human conduct can only meaningfully be understood in its relational and temporal context (Dewey, 1922) and that thinking and action can't meaningfully be separated (Dewey, 1896, 1910). Dewey argued for the primacy of experience, meaning that we can only access the world through our experience, which relies on socially produced habits of thought and action. This idea leads to a focus on reflection in inquiry processes. Another important idea in Dewey's thinking is the notion that we develop new ideas and practices through inquiry that begin with moments of breakdown. This leads to a focus on abductive reasoning (Peirce, 1877), which is a form of reasoning that we employ in uncertain situations where we don't know how to go on. It is the process of generating hypotheses that, for now, form the most plausible explanation for a set of observations. These ideas offer a valuable starting point for considering how both management research and management education can be carried out in ways that are more consistent with the complexity, ambiguity and uncertainty of experience.

For academic research, this is the foundation of methodological coherence, or in other words, consistency between the object of study and the methods involved (Tracy, 2010, Cunliffe, 2011). So, how can reflexivity and abductive inquiry be mobilised in service of inquiring into organisational phenomena in their complex relational and temporal embeddedness?

This chapter engages with the possibilities within *experiential methods* as one of the methodological resources that can be drawn upon in the pursuit of this agenda and addresses the following question: how can experiential methods be mobilised with an attempt to inquire into organisational phenomena in ways that are coherent with the complexity and uncertainty of lived experience?

I will begin with a more thorough introduction to some key ideas within Dewey's psychology. This will lead to an introduction to and critical evaluation of experiential methods in the light of the Deweyan attempt to take the complexity of experience seriously. The case of the Doctor of Management (DMan) programme at the University of Hertfordshire is offered as an example of a research tradition, which draws on experiential methods in the pursuit of reflexive and abductive inquiry. Finally, I will consider the possibilities and limitations of this form of abductive and reflexive inquiry.

John Dewey's psychology

From John Dewey's extensive writing, I will highlight two key ideas that are particularly relevant to this chapter: Dewey's understanding of the relationship between habit and inquiry, and his understanding of how we engage with doubt.

Habit and inquiry

In 1896, Dewey wrote his famous 'reflex arc' paper in which he argued against the behaviouristic idea that human behaviour can be understood as serial connections between stimulus, mental operation and response; an idea that keeps subject and object, body and soul separated. For Dewey, people don't respond to raw and isolated stimuli, but to the *meaning* that arises through engagement in social activity in the material world. Over time, these responses become recognisable as patterns – what Dewey calls *habits* – and because they are formed through our intercourse with other people, they are socially produced. Habits are not purely cognitive but fundamentally corporeal, which is to say that they concern the actions of bodies. Indeed, Dewey goes as far as to say that the self is constituted by habits (Dewey, 1922, p25) and it is through habits that the world comes to feel like home to us – we in-*habit* the world.

Dewey advocates an experiential ontology (Martela, 2015), meaning that as human beings, we live in a world where we need to respond or to act, rather than to observe. This means that 'experience' is primary and an important consequence of this ontology is the impossibility of detaching the subject from temporal and social relations. This is the basis for Dewey's rejection of spectator theories of knowledge (Dewey, 1929), which assume that people – for example, managers – can detach from whatever is going on and have some analytic overview of what is actually happening. With this rejection, Dewey places humans in a realm of uncertainty exactly because of our relationality. He draws attention to the way in which we are caught up in relational processes of emergent meaning making and mutual identity forming that no-one can control or predict.

Inevitably, humans encounter indeterminate situations where meaning, and therefore the appropriate response, is unclear. For Dewey, the experience of finding oneself in an indeterminate situation emerges because of one's habits:

> We do not approach any problem with a wholly naïve or virgin mind; we approach it with certain acquired habitual modes of understanding, with a certain store of previously evolved meanings, or at least of experiences from which meanings may be educed.
>
> (Dewey, 1910, p106)

Importantly, *inquiry* is the activity that holds the potential of transforming a situation – and therefore includes the possibility of novelty. Inquiry is the process of engaging with indeterminate situations, where we don't know how to go on. Through inquiry, we attempt to stabilise the situation.

However, these moments of perplexity are not simply cognitive puzzles because habits are corporeal. As such, they can be full of intense emotions, and the world can appear to have no direct meaning (Brinkmann, 2013, p97). Dewey understands the emotional quality of such situations as 'the release of impulse' which drives the inquiry:

> In the course of time custom becomes intolerable because of what it suppresses and some accident of war or inner catastrophe releases impulses for unrestrained expression.
>
> (Dewey, 1922, p68)

We find ourselves wanting to understand what is going on; wanting to find out how it is possible to think and act differently. It is following this impulse that leads to the:

> transformation of an indeterminate situation into one that is so determinate in its constituent distinctions and relations as to convert the elements of the original situation into a unified whole.
>
> (Dewey, 1938, pp104–105)

So, through processes of inquiry into indeterminate situations, we can transform the situation into a 'unified whole', which for Dewey means that we have found a way of acting meaningfully into it (Brinkmann, 2013).

Through these concepts of habit, breakdown, release of impulse and inquiry, Dewey describes an ongoing dialectical process in so far as inquiries transform habits, which lead to new inquiries and so on.

The scientific attitude: reflection and reflexivity

Dewey also describes different ways in which the release of impulse can be satisfied. In everyday life, inquiry may be resolved quickly: if we are walking on an unsteady path for example, we may make decisions quickly and unreflectively about how to adjust our posture to feel secure and able to go on. In cases where other people are concerned, however, Dewey warns against the temptation to rush to action:

> The moral correlate of liberated impulse is not immediate activity, but reflection upon the way in which to use impulse to renew disposition and reorganize habit.
>
> (Dewey, 1922, p68)

Here, Dewey advocates instead *inquiry with a scientific attitude*, by which he means reflection with a disciplined mind that suspends judgment in favour of further investigation. Through such inquiries into breakdowns of habit, new hypotheses can form that enable the emergence of more helpful or sophisticated habits. For Dewey, scientific inquiries are animated by a delight in the problematic and the ability to cherish uncertainty until one has found a way forward that proves useful.

> The scientific attitude may almost be defined as that which is capable of enjoying the doubtful; scientific method is, in one aspect, a technique for making a productive use of doubt by converting it into operations of infinite inquiry.
>
> (Dewey, 1929, p227)

As the quotation suggests, inquiry into breakdowns can be a demanding process, which requires a capacity to endure a prolonged state of being in doubt. This fits well with Dewey's understanding of reflection, which he describes as "the painful effort of disturbed habits to readjust themselves" (Dewey, 1922, p76).

Dewey doesn't make a conceptual distinction between reflection and reflexivity, but he does draw attention to the way in which our habits of understanding are full of taken-for-granted assumptions, which mostly go unnoticed.

> The things of primary experience are so arresting and engrossing that we tend to accept them just as they are – the flat earth, the march of the sun from east to west, and its sinking under the earth. Current beliefs in morals, religion, and politics similarly reflect the social conditions, which present themselves. Only analysis shows that the ways in which we believe and expect have a tremendous affect upon what we believe and expect.
>
> (Dewey, 1958, p14)

Thus, for Dewey, it is important to develop a critical awareness of our beliefs and prejudices, because they can obfuscate and distort our inquiry processes if they are not detected (Dewey, 1958, p14). In the quote above, Dewey emphasises the pragmatic doctrine of *fallibilism* – that what we call knowledge is always fallible and provisional – that Bernstein also emphasises. There is no final truth about the world. Therefore, the ability to call into question our taken-for-granted assumptions becomes important, so that our thinking continues to develop. This calling of assumptions and beliefs into question is what is often conceived of as critical and self-reflexivity in the management literature (Cunliffe, 2002).

Researching with Dewey: experiential methods

Dewey's theory of human conduct continually sought to reunify concepts that tend to be split. As described above, one example is habit and inquiry; another is the self and the social – habits as the practices of selfhood emerge through social encounters; another is knowledge and experience – experience unifies the subject with the world so there can be no knowing the world without engagement with it.

In a management context, taking up Dewey's ideas mean trying to understand experience in organisations more fully, in all its contradictory and confusing richness, and with an emphasis on the moral horizon around all social interaction. So how can management research and education encourage this kind of engagement, recognising the social and temporal complexity of organisational life? One way of holding on to Dewey's ontological experientialism (Martela, 2015) is by drawing on methods that take people's lived experience as the starting point for exploring the social world.

The need to close the gap between the simplifications of theory and the complexity of practice is increasingly noticed in higher education where there is a calling for an increased experiential pedagogy as a central approach in the pursuit of lasting and effective learning outcomes (Dean et al., 2020). In management education, experiential methods are "considered helpful because they approximate the mess and ambiguity of everyday organisational life and encourage critical reflection" (Mowles, 2017, p3). There are different approaches to experiential methods, and in the following, I will explore how *experiential learning* can allow for reflexive and abductive theorising in ways that are consistent with pragmatist ideas.

Experiential learning

Experiential learning is often identified with the work of David Kolb in the 1980s, through which he brought together ideas from John Dewey, Jean Piaget and Kurt Lewin to develop a theory where learning is seen as "the process whereby knowledge is created through the transformation of experience" (Kolb, 1984, p38). Learning is seen as effective when it follows a cycle of four stages of (1) concrete experience, (2) reflective observation, (3) formation of abstract concepts and (4) active experimentation leading to new concrete experience. Engagement in activities where students are actively involved in situations where learning is stimulated by direct experience is considered essential (Reynolds, 2009) and so learning situations are explicitly designed to create emotional engagement similar to the kind of engagement that people experience outside the classroom. Through such emotional engagement, the reflective and critical observations can arise.

Experiential learning in management education and research

In the realm of management education and research, students are introduced to learning situations, which have similarities with the situations one might encounter at a workplace, and here, experiential learning is often seen as "the most appropriate modality by which to help students learn essential management competencies and make impactful, intelligent organisational decisions as leaders" (Dean et al., 2020, p571). Experiential teaching activities include role-plays, fishbowl discussions, in-class interpersonal simulations and self-assessments (Dean et al., 2020, p571).

Experiential learning has become so widespread in management education over recent decades that in 2019, the *Journal of Management Education* dedicated a Special Issue to its shadow sides. Contributions drew attention to the practical, psychological and pedagogical aspects of teaching experientially (Wright et al., 2019) and noted that while they hold great potential for rich reflexive insights, these approaches require careful handling and ethical consideration (Bradford, 2019, Edelson et al., 2019). This is because they can elicit powerful emotional responses amongst students and instructors (Taylor, 2018, Clancy and Vince, 2019), surfacing shadow dynamics that can take over a classroom (Elmes, 2019). The 2019 Special Issue attracted much attention and a second Special Issue on experiential learning was published in 2021, this time focusing on the perspective of the instructors, and exploring challenges and barriers arising post-pandemic in large class settings (Clancy et al., 2021).

Evaluating experiential learning trends in the light of pragmatism

There is an important question about whether experiential learning following Kolb holds on to the relational and temporal complexity key to Dewey's pragmatism. Brandi and Elkjær (2016), for example, notice a tendency in management education theory taking up experiential learning, to individualise the process of learning. The quote above by Dean et al. is an example of the way in which the end-in-view of experiential learning is around (individual) students learning essential competencies and becoming able to make "impactful, intelligent organisational decisions as leaders". The implicit individualism shines through this description where it is clear that the learning process takes place within the individual mind.

Critics of this style of thinking argue that what gets ignored then is the way in which learning processes are embedded in unique cultures and social practices (e.g. Kayes, 2002, Reynolds, 2009, Brandi and Elkjær, 2016). This accords with Miettinen (2000), who critiqued Kolb's interpretation of Dewey's concept of experience as being inadequate and narrow. For if reflective thought is an activity involving evolution of habit and inquiry – both of which are social processes – then experience cannot be reduced to anything simply in the minds of individuals. Miettinen concludes that Kolb's work and the adult education tradition more generally "represents the kind of psychological reductionism that Dewey considered a misinterpretation of his anti-dualist conception of experience" (Miettinen, 2000, p70).

The central issue here is that bringing experiential learning exercises such as role-plays and simulations to life with an attempt to equip the individual manager with idealised and instrumentalised insights about how to be effective, how to achieve targets in a particular area and how to reach one's targets through interactions with other people would be a narrow, individualistic and instrumental use of experiential learning. Alternatively, experiential learning can be brought to life in a way that is less instrumental, and more reflective of the competing values (Mead, 1934) at stake in any social situation. This would be using experiential learning with an attempt to sensitise managers to more of the complexity and uncertainty of what is going on between people as they interact to get something done. It would mean an emphasis a deepening the understanding of relational dynamics involved in breakdown and joint inquiry processes, which speaks directly to the opening of this chapter.

The breakdowns (not to say crises) we have encountered in recent years have shown the shortcomings of applying the simplifying ideal of the natural sciences to the social world (Rosa, 2020). Predictability and control are lauded, particularly the case in corporate contexts where individualistic and instrumental tendencies dominate the everyday practice of people. This is exactly where it becomes important to dwell on Dewey's warning about the tendency to respond to breakdowns and liberated impulse through a rush to action. Dewey encourages inquiry with a scientific attitude and taking relational complexity seriously.

Returning to the 'bad manager students' in the study by Larsen et al., perhaps we gain some insight into why they were more successful after the end of the leadership development programme: They attended the course with a 'disciplined mind', exercising critical and reflective thinking, taking into consideration their experience of engagement with a plurality of different people, a plurality of values.

Mobilising experiential learning in management education

So what might experiential learning taken up in ways that are less instrumental and more reflective of relational complexity look like? Further, how can they be mobilised with an attempt to inquire and theorise abductively and reflexively about organisational phenomena in ways that are coherent with the complexity and uncertainty of everyday lived experience? I address these questions using the example of the University of Hertfordshire's DMan programme.

The Doctor of Management programme

As described in the introduction to this volume, this programme is a group-based research degree that draws on the perspective of human interaction as complex responsive processes. Students offer contributions to theory and practice based on a series of projects that investigate their work practice beginning with narrative accounts of a breakdown that has puzzled or intrigued them. The programme relies on experiential methods as key resources in the learning process; these are used particularly during the quarterly themed residential weekends.

Showing its roots in pragmatist philosophy, the complex responsive processes perspective is a critique of the widespread tendency to think about organisations as 'things' (systems, wholes) that can be observed from a detached, rational and analytical perspective. The alternative offered aims to start engaging with the blooming, buzzing confusion of experience (James, 1890): to 'take experience seriously' is an encouragement to attend to the lived experience of interacting with others in organisational groups, and exploring the wider patterns of interaction through one's own involvement (Stacey and Griffin, 2005). This approach to inquiry processes is based on abductive reasoning (Peirce, 1877), where experiences of breakdown of habit and the release of impulse are the starting points for inquiry processes, as I have explored previously. Through the inquiry, explanations for the breakdown are generated, leading to a transformation of the indeterminate situation, meaning that it is again possible to act in a meaningful way.

The DMan therefore uses the iterative writing of projects as a way of capturing this process. Each project begins with a narrative account of a breakdown that the abductive theorising seeks to resolve. The breakdown is written autoethnographically through a narrative that describes the interactions in which something unexpected or intriguing occurs these moments of perplexity illuminate the taken-for-granted habits that are breaking down. The narrative is followed by reflections leading to a research question that animates the reflexive and critical inquiry.

Since researchers on the DMan study the breakdown of habits of practice arising in their engagement with others, their own patterns of feeling, relating and thinking are fundamentally a part of the research (see chapters in Part 1 of this volume). Therefore, inquiring into such breakdowns involves a reflexive turn, where the manager becomes aware of the way in which their own patterns of thinking, acting and feeling in interactions with others impact their experience and interpretations of experience.

Such a reflexive approach is widely acknowledged as important when it comes to management education. Cunliffe (2002) describes management learning as a "reflexive dialogic practice" (p36). For Cunliffe, critical reflexivity is about questioning the taken-for-granted aspects of everyday experience. Likewise, Corlett (2012) draws attention to the importance of offering dialogic opportunities within which managers can engage in critical discussion of problematic aspects within their own practice. A crucial question, however, is about how such a reflexive practice can be achieved.

Since critical reflexivity involves an active questioning of taken-for-granted assumptions, there is a tendency in leadership development for people to shy away from this critical engagement due to a value of respecting peer-students as expert in their own field, not wanting to destabilise the socio-moral order of the learning situations (Larsson and Knudsen, 2022).

Three examples of experiential methods on the DMan

In many ways, the every interaction to do with the programme is an opportunity for experiential learning: how students engage with the application process, or how they feel about the mandatory attendance at residentials, or how they go about negotiating their way into a learning set, or their relationship to meeting submission deadlines, or how they respond to critique or encouragement, all provide rich material for inquiring into both their own habits, but also the norms of their social worlds. Any of these topics (and anything else relating to the programme) can be explored through project work or in conversions at residential weekends.

The programme also employs some more specific approaches to support the kind of abductive and reflexive inquiry that – according to the Deweyan perspective introduced in this chapter – is of great value when it comes to the development of a capacity of managers to respond skilfully to complex situations. I will now describe three of these: learning sets, the community meeting and the use of experiential learning exercises.

Learning sets

Researchers work in groups of two to four students and a supervisor, submitting draft projects and meeting roughly every six weeks. Projects are typically iterated four to six times, and each iteration is reviewed by the student's learning set members, who respond in whichever way feels most helpful at the time, of course reflecting their own histories of sociality. This may include offering different interpretations of what they understand to be happening in the narrative material being presented, or drawing attention to the author's interpretive or responsive patterns. They may also highlight particular developments of deficiencies in the quality of the project: for example, supervisors or more senior students may more readily comment on academic or critical rigor due to their greater experience, whereas all members may convey whether they find the project interesting or relevant to their own working lives.

Importantly, it is usually only when the group judges the impulse that initiated the inquiry to have been resolved in a way that is both resonant and plausible, that students move onto the next phase of their work. As such, the function of the learning set is to form a community of inquiry (Peirce, 1877, see also Larsen, Chapter 3 this volume) within which the abductive process takes place (for a more elaborate account of the way in which reflexive and abductive theorising leads to contributions to practice and knowledge, see Rasmussen, Chapter 9 this volume).

The work in the learning set offers opportunities for experiential learning to the extent that the themes that researchers write about often show up in the lived interaction between learning set members. The learning set is a group in the wider research community, and the dynamics of group life relating to interdependence, power and ethics show up just as they do in organisations. Perhaps different from organisational life is the opportunity to inquire into what happens in learning sets, which may be more constrained when managers are at work.

To illustrate this, here is the example of David,[1] a student and researcher on the programme inquiring into his leadership practice as a headteacher. For David, research themes of responsibility and ethics came up again and again in lively ways during the residential weekends, in small moments of breakdown leading to release of impulse experienced as guilt and frustration in his interactions with his fellow students. This was typically related to a question about what it means to take responsibility for what happens in a group of people. David's tendency was to take a lot of responsibility through highly engaged participation – often leading to frustration with others who participate less actively – seemingly taking less responsibility.

For example, at one residential he criticised a presentation made by his supervisor in front of the community. After his questioning, he was burdened with guilt while at the same time frustrated with himself for feeling guilty. The experience was then turned into an inquiry in the learning set – along the tradition of the experiential group – where the plurality of experiences amongst learning set members was explored and discussed in the light of the set members' interpretation of the situation. For example, one learning set member said that he hadn't even noticed the criticism in what David had said, while another member said that she had been curious about why he had felt so guilty about it because she thought the criticism was relevant.

The learning set thus becomes a social arena in which group members' patterns of relationship and habits of thought and action inevitably get played out in ways that can become a resource for researching organisational life. In this way, while conversations in the learning set aren't experiential learning exercises as described above, qualities of the style of relating in experiential learning methods are enacted through the reflexive inquiry into the lived experience of relational complexity during the residential weekend.

The community meeting

When being interviewed before joining the programme, researchers are told about the reliance on experiential methods on the programme. The most obvious and ritualised use of experiential methods is called 'the community meeting'. On the quarterly residential weekends which last from Friday afternoon to Monday afternoon, each morning begins with a community meeting. This is an experiential group in the group analytic tradition (Foulkes, 1975; Mowles, 2017; see also the introduction in this volume).

The community meeting lasts for an hour and a half with no other agenda than the task of exploring what is happening for and between group members. Faculty members working on the programme participate in the group, disclosing some of their experience as other members do. They are of course in a position of authority in relation to students, which is likely to influence their participation; however, they are not conductors, which is a key difference from therapeutic groups. Topics arising in the conversation are, for example, community members' senses of belonging (e.g. affection or conflict amongst learning set members), or experience of hierarchy and discipline (e.g. the roles of senior and junior students, or students and faculty), surprising emotional reactions to particular events such as loyalty, betrayal, anxiety, guilt, shame, envy and other complex feelings, arrivals to and departures from the group, and many other topics. As such, these meetings can bring up the kinds of uncomfortable aspects of experience within the community which are often under-attended to in research processes and indeed in organisational life (Kanov, 2021).

The topics emerging at community meetings tend to reflect the themes that researchers write about in their projects, but unlike how they show up in organisational life, here they can be explored in ways that may not be possible in typical work settings. The community meeting thus offers a unique possibility for reflexive insight for students on the programme, for as they engage with their research themes through their embodied participation with others in the group, they are likely to call out responses from others through which patterns in their own organisation tend to be brought to life.

In David's case, for example, this meant raising in the community meeting the experience described above of his feeling critical towards his supervisor about her presentation and dealing with the guilt and shame that he immediately felt when articulating his critique. David reflected on the way in which these feelings are very familiar to him, and thus very related to the kinds of breakdowns that his research focussed on. Others could then respond to David, for example, by saying that they hadn't really noticed the degree of criticality in his response to the presentation, and how listening to him in the community meeting led them to think about their capacity to notice when others around them go through something emotionally demanding. Others, however, had clearly noticed the sense of critique leading for them to a sense of anxiety related to open critique of authority figures, reflecting assumptions and habits within their own practice and organisations about relationships across hierarchical boundaries. The conversation in this community meeting thus led to wider exploration of how power relations in organisations and society more widely are produced and reproduced through the suppression of expressions of frustration towards authority figures in public.

In this way, the community meeting offers an opportunity for experiential learning that can help researchers to become (or practice becoming) reflexive about their own habitual ways of being with others in groups – a key requirement in writing autoethnographic projects. Through the ongoing use of experiential methods, both in the learning sets and in the larger group, researchers become aware and reflexive about the patterns of relating that they write about in their narratives, and they become able to generalise from their own practice, drawing on their sociological imagination (Mills, 2000) to notice how the pattern of thought and action are reflective not just of their own practice, but of wider habits in organisations. This is not done with the narrow focus on the individual becoming more skilful in order to reach his or her goals. Rather, it is done in a way which involves an ongoing inquiry into the plurality of perspectives and values that emerge as important during the inquiry.

Returning to David, he came to theorise about how the breakdowns he encountered in his practice as a headteacher seemed to centre around a theme of struggling to feel good enough, and struggling to feel that he was doing well enough to look after the competing needs of the variety of people at the school. From becoming reflexive about his tendencies to feel guilty, absorb responsibility, and struggle to make demands on others, he came to theorise about how – in the literature on school leadership – leaders are idealised and portrayed in heroic and omnipotent ways, reflecting individualistic discourses in the wider management literature. David argued in his thesis that this individualised discourse can leave leaders with a nagging sense of inadequacy and self-critique that goes hand in hand with the social context of a prescriptive national schools inspectorate system. His contribution focused on the relational processes involved in the emergence of such patterns, which moved the responsibility away from only being an issue for single individuals.

Experiential learning exercises

The DMan also sometimes employs practices that are more formally recognisable within the experiential learning tradition. This could be in the shape of, for example, experiential games, role-plays or fishbowl dialogue relevant to the theme of the weekend.

When they happen, exercises typically take place early on in the residential weekend, because such games often lead to quite powerful experiences which can be explored in depth after the exercise has ended. The quality of the post-game reflection is crucial, thinking about the critique raised above about the tendency to individualise and instrumentalise learning. Rather than focusing on what individual managers can learn from the exercise in terms of being more effective in reaching their targets, the focus is more on the plurality of experience, allowing for reflexive insight. This timing also means that what happens in experiential learning games can be explored community meetings, where it becomes possible to notice potential links between what happened in the exercise, and one or more students' research themes. In this way, experiential learning is mobilised to stimulate the reflexive inquiry into the breakdowns that students' inquiries are about, and the whole weekend becomes an opportunity for experiential learning, as students reflect together on how they relate to each other and faculty.

Thus, the aim is to complexify rather than simplify the understanding of what happened in the game, thus offering opportunities to enrich students' sensitivities and ability to hypothesise about what happens in organisational life. For David, inquiring reflexively into moments of breakdown allowed him to become more aware of his own patterned tendencies, but also to realise how the responses of others reflect their histories of sociality. He became able to detach more from the heat of emotion when dilemmas or difficulties emerge in his leadership practice. As such, abductive and reflexive inquiry holds a potential for a deepened understanding of the complexity of social and institutionalised action; an understanding which can lead to a development of practical judgment. Stacey (2012) understands practical judgment as:

> … the experience-based ability to notice more of what is going on and intuit what is most important about a situation. It is the ability to cope with the ambiguity and uncertainty, as well as the anxiety it generates.
> (Stacey, 2012, p108)

Holding on to Dewey's relational and temporal outlook, Stacey emphasises that practical judgment is not an individual possession, but rather a social process of responding to the ongoing emergent meaning that arises in social interaction.

Limitations

As already noted, there are limitations or shadow sides to the use of experiential methods in reflexive and abductive inquiry (see also Mowles on reflexivity, this volume). One of these relates to the identity destabilising processes that is often associated with the use of experiential methods in the pursuit of reflexive inquiry. Since manager students on the DMan are inquiring into their own experience, the projects that they write unavoidably touch on themes and questions that are closely connected to their sense of self. If the self can be understood as a collection of habits as Dewey suggests, then inquiry processes directed towards breakdowns of habit are likely to feel disturbing to some degree. The continuous joint work in the learning set and in the community to pursue the inquiry with a disciplined mind is just what Dewey advocated and is what often leads to profound insight and identity shifts.

However, equally painful, disappointing or difficult is the experience, if – for some reason – the student can't seem to work his or her way through the reflexive destabilisation, despite a joint effort to work through the process. Occasionally, students leave the without having stabilised the indeterminate situation that brought them to the DMan in the first place. The fact that this is a possible outcome of one's work on the programme is raised with all students in the interviewing process before commencing their studies. However, this doesn't take away the moral obligation to continue to respond to the dilemmas and difficulties that arise. In moments where students struggle, the struggle typically becomes a social one for all involved who must work their way through the process with as much care and thoughtfulness as possible – another opportunity to pay attention to relational complexity and under-attended to parallels in organisational life.

Experiential learning in organisational settings

This chapter has focused on the use of experiential learning in educational settings. What possibilities may there be for mobilising experiential methods in work settings – either as a consultant or as a manager?

As noted at the outset, groups in organisations face plenty of breakdowns that require some form of response, and all too often, the push for swift plans, actions and solutions come to limit the possibilities for the use of the reflective intelligence with a disciplined mind, as Dewey advocates. However, due to the rhetoric around increasing complexity in society and organisations, there is also (at least in some organisations) a growing awareness of the need for reflective thinking and joint sense-making, for example, in (management) team development (Drath et al., 2008). Here, managers increasingly acknowledge that the capacity to work collaboratively together across different areas of expertise requires some space for joint reflection on the ways in which the interdependency between people and groups enables and constrains the capacity to work together in productive ways (Bartle, 2020). Similarly, in the field of working with change, the recognition of the inherent unpredictability and uncertainty of the future has led to a focus on approaching change through learning processes (Gherardi, 2011, Garud et al. 2015), which involves spaces for joint reflection.

The question (for managers and consultants) becomes one of noticing when the breakdown facing a group involves qualities which may benefit from being approached through experiential methods. Kayes et al. (2005) suggest that group patterns such as groupthink, overdependence on a dominant leader, over-commitment to goals and diffusion of responsibility are amenable to learning approaches where team members reflect on their actual experience of working together in order for them to establish more productive working patterns.

Fundamentally, experiential learning is about reflecting on actual experience. It is about the emergence of opportunities for people become reflective about their involvement and the release of impulse that arises from breakdown. While experiential learning can involve games and exercises, it can also 'just' involve a practice of asking questions like: "what is happening in this room right now?" As has been mentioned above, as with everything else, working with experiential methods involves practical judgment (Stacey, 2012), and becoming skilful in working with experiential methods is a practice that needs ongoing development.

I have described how such experiential methods are integrated into the DMan programme through rituals like learning set meetings, community meetings and through the use of exercises. It is worth thinking about what kinds of rituals one might need to create in organisations to allow for the use of experiential methods. As has become clear in this chapter, experiential learning can have a destabilising quality, which raises important ethical considerations. Therefore, careful thought must be given to how experiential methods can be introduced so that the aim for deepened reflexive insight into a variety of interpretations and feelings can emerge.

Conclusion

This chapter opened with reflections on the widespread tendencies in organisations to simplify the complexity of everyday interactions in organisations and how these simplifying tendencies may be counterproductive when it comes to stabilising the uncertainty of the world. A radical alternative is found drawing on the work of John Dewey, who insisted on the importance of an understanding of interaction that resonates with everyday experience. Dewey's ideas lead to a perspective on inquiries into organisational contexts which emphasise *reflexivity* and *abduction*: starting inquiry processes in moments of breakdown, and sustaining such inquires with a disciplined mind willing to reevaluate beliefs and prejudice. Pursuing such reflexive and abductive inquiries is not an easy task. It is one that requires the creation of practices and routines which support the sustaining of the disciplined mind.

Here, experiential methods prove useful due to the primacy of experience and due to the open-endedness of the approach, which fit well with the abductive logic of pragmatism. Just as powerful and significant experiential methods can be in terms of the emergence of radical reflexive insights, just as destabilising can the process be in terms of identity. Here, what is called for is a moral stance, where managers as well as people more generally continue to develop their ability to respond to the variety of ways in which the inquiry process manifests itself. As with most of the situations that involve breakdown or crisis, what is key is the question of how we respond to plurality; to the otherness of the other (Bernstein, 1991). This chapter has argued for the importance of an engaged fallibilistic pluralism; a pluralism where we struggle to stay in relation, despite our differences. This requires a capacity to complexify rather than simplify our thinking about what we are doing together with others.

Note

1 David is a former student on the programme, who has been anonymized but has read and agreed to his inclusion in this chapter.

References

Bartle, K. (2020) *The Struggle for Plurality and Politics in School Leadership Practice: Exploring the Importance of Thoughtful Action in Conditions of Uncertainty*. Available at: https://doi.org/10.18745/th.24596

Bernstein, R.J. (1991) *The New Constellation*. Cambridge: Polity Press.

Bradford, D.L. (2019) Ethical Issues in Experiential Learning. *Journal of Management Education*, *43*(1), pp. 89–98.

Brandi, U., and Elkjaer, B. (2016) Management Education in a Pragmatist Perspective after Dewey's Experimentalism. In Steyaert, C., Beyes, T., and Parker, M. (Eds.), *The Routledge Companion to Reinventing Management Education* (pp. 193–205). London: Routledge.

Brinkmann, S. (2013) *John Dewey: Sciences for a Changing World.* London: Routledge.

Brown, B. (2018) *Dare to Lead. Brave Work. Tough Conversations. Whole Hearts.* New York: Random House.

Clancy, A., Cullen, J.G., and Hood, A. (2021) Teaching Perspectives on Experiential Learning in Large Classes. *Journal of Management Education, 45*(5), pp. 685–689.

Clancy, A., and Vince, R. (2019) Theory as Fantasy: Emotional Dimensions to Grounded Theory. *British Journal of Management, 30*(1), pp. 203–216.

Corlett, S. (2012) Participant Learning in and through Research as Reflexive Dialogue: Being 'Struck' and the Effects of Recall. *Management Learning, 44*(5), pp. 453–469.

Cunliffe, A. (2011) Crafting Qualitative Research: Morgan and Smircich 30 Years On. *Organizational Research Methods, 14*(4), pp. 647–673.

Cunliffe, A. (2022) Must I Grow a Pair of Balls to Theorize about Theory in Organization and Management Studies? *Organization Theory, 3*(3), pp. 1–28.

Cunliffe, A.L. (2002) Reflexive Dialogical Practice in Management Learning. *Management Learning, 33*(1), pp. 35–61.

Dean, K.L., Wright, S., and Forray, J.M. (2020) Experiential Learning and the Moral Duty of Business Schools. *Academy of Management Learning and Education, 19*(4), pp. 569–583.

Dewey, J. (1896) The Reflex Arc Concept in Psychology. *Psychological Review, 3*, pp. 357–370.

Dewey, J. (1910) *How We Think*. Boston, MA: D.C. Heath and Co.

Dewey, J. (1922/2019) *Human Nature and Conduct. An Introduction to Social Psychology.* Whithorn: Anodos books.

Dewey, J. (1929) The Quest for Certainty. In Boydston, J.A. (Ed.), *John Dewey: Later Works, 1925–1953* (vol. 4). Carbondale: Southern Illinois University Press.

Dewey, J. (1938) Logic: The Theory of Inquiry. In Boydston, J.A. (Ed.), *John Dewey: Later Works, 1925–1953* (vol. 12). Carbondale: Southern Illinois University Press.

Dewey, J. (1958) *Experience and Nature.* Chicago, IL: Open Court Publishing Company.

Drath, W.H., McCauley, C.D., Palus, C.J., Velson, E.V., O'Connor, P.M.G. and McGuire, J.B. (2008) Direction, Alignment, Commitment: Toward a More Integrative Ontology of Leadership. *Leadership Quarterly,* 19, pp. 635–653.

Garud, R., Simpson, B., Langley, A. and Tsoukas, H. (2015) Introduction: How Does Novelty Emerge? In Garud, I.R., Simpson, B., Langley, A. and Tsoukas, H. (Red.), *The Emergence of Novelty in Organizations* (s. 1–26, pp. 1–24). Oxford: Oxford University Press.

Gherardi, S. (2011). Organizational Learning: The Sociology of Practice. In Easterby-Smith, I.M. and Lyles, M.A. (Red.), *Handbook of Organizational Learning and Knowledge Management* (2. udg., s. 43–65). Chichester: John Wiley and Sons.

Edelson, S.A., Lo, K.D., Nelson, T., Stark, G., Stratton, M.T. and van Esch, C. (2019) From the Shadow of Overconfidence into the Light of Humility: Reflections on Experiential Learning Activities Gone Awry. *Journal of Management Education,* 43(2), pp. 200–211.

Edmondson, A. (2018) *The Fearless Organization. Creating Psychological Safety in the Workplace for Learning, Innovation and Growth.* Boston, MA: Harvard Business School.

Elmes, M.B. (2019) Working with(in) the Shadow of Experiential Learning. *Journal of Management Education,* 43(1), pp. 99–107.

Flyvbjerg, B. (2001) *Making Social Science Matter. Why Social Inquiry Fails and How It Can Succeed Again.* Cambridge: Cambridge University Press.

Follett, M.P. (2013/1924) *Creative Experience.* Mansfield Centre, CT: Martino Publishing.

Foulkes, S.H. (1975) *Group Analytic Psychotherapy: Method and Principles.* London: Karnac Books.

Griffin, D. (2002) *The Emergence of Leadership. Linking Self-organization and Ethics.* London: Routledge.

James, W. (1890) *The Principles of Psychology.* Cambridge, MA: Harvard University Press.

Kanov, J. (2021) Why Suffering Matters! *Journal of Management Inquiry,* 30(1), pp. 85–90.

Kayes, A.B., Kayes, D.C. and Kolb, D.A. (2005) Experiential Learning in Teams. *Simulation and Gaming,* 36(3), pp. 330–354.

Kayes, D.C. (2002) Experiential Learning and Its Critics: Preserving the Role of Experience in Management Learning and Education. *Academy of Management Learning and Education*, 1(2), pp. 137–149.

Kolb, D.A. (1984) *Experiential Learning: Experience as the Source of Learning and Development*. Englewood Cliffs, NJ: Prentice-Hall.

Kotter, J. (1996) *Leading Change*. Cambridge, MA: Harvard Business School Press.

Larsson, M., Carsten, M. and Knudsen, M. (2020) Good Intentions Gone Awry: Investigating a Strategically Oriented MLD Program. *Journal of Management Development*, 39(3), pp. 334–354.

Larsson, M. and Knudsen, M. (2022) Conditinos for Reflexive Practices in Leadership Learning: The Regulating Role of a Socio-moral Order of Peer Interactions. *Management Learning*, 53(2), pp. 291–309.

Martela, F. (2015) Fallible Inquiry with Ethical Ends-in-View: A Pragmatist Philosophy of Science for Organizational Research. *Organization Studies*, 36(4), pp. 537–563.

Mead, G.H. (1934) *Mind, Self and Society: from the Standpoint of a Social Behaviorist*. Chicago, IL: University of Chicago Press, 2015.

Miettinen, R. (2000) The Concept of Experiential Learning and John Dewey's Theory of Reflective Thought and Action. *International Journal of Lifelong Education*, 19(1), pp. 54–72.

Mills, C.W. (2000/1959) *The Sociological Imagination*. Oxford: Oxford University Press.

Mowles, C. (2015) *Managing in Uncertainty: Complexity and the Paradoxes of Everyday Organizational Life*. London: Routledge.

Mowles, C. (2021) *Complexity – A Key Idea for Business and Society*. London: Routledge.

Mowles, C. (2017) Experiencing Uncertainty: On the Potential of Groups and a Group Analytic Approach for Making Management Education More Critical. *Management Learning*, 48(5), pp. 505–519.

Nicolini, D. (2012) *Practice Theory, Work and Organization. An Introduction*. Oxford: Oxford University Press.

Peirce, C.S. (1877) The Fixation of Belief. *Popular Science Monthly*, 12, pp. 1–15.

Reynolds, M. (2009) Wild Frontiers – Reflections on Experiential Learning. *Management Learning*, 40(4), pp. 387–392.

Rosa, H. (2020) *The Uncontrollability of the World*. Cambridge: Polity Press.

Solsø, K. (2024) *Dømmekraft – ledelse i social kompleksitet*. Frederiksberg: Samfundslitteratur.

Stacey, R., and Griffin, D. (2005) *A Complexity Perspective on Researching Organizations. Taking Experience Seriously*. London: Routledge.

Stacey, R.D. (2012) *Tools and Techniques of Leadership and Management – Meeting the Challenge of Complexity*. London: Routledge.

Stacey, R.D. and Mowles, C. (2016) *Strategic Management and Organisational Dynamics. The Challenge of Complexity to Ways of Thinking about Organisations*. Harlow: Pearson.

Taylor, V.F. (2018) Afraid of the Deep: Reflections and Analysis of a Role-Play Exercise Gone Wrong. *Journal of Management Education, 42*(6), pp. 772–782.

Tracy, S.J. (2010) Qualitative Quality: Eight "Big-Tent" Criteria for Excellent Qualitative Research. *Qualitative Inquiry, 16*(10), pp. 837–851.

Tsoukas, H. (2019) *Philosophical Organization Theory*. Oxford: Oxford University Press.

Wright, S., Forray, J.M., and Lund Dean, K. (2019). From Advocacy to Accountability in Experiential Learning Practices. *Management Learning, 50*(3), pp. 261–281.

7

PROCESS AND POLITICS

Negotiating the Roles of Human and Non-Human Actors

MIKKEL HAUGSTED BRAHM

Introduction

I am the leader of an architecture unit in a large bank. Architecture as a practice involves mediating between building owners and builders to ensure the owners get the buildings they want (Vitruvius, 50BC/2009). The architecture practice has evolved over time and exists today in many variants. Anything which is constructed has an architecture, i.e., structural properties. This includes buildings, information systems, and enterprises (a business, company, or bold undertaking), i.e., physical constructs *and* social constructs. My unit employs architects with various specialisations within business, enterprise, and IT architecture, and I label our work 'technology-enabled business transformation'; in other words, finding innovative uses of technology to evolve what an enterprise does or how it does it. The constructions we design can sometimes be mechanical, such as IT solutions, and sometimes be social, such as business processes. Throughout my career, I have experienced shortcomings in the ability

DOI: 10.4324/9781003410522-9

of orthodox theories within my field (enterprise architecture, and more broadly change management) to explain practice satisfactorily and to guide practitioners in a useful way. When I asked more experienced colleagues why that may be, I often got the question back: "Don't you know that there is a difference between theory and practice?"

This chapter is my contribution to leaders, practitioners, and researchers working with technology-enabled business transformations to take steps towards a theoretical basis for our practice better able to explain practice and guide practitioners. I provide a process-theory-based description of how the organisation I am part of works with developing and adopting non-human actors[1] and social constructs. This perspective means I understand human and non-human actors as being entangled in an ongoing process of becoming. This contrasts with a systems-theory-based understanding of organisation, i.e., organisation as a system consisting of sub-systems. Together with scholars like Michel Callon, Madeleine Akrich, John Law, and others, Bruno Latour developed Actor-Network Theory as a science and technology studies theory to better understand the role and influence of non-human actors on society. In this chapter, I draw particularly on Latour (1988, 2005) and Akrich (1992) to define a few concepts: *delegation*, *translation/transcription*, *scripted action*, and *prescription* and more broadly on what Latour calls the 'sociology of associations' as something distinct from 'sociology of the social' (2005).

My aim is to draw attention to how paying attention to both the social and the technical aspects of technology-enabled business transformation can provide different interpretations of resistances and powerplays which in turn can provide new options for change managers and researchers.

A process perspective on change

Actors, punctuation and unpredictability

When I say that non-human actors perform actions, I do not imply that they have agency but merely that they perform what is equivalent to some human work. Latour (1988) uses the example of a door in a wall to illustrate this phenomenon. The wall has a purpose of keeping out the cold, or the heat, or other things unwanted by the human occupants. People need to pass through the wall, so we have invented doors on hinges, and, since not everyone remembers to close the door after themselves, we have invented the automatic door closer (groom). To understand the action or work done by doors and their hinges, Latour suggests that you

> simply have to imagine that every time you want to get in or out of the building you have to do the same work as a prisoner trying to escape or a gangster trying to rob a bank, plus the work of those who rebuild either the prison's or bank's walls.
>
> (1988, p299)

Latour defines "this transformation of a major effort into a minor one by the word translation or delegation" (Latour, 1988, p299) which means that we *translate* or *delegate* to the door and hinges the work equivalent to tearing down and rebuilding the wall, and similarly, if we add a door groom, we delegate to this mechanical door closer the work of closing the door behind the person entering or leaving the room. The door, hinges, and groom are not alive and as such have no intentionality nor preferences. They simply perform what Latour calls *scripted action*, i.e., they always (until they break at least) do the same thing and perform the same scripted action, given the same circumstances. This happens to be to close the door by default which reflects the intentionality of the human creators of these non-human actors, not intentionality of the non-human actors themselves. With discipline exceeding any human, the door, hinges, and groom will continue to carry out this scripted action unless some other human actor intervenes and for example jams the door open or the mechanical actors eventually deteriorate and break down.

For the human users of doors, the addition of an automatic door groom has consequences. It alters the experience of using the door. Latour adduces Akrich to define *prescription* as "the behaviour imposed back onto the human by non-human delegates" (1988, p301), remarking that a groom has different prescription than for example a spring would have, since springs simply slam the door shut. Even so, a door groom can be difficult to use for some and can be said to "discriminate against the very little and very old persons" (1988, pp301–302). Prescription does not imply that non-human actors have intentionality or preferences. It is simply the consequence of the scripted action which has been transcribed into the non-human actor by its human creator. This implies that the creation of non-human actors by human actors has consequences for other human actors: those who interact with a non-human actor are subject to the function of the scripted action transcribed into it and the prescription its behaviour imposes. Human creators may intend the functions of non-human actors, but the planned change will have many effects; some effects may have been part of our designs, and some may surprise the designers, planners, and change leaders. The outcomes of the design are predictably unpredictable.

So, how does all of this relate to enterprise architecture? Here is an example I experienced in my job some years ago. Working on designing a new core banking solution, I was engaged in direct observation of users of a core banking solution we were looking to replace to find out what it did well and what could be better. I noticed something odd. The user I was observing was using physical filing cabinets, folders, and papers but I was sure we had introduced electronic document management, so I asked what these folders and papers were. She told me that I was right. When the electronic document management solution was adopted, their old filing cabinets had been removed; the delegation of work to the new system had imagined the paper cabinets as redundant. However, the current solution for core banking had some shortcomings and its prescriptions created some peculiar problems for the human actors involved.

One such example concerned interest calculations. When a loan had an intertest that changed periodically, say every quarter, but the first period was less than a full quarter, the scripted action of the core banking solution would calculate the interest incorrectly for the first period. Human actors would then have to compensate for that by altering the margin (what we add as a bank to the base interest rate) and then the interest rate for the first period would become correct, but next period the loan would again have a wrong interest rate until she returned the margin to its original value. She and her colleagues had created an intricate system of paper records with a folder which they called their 'date archive' with paper notes telling them what they had to change back on that date. If they forgot to change the values when they needed to, the customer could be paying the wrong interest. Informing customers of mistakes like that when eventually discovered was what she hated the most about her job. To deal with these problems, they had been allowed by her manager to buy new cabinets to contain all this extra paper. I was ashamed that we in IT could not provide a solution that just worked, but I could also see that these errors were difficult, time-consuming, and thus expensive to fix. I could not even say that fixing this would be prioritised if brought up in the relevant decision forums. That realisation was even more shameful.

So, you could see the introduction of the electronic document management and core banking solutions as some parts of a change – the parts that were included in our change management plans. The introduction by users of what they called their date archive and a practice of working around errors in the system wer other parts of the change, ones that hadn't been envisioned in our designs nor included in our change management plans.

Akrich notes,

> we are able to say that technical objects changed, stabilized, naturalized, or depoliticized social relations only with the benefit of hindsight… technical objects and people are brought into being in a process of reciprocal definition in which objects are defined by subjects and subjects by objects. It is only after the event that causes are stabilized.
>
> (1992, p222)

So, when did the change to how core banking was done happen? And who gets to decide? Was it when the project team celebrated the success of delivering new solutions to the users, or when the users had finally adopted sufficient workarounds to make the new solutions work as well as they practically could? Arguably, these *punctuations* are in themselves arbitrary, but the declarations may be political – e.g. by declaring that this is the day when solutions are shipped suppliers may be wanting to signal that the cost of further work is not covered by the project (as I worried about when considering the time and effort needed to address the workaround); these decisions may draw attention to some things and away from others, potentially leading to ignorance about a great many aspects and effects of changes that occur after solutions are received and adopted by users into their organisation.

Further, it would be easy to see the complications I described in my example simply as unintended consequences of a well-intentioned change initiative. However, my moral feelings draw attention to how prescription points to "the moral and ethical dimension of mechanisms" (Latour, 1988, p301); if we understand transcription as the expression of the intentions of humans, these can also be seen as the moral and ethical dimension of one group of humans, the creators of non-human actors, influencing organisation of another group of humans, the users of these non-human actors. Human designers try to envision how human users will use the designed non-human actor. They transcribe scripted action into it which will result in prescription that could be meaningful if the envisioned usage matches the actual usage which emerges when the non-human actor is taken into use. If you perceive what non-human actors such as new solutions do as gestures which users respond to, there had been a long process of gestures and responses (Mead, 1934) between celebrating the project's success and the users accepting that now it is as good as it gets. This ultimately led to a different change than the change envisioned, designed, and planned by the project.

We are starting to see, then, that we cannot know the (full) meaning of gestures such as introducing an architectural design, introducing a non-human actor, or introducing a new social construction until users and other stakeholders have responded to these. The future usage of these constructions is paradoxically predictably unpredictable. We also see how the design of non-human actors is social as well as technical. This means that changes are the results of many gestures and responses, where responses are themselves new gestures made by everyone involved. Users will respond in some way to what we change and we can't really know what their responses will be. Those responses are part of the change and affect the outcome of making the change, but they are typically not part of any plan nor design for the change. All of this is worth paying attention to in trying to understand change from a process-theory perspective.

Creativity, resistance and limits

A key difference between human and non-human actors concerns their respective abilities to respond to change creatively. As the example I gave illustrates, while human actors often act habitually, they also have the potential for acting spontaneously and surprisingly, responding to others and adapting to the unexpected and unusual: the people I was observing had invented workarounds to problems created by the core banking system and negotiated the reintroduction of filing cabinets. So, when human actors re-enact something, e.g., reiterate an earlier agreement, there is an opportunity for renegotiation and change.

By contrast, non-human actors can only enact previously transcribed scripted action – the core banking system in the example couldn't itself notice and respond to the interest calculation issue, only reproduce it. Where non-human actors can cope with changes, this is only to the extent that this coping ability was transcribed into them at their creation, i.e., was anticipated and handled by their creator. Further, non-human actors can interact with other non-human actors but only as long as the responses of the other are still within the set of pre-determined potential responses, the non-human actor is designed to cope with. Inevitably failures occur as we try to shape materiality into doing what we want it to do, but still, it does not – what Pickering calls *material resistance*. From the perspective of the designer and constructor of the non-human actor, this is experienced as a form of resistance, albeit different from human resistance.

When we work with IT solutions, we use the term 'breaking changes' to denote a change in the response of one non-human actor which cannot be coped with by other dependent non-human actors. Breaking changes are problematic because they cause a ripple effect of required redesigns throughout a chain of interdependent non-human actors all of which requires careful deliberation (design) and construction work which can be extensive and expensive. Non-human actors' repertoires of scripted actions and interactions are fundamentally non-complex although they can be very complicated. Thus, designers of non-human actors often seek to devise a set of simple scripted actions that have appreciated function for their human users without too onerous prescription, or designers simply choose a role for the non-human actor which is simple. Designers inevitably make assumptions about users which may be true or false or in other words:

> we have to go back and forth continually between the designer and the user, between the designer's projected user and the real user, between the world inscribed in the object and the world described by its displacement. For it is in this incessant variation that we obtain access to the crucial relationships: the user's reactions that give body to the designer's project, and the way in which the user's real environment is in part specified by the introduction of a new piece of equipment.
>
> (Akrich, 1992, pp208–209)

What I am trying to draw attention to is that users who accept prescription implicitly accept a standardisation of work with the roles the designer has delegated to both user and non-human actor acted out in a simplistic way. Users accept in other words a loss of optionality and are typically just expected to cope with any changes (and problems) transcribed into their non-human delegates. You could say that through this form of delegation from manual to automated work, we may replace the work of a flexible and responsive human actor with the roughly equivalent work of an obstinate and inflexible non-human actor. Thus, including non-human actors in organisations tends to make the repertoire of actions more durable and less flexible (Latour, 1988, p306), i.e., often non-human actors render work more standardised which may be perceived as detrimental to some actors while beneficial to others.

I also want to draw attention to how delegating work to non-human actors changes the organisation also for the human actors, i.e., IT changes inevitably cause organisational changes to some extent. Since we can rely on human actors to cope with imposed changes, we typically spend relatively less resources on producing knowledge about users and organisation and relatively more resources on producing knowledge about non-human actors and the scripted action which we have to transcribe into them, since they cannot on their own improve after the end of the change initiative. This only works to the extent that human users accept that they must compensate for the lack of responsiveness and other shortcomings of their non-human actor delegates. Accepting this may not be in the users' interest, and the changes may be associated with a degree of loss or weakening of valued social relations, feelings of competence, status, etc. which can lead to legitimate resistance and grief (see also, Askeland, this volume) or at least can lead to anxiety since losses may potentially occur. Refusals to accept changes for any of these reasons may be seen as resistance to change.

Acts of resistance towards the most well-intentioned changes may be legitimate, and if the intended effects are sufficiently positive from the leaders' perspective, and if positive collaboration during adoption by user communities is important, it may be a net positive to find better ways to accommodate resistance to some extent into compromises. Users may have their own interests and intentions about how the actions should be done, but if they do not have the ability to change the scripted action which has been transcribed into the non-human actor, then they also cannot change the prescription which the non-human actor imposes on its users. That basically leaves users with the choice to either reject and attempt to resist or else to accept and accommodate the imposed prescription.

I find it interesting that we who deliver IT solutions – non-human actors – to our business colleagues know (but rarely discuss) the many workarounds and other actions we rely on our user colleagues to invent to ensure that the enterprise still does what it needs to do. This includes when our non-human actors do not do what we originally intended them to do as exemplified in the previous section with an elaborate 'date archive' workaround to a flawed core banking solution. And yet, it falls to users as representatives of the enterprise, to apologise and compensate for our (human and non-human actors') collective failures – an unintended effect of a change may include shameful awkwardness towards customers if our non-human actors are flawed and users fail to compensate. Often, users do take responsibility and ownership of something which is beyond their ability to influence, but as an enterprise architect, I feel that it *should* be within my ability to influence. If designed and engineered properly, non-human actors should do what they were designed to do and solve the problems they were designed to solve. However, whenever I talk to users about their experiences with what we deliver to them I grow humbler, and not rarely also shameful.

Of course, I must accept that there are limits to what we can be engaged in both for individuals like me in my role as enterprise architect, and for the organisation. Sometimes limits are self-imposed, like organisational budgets for investing in changes, which means that they are agreed by some decision makers and could be renegotiated. Other times, when we attempt to achieve a specific change, it can fail because we make mistakes, because we attempt to do something which cannot be done, or because we attempt something we do not have the capacity or competence to do well; in these cases, we risk getting things done in ways we later regret. For example, creating a useful mechanism or an effective and efficient standardised process may still end up with something which we later realise has negative consequences for many. Further, engaging in more than we have the capacity to do well can be stressful and have negative consequences for others; sometimes it may be better to not engage at all.

The perspective of the eminent enterprise architect Chris Potts resonates with me. He says:

> … opportunities are constantly bubbling up everywhere… The most important decision every Enterprise Architect has to keep making is which opportunities to play in – and how – and which to pass on. Either way, the decision will have an impact on what happens next.
>
> (Potts, 2010, p164)

When confronted with negative consequences of something we have done with good intentions, I wish that we could spend the time needed to fix the problems. In the greater prioritisation however, the pain caused is often not sufficient to warrant spending our limited resources on such improvements – hence another part of my shame. I wish we could fix the problems we have caused, but I accept that in practice we cannot avoid making mistakes, nor can we always prioritise fixing the problems this causes. Decisions such as when to play and when to pass, how ambitious to be, what to attempt to achieve – these are judgement calls. Our feelings of shame, regret, and pain do not have to be seen as only negative or useless. They can also be seen as something which, if we develop a different way of noticing and a reflexive practice, can help us hone our ability to make useful judgement calls.

The implications of these observations for researching organisations are that if we start to pay more attention to effects of and responses to changes, not only those that are intended, but any effects from the perspective of any actor and stakeholder, we can start to think about what changes during change processes differently. We may consider an iterative approach to change management which incorporates some form of research conducted after solution delivery into what emerges as non-human actors are adopted and workarounds are potentially introduced by users.

We may also become quite interested in what forms of resistance emerge, and who is interpreting them as such: what one person interprets as resistance to change, others may interpret as standing up for something important. Resistance can also be considered a valuable political influence into that which is in the process of becoming. Perceiving organisation as a compromise of countless mutual adjustments of players allows acts of resistance to be seen as legitimate renegotiations of a complex compromise across the organisation. Acknowledging resistance as legitimate and allowing open conversations about resistances can contribute to achieving 'good enough holding' of anxiety (Stacey and Mowles, 2016, pp356–357) to enable coping with changes, where coping is holding, not closing down, not fixing, but taking accountability and accepting that leaders of change are in charge but not in control of what emerges.

Lastly, by paying attention to limits, and whether they are self-imposed or natural, we may enrich our ability to anticipate, negotiate, and manage ambitions accordingly. Seeking to understand the limits of ourselves and our organisations is therefore an important research task and brings into view the interplay of moral considerations as involving human and non-human actors. While we may not be able to predict with certainty how things will go, we may begin to see more of potential implications for the people who are affected by the changes we attempt to introduce, and for ourselves and our co-workers.

In systems-theory-based enterprise architecture and change management methods, I often encounter assumptions that everything which is important should and can be modelled and planned, which implies limitless resources. It is also often stated that agreement and unambiguity is necessary to proceed according to the intentionality of the enterprise, where the latter implies that the enterprise as such is an entity (a system) with intentionality and that unaligned individual goals are illegitimate. I have tried to offer a process-theory-based alternative where organisation is the process of doing what we do together, where there is a web of intentionality formed by participants, and where punctuation is arbitrary since process – unlike systems – have no natural boundaries. This challenges some habitual ways of thinking about change management such as when a change 'ends' and why resistance to change occurs. In the next section, I will explore further what options the process-based approach opens.

Ethical architecting

Uncertainty and partial knowledge

In contemporary Lean and Agile methods, it is common to find encouragements to conduct research and development using what is often referred to as 'fail fast' approaches. For example, Ries (2017) recommends making assumptions and formulating hypotheses based on these assumptions that can be tested; prescribes prioritising hypotheses by their potential impact on your objectives; and prescribes conducting a series of tests of their validity starting with the most impactful hypothesis. The idea is that some of your assumptions will be proven wrong, and the earlier you fail, the faster you learn and improve. I see this prescriptive method as quite useful, but not without challenges when trying to take a process-theory perspective.

One challenge is the assumption that objectives are clear and unambiguous, so that experiments can be unequivocally judged as having succeeded or failed. Understanding organisation as the process of organising how actors together do something, and changes as the evolving meanings of many gestures and responses by the actors involved, makes things less clear. Many actors will have interests and intentions with regard to how they would prefer the organisation to evolve. In my work, executives, regional and local managers, users, customers, bank regulators, and myself and my colleagues who work with design and construction of non-human actors and social constructs all have interests, legitimate concerns and preferences with regard to what is to be achieved, and so objectives are often unclear, ambiguous, and challenged by various stakeholders to some extent; these conflicting interests form what I call a *web of intentionality*. Exploring the range of objectives actors may have, and how the pursuit of certain objectives may be impacted by opposing objectives of other actors is one way of explicating the web of intentionally.

A second and related challenge arises from the assumption that learning and knowledge production is a linear process. Pickering (1993) uses the story of Donald Glaser's development of the bubble chamber – an instrument for the study of atomic particles – to explore the scientific development of knowledge and non-human actors as a non-linear process with many setbacks and many incremental improvements in what he calls the *mangle of practice*. Glaser experimented to find out which configuration of the instrument produced (the desired) tracks in a bubble chamber and which did not; Pickering describes this as a 'learning by doing' approach where the learning is production of knowledge. Generally, transcribing action into non-human actors with a desired function requires a lot of such knowledge to be created, and a lot of tests of work in progress to be conducted. This accords with the perspective offered by Karl Mannheim who, drawing on insights from statecraft and sociology in national contexts, suggested that we can only ever gain partial knowledge of that which is "in the process of becoming" (Mannheim, 1936). Further, this partial knowledge itself only emerges by "acting in the situation" and deriving answers "in the form of the success or failure of the action" (Mannheim, 1936, p133).

In enterprise architecture, what is in the process of becoming is the organisation that will include action delegated to non-human actors such as IT solutions that are still under design and construction. IT solutions are generally unique designs, which means that they solve problems in a specific context (Alexander, 1979) that may never have been solved before. Even when solving a deterministic problem for which there is an unambiguous theoretically correct solution, such as calculating and accruing interest on a loan, designers may run out of time to learn and improve sufficiently to get it right and may fail. The choices made in response to these problems are therefore judgements about competing goods – and in the web of intentionality, any actions you take when attempting to produce knowledge, clarify, and deliberate are always in the words of Mannheim acts of politicking.

These observations have some important implications. First, it problematises Reis's prescriptive method: fail-fast approaches do have value and knowledge production of this kind can be very useful; however, the method is not a silver bullet, and conclusions drawn may be challenged. Constructing useful non-human actors requires a lot of knowledge both of a social nature (e.g. about likely human resistance, powerplays, perceptions of utility or potential pain and inconvenience) and of a technical nature (e.g. about likely material resistance, or how to transcribe the intended scripted action with reasonable prescriptions on human actors); only some of this will be able to be planned for, while the rest will be learned by doing. Decisions about how much knowledge production of this kind we can perform before we must make decisions about what to change and how are judgements, which will always be based on partial knowledge about that which is in the process of becoming. A corollary of accepting this is that we are therefore always dealing in acts of politicking in the context of a web of intentionality. So how we go about trying to understand differences in stakeholders' views, how we judge their relative importance, and how we act in response, all become useful routes into understanding organisational life. This leaves us with the question of how people in my field can become better at politicking both effectively and ethically.

Power and politicking

Non-human actors have a very high degree of influence when action is delegated to them exactly as transcribed and prescribed due to their very innate differences from human actors including their durability and inability to respond in a humanly meaningful way. This gives designers of non-human actors – as political players – a high degree of influence over organisation (in the process of becoming), and leaders who want to influence organisation may exercise influence over these designers as a means towards that end. Leaders are not unconstrained however, as any individual, group, or tier may attempt to influence decisions about stability and change.

In the bank I work for, my unit consists of a few dozen people who design (architect) and indirectly lead thousands of engineers of non-human actors and social constructs adopted by millions of users. This split of responsibilities provides its own challenges which is mentioned as early as 50 BC by Vitruvius and is still debated:

> Architects who have struggled to achieve practical proficiency without an education have not been able to achieve recognition commensurate with their efforts; by contrast, those who have relied only on theory and book-learning were evidently chasing shadows rather than reality. But those who have mastered both… have achieved recognition and fulfilled their ambitions more quickly. For all fields, and especially architecture, comprises two aspects: that which is signified and that which signifies it. That which is signified is the object under discussion, while that which signifies it an explanation of it conducted according to scientific principles.
>
> (50BC/2009, pp4–5)

Vitruvius articulates the dual challenge that architects seeking to influence engineers and decision makers must be recognised by those as authorities to convince them. Recognition from engineers is difficult to obtain without demonstrable mastery of engineering practices, and prior engineering experience helps. Recognition from leaders politicking about that which is in the process of becoming is difficult to gain without the ability to express design deliberations by producing scientific knowledge, and academic training helps. Thus, ideally architects should to some extent be both engineering practitioners and politicking academics. Individuals that master both are difficult to come by, and since this has been articulated as a challenge literally for millennia, it is unlikely to be something which can be resolved quickly. In my organisation, I work deliberately with team composition and collaboration models to bring together the necessary competences to get the job done, rather than relying on individuals who embody all of this.

Some leaders may see opportunities in the fact that introduction of non-human actors tends to lead to an increase in robustness and standardisation of processes. If leaders can control those few who can change what is transcribed into non-human actors and can control the standards that accompany their adoption, they may have a high degree of influence on that which is in the process of becoming. That is a big if, and I am not saying that this can be done completely and perfectly. However, I do see a tendency towards executives either seeking a high degree of influence over internal staff with these competences and accountabilities, or towards purchasing such competences in the form of management consultant services or similar which the executives feel that they can control to an above average degree since they are paying for them. The competition amongst leaders of who gets to control those who can transcribe action into non-human actors can be seen as a competition by proxy of who gets to control future standardised processes of the organisation, i.e., control over *what* the organisation will do in the future and *how* it will be done.

In the introduction, I stated that I work with technology-enabled business transformations where we delegate action to non-human actors (typically IT solutions) to change the resulting organisation. Many leaders want to influence the design decisions my colleagues and I make and a common organisational pattern for managing this is to establish design or decision committees or forums with clearly defined mandates for making certain decisions and clearly defined participation by certain executives. These constitute tiers in the organisation where "at least three, if not four, different balances of power may be distinguished… [and] people who are enemies on one level may be allies on another" (Elias, 1978, pp86–88). This makes it complicated and difficult for each individual player to grasp the many potential coalitions and conflicts that may emerge temporarily, and it makes it difficult for a single player to use "strategy to force them to make the moves which seem desirable to him" (Elias, 1978, pp86–88).

I sense clear conflicting needs and intentions between different local, regional, and group-level groupings within my organisation. Sometimes, people with conflicting needs and intentions can meet and agree a course of action, but in large organisations, it is not a given that everyone who has conflicting needs and intentions can meet or feel adequately represented. Paying attention to powerplays, potential conflicts and potential alliances with other political players in the organisation adds a further depth to the available social knowledge. This may help to anticipate what resistance may emerge as users are asked to accept non-human actors into their workflows.

Taking responsibility

In the previous section, I describe that architects seek to influence decision makers to make decisions based on the information and knowledge produced by architects, and I also describe how decision makers and executives seek to influence architects to (by proxy) influence engineers and via prescription of non-human actors that which is in the process of becoming. The attempt at influencing goes both ways and both parties need the function of the other to legitimise and support their attempts to influence that which is in the process of becoming. In conversations with colleagues, I often hear arguments like 'there was no other option than...' or 'we simply had to...' which I tend not to accept at face value. My experience is that there are always multiple options and never anything we 'have to' unless we 'choose to'.

However, I do recognise that the politicking which we are engaged in can feel overwhelming and it may be easier to accept conclusions and decisions of others rather than to insist on producing more knowledge and engaging in further deliberation when we are not sure we have yet drawn the best possible conclusion or made the best possible decision. Drawing on Foucault, I would argue that regardless of the relative strength of others in the politicking we participate in, we always have the possibility to resist and provide counter arguments:

> ...at the heart of power relations and as a permanent condition of their existence there is an insubordination and a certain essential obstinacy on the part of the principles of freedom, then there is no relationship of power without the means of escape or possible flight.
>
> (Foucault, 1982, p794)

The freedom Foucault speaks of does not imply parity or equality. When someone with relatively little positional power attempts to resists the very powerful, it is generally done delicately and with finesse. Scott (1990) remarks that resistance against this kind of control and influence can take many forms but rarely will resistance against the most powerful individuals in an organisation be entirely clear and direct. Scott describes human resistance when power imbalances are great as more art than science where the less powerful may adopt strategies such as the use of humour to diffuse a conflict and limit repercussions. Scott also introduces the term 'hidden transcript' to denote the topics and stories the less powerful may only reveal when the more powerful are not present, and 'public transcript' as the topics and stories we all tell when we are all present together. Since the hidden transcript is not generally talked about openly for example in the recurring decision meeting forums I mention above, it contributes to the formation of what Elias refers to as tiers where a certain understanding of the organisation dominates, and other understandings dominate other tiers. This can lead to prolonging conflicts since they are not coped with openly or directly. Since architects work with users, engineers, decision makers, and executives, they tend to navigate several tiers and may occasionally have the opportunity to use knowledge from one tier to challenge unresolved conflicts on another tier, but as Scott says, this should be carefully considered and done artfully since it carries a political risk to say that which is not spoken about according to corporate culture on a given tier of the organisation.

When we deliberate about designing and constructing non-human actors and taking these into use in our future organisation, we are attempting to simultaneously produce knowledge about and influence that which is in the process of becoming. Orthodox enterprise architecture theories like TOGAF ADM[2] often prescribe fully modelling and describing different stakeholder's goals and strategic drivers (Open Group, 2013, p70), but as I describe above, some of this is part of hidden transcripts and it would have severe political implications to describe this and share it openly. Elias (1956) argues that in such situations, it is important to be aware of the role oneself plays in the politicking by becoming observant of one's own relations to others, since power and influence are relational in nature. This is what I mentioned before as a different way of noticing and developing a reflexive practice. Elias counsels greater detachment as a means to become more aware of the politicking both of others and one's own.

These others can be other players in the politicking we are engaged in, but it can also for example be people we feel that we represent like users. The shame I feel when I acknowledge that the IT solutions we provide are far from ideal drives me to seek to do better in the future and to some extent to represent users that are not directly involved in deliberating about future IT solutions and the future organisation, so that it becomes less awkward and annoying for them. Other players in this politicking may represent other interests and intentions they bring into the deliberations and design decisions we engage in. Ultimately, I see decision forum meetings and other design meetings we participate in as mediums for this politicking. There is of course a history and structures in place already. Some stakeholders have more formal power than others, different forums have different officially defined mandates, but it is still at the end of the day the skill with which different stakeholders participate in this politicking which ultimately determines what we conclude and design, or in the words of Foucault: "Power exists only when it is put into action, even if, of course, it is integrated into a disparate field of possibilities brought to bear upon permanent structures" (1982, p788).

If we are not aware of the sources of the web of intentionality, we can be tempted to personify the influence we experience. The influence can feel like compulsion, and we may assume that 'someone' must 'have that power' over us (Elias, 1978, pp93–94). However, by becoming more aware of how this web of intentionality is brought about via a multitude of powerplays and influencing moves by others we open up possibilities not only of better understanding our options, but also of finding other players who may be willing to pursue some of the objectives we also pursue, i.e., forming a coalition of those willing to take action to achieve a certain objective. Coming back to Elias's point about detachment as a means towards greater awareness, I find that it is precisely by taking your own role and relationships, the people and interests you represent in the negotiations seriously, the politicking and powerplays of others and yourself, by noticing all of these differently – more thoroughly, that you can become more effective at negotiating about what is in the process of becoming. Mannheim (under whom Elias studied) concludes that

> ... action should not only be in accord with the dictates of conscience, but should take into consideration the possible consequences of the

> action in so far as they are calculable ... conscience itself should be subjected to critical self-examination in order to eliminate all the blindly and compulsively operating factors. ... the knowledge of everything knowable becomes the obligation of the acting person. ... out of the new ethics a point of view emerges which regards knowledge not as a passive contemplation but as critical self-examination, and in this sense prepares the road for political action.
>
> (1936, p191)

We are responsible for our own responses to power and for our responses towards the resistances of others. Towards the most powerful, resistance may have to be artful to succeed. If success with changes depend on responses by users and other stakeholders like their willingness to make contributions in the form of adoption and workarounds, then developing a greater empathy with the wider organisation is important. When Mannheim states that conscience itself should be subjected to critical self-examination, I see this as an example of what I alluded to earlier as developing a reflexive practice where among other things you acknowledge your emotional responses to the consequences your actions and choices have for others, and you become more aware of how past experiences are influencing your judgement calls.

Conclusion

In this chapter, I have tried to provide a process-theory-based description of how, in the world of enterprise architecture, we go about developing and adopting non-human actors as technical and social constructs. A lot has happened since the hunter/gatherer society introduced rudimentary spear and spear thrower non-human actors into their hunting practice and wicker baskets into their gathering practice. Many modern practices like banking would be impossible to conduct at the scale required in modern-day society without the help of a great many sophisticated and complicated non-human actors and social constructs. These non-human actors and the way they act are very unlike their human counterparts who delegate action to them. Their actions and interactions with human users are not complex in the human sense of the word, regardless of how sophisticated and complicated we make them. This has consequences for individual human users who must either resist changes or accept that they must compensate for the shortcomings of their non-human delegates via workarounds and other changes to their work lives. Many believe that although the technological growth rate has fluctuations it is generally increasing. The cumulative effect of these workarounds and compensations may have consequences on a societal level where stress and 'the Great Resignation' (Serenko, 2023) could be signs that human actors are approaching the limit of their ability to cope with and compensate for the shortcomings of non-human actors.

It is a wonder that we have over the millennia become so willing and adept at including these simpler delegates and intermediaries into our organising. We do this of course because their actions have function and value for us. And yet, it is common place to keep the two implicated fields or schools of science isolated from each other: often, one focuses on the organisation of human actors and organisational changes from sociological and psychological perspectives and tends to treat non-humans as inconsequential since non-humans have neither intentionality nor agency; or one focuses on organisations as systems of sub-systems from technological and engineering perspectives and tends to treat organisations as more predictable and controllable than they are and tends to ignore resistances or perceives these as illegitimate. I argue that understanding organisations needs us to combine the two, so that we can explore the emergent consequences for the human actors of introducing non-human actors into processes of organising.

In addition, if we start paying attention to what is in the process of becoming, we can become more able to notice certain fundamental assumptions and habitual ways of thinking that may limit which options are available to us when navigating transformational changes. Those in charge of transformations may benefit from greater detachment (observing themselves and their relations to others) to deepen their understanding of relationships, power differentials in relationships, the intentionality of other players, and their own role in powerplays, i.e., increasing their level of empathy and noticing differently. For those who deliberate and make design decisions for construction of non-human actors, a combination of practical knowledge of construction and scientific knowledge production can help ensure both recognition as a figure of authority among those engineers who construct non-human actors and those stakeholders who participate in politicking about that which is in the process of becoming.

Paying attention to emotions as indicators of the moral concerns at play can help direct us back to the people whose interests are satisfied in the delegation of work to non-human actors, and so help us navigate in the web of intentionality. This may better inform our own decisions about when to play and when to pass and help us evolve a reflexive practice.

I hope that my chapter will contribute to making practitioners curious about this different way of noticing, and to sociologists becoming more curious about the role of non-human actors and those who use them and those who create them in our organisations. A vast body of literature (from an engineering culture) exists about how to construct non-human actors, but less literature exists (from a sociology culture) about the effect of introducing these non-human delegates into our organisations. I believe that ignoring non-human actors while studying organisation and sociology is to ignore something profound about almost any organisational or societal change that has occurred since the age of the hunter/gatherer society.

Notes

1 Different authors use different terms with subtly different meanings such as actant (Latour, 2005) and material agent (Pickering, 1993). I have chosen to use the term non-human actor to mean anything which is not human (mechanism, domesticated animal, etc.) but performs action which is recognised as having function for someone (human). When I refer to the works of others in this chapter, I use my own terms (except in direct quotes) for the sake of consistency.

2 The Open Group Architecture Framework Architecture Development Method

References

Akrich, M. (1992) The De-Scription of Technical Objects. In Bijker W.E. and Law J. (eds.), *Shaping Technology / Building Society, Studies in Sociotechnical Change*. London: The MIT Press, pp. 205–224.

Alexander, C. (1979) *The Timeless way of Building*. New York: Oxford University Press.

Elias, N. (1956) Problems of involvement and detachment. *The British Journal of Sociology*, 7(3), pp. 226–252.

Elias, N. (1978) *What Is Sociology?* New York: Columbia University Press.

Foucault, M. (1982) Subject and Power. *Critical Inquiry*, 8(4) (Summer, 1982), pp. 777–795.

Latour, B. (writing under the pseudonym Jim Johnson) (1988) Mixing Humans and Nonhumans Together: The Sociology of a Door-Closer. Social Problems. Special Issue: *The Sociology of Science and Technology*, 35(3), pp. 298–310.

Latour, B. (2005) *Reassembling the Social – An Introduction to Actor-Network-Theory*. Oxford: Oxford University Press.

Mannheim, K. (1936/1955) *Ideology and Utopia: An Introduction to the Sociology of Knowledge*. San Diego: Harcourt Brace Jovanovich. First published in 1936.

Mead, G.H. (1934) *Mind, Self and Society: from the Standpoint of a Social Behaviorist*, 17th ed. Chicago, IL: The University of Chicago Press, 2015.

Open Group, The (2013) *TOGAF® Version 9.1*. Zaltbommel: Van Haren Publishing.

Pickering, A. (1993) The mangle of practice: Agency and emergence in the sociology of science. *American Journal of Sociology*, 99(3), pp. 559–589.

Potts, C. (2010) *Recreation – Realizing the Extraordinary Contribution of Your Enterprise Architects*. Denville, NJ: Technics Publications.

Ries, E. (2017) *The Lean Startup: How Today's Entrepreneurs Use Continuous Innovation to Create Radically Successful Businesses*. New York: Random House USA Inc.

Scott, J.C. (1990) *Domination and the Arts of Resistance – Hidden Transcripts*. New Haven, CT: Yale University Press.

Serenko, A. (2023) The Great Resignation: the great knowledge exodus or the onset of the Great Knowledge Revolution?. *Journal of Knowledge Management*, 27(4), pp. 1042–1055.

Stacey, R.D. and Mowles, C. (2016) *Strategic Management and Organisational Dynamics: The Challenge of Complexity to Ways of Thinking about Organisations*. 7th ed. England: Pearson Education.

Vitruvius, M.P. (50BC/2009) *On Architecture*. London: Penguin Classics. First published circa 50 BC.

8

COMPROMISING IN RESEARCH PROCESSES

HELLE THERKELSEN STOLTZ

Introduction

When participating in a research process, there are always agreements to be negotiated or decisions to be made between going with the dominant views of the group or speaking up and taking a stand that differs from those of others. In research settings, compromising might emerge, for example, when agreeing on the focus of the research, when selecting which research method is to be used, when agreeing on the composition of the research team for data collection, and in the interactions with fellow researchers and/or other team members during the analysis of research data. In work situations, compromising might emerge, for example, when we meet with an important representative of a client for the first time, or join a new team, and we discover that there are substantial differences in our views on the most appropriate ways to complete the tasks at hand.

A focus on consensus and harmony might mean that we do not raise critique or voice a view that differs from the dominant views or thought style

DOI: 10.4324/9781003410522-10

because it is easiest not to, or out of fear of exclusion from the group if the expressed view is too unorthodox (Mowles, 2022, p111). Going with the dominant views might be in the form of submission to or collusion with these views and might happen more frequently when being a newcomer in a group. An idealisation of consensus and harmony has also been described as a limitation in people's legitimate right to disagree and present different views; a limitation that can be oppressive (Solsø and Thorup, 2015, p69). Such idealisation might thus result in us not talking about the conflicts and conflictual feelings which inevitably evolve in interactions between people (for further explication of reasons for playing the game in research, see Rasmussen's chapter in this volume) nor about how it might be possible to move on in conflictual situations through negotiation and compromise.

This chapter outlines an alternative to a consensus and harmony perspective within research groups, and in other work situations, by paying attention to compromise. Some organisational scholars claim that organisational conflicts, which I see as including conflicts within research groups, can be managed through different strategies or tools, one of which might be compromise. M. Afzalur Rahim is among these authors. Part of his proposed management strategy is to deal with conflicts by using one or several of the following management styles: integrating, obliging, dominating, avoiding, and compromising (Rahim, 2002). He considers it possible to use these styles to either minimise so-called dysfunctional conflicts or attain so-called functional conflicts. Rahim provides an overview of situations in which the different styles of handling conflicts are, in his view, more – or less – appropriate. He indicates that compromising is an appropriate style in conflictual situations where the goals of the parties involved in a conflict are mutually exclusive, parties are equally powerful, and consensus cannot be reached (Rahim, 2002, pp218–221). Rahim suggests, in other words, that compromising can be devised, as a tool, and should be used in some conflictual situations and not in others.

Similarly, the conflict management instruments developed by Ken Thomas and Ralph Kilmann include compromising as one of the strategies, or tools, to resolve organisational conflicts.[1]

These perspectives of compromise are in stark contrast to my understanding of compromise as a process which involve negotiating with others and in our private conversations with ourselves, influenced by the power relations between the parties involved. For if the future, including the outcomes of intending to compromise, cannot be predicted, then compromise cannot be devised and used as a tool – rather it evolves as we interact with each other. Here is an illustrative example of such an evolution in the interactions of a research group.

At the start of my research studies, I joined a small group consisting of three other research students and our supervisor. The three other researchers had entered the research programme between two and three years before me and were therefore far advanced in their research. Along with our supervisor, they gave me a warm welcome and were eager to ensure that I had a good start on the programme. After some months, it was time for me to start preparing a research proposal with a description of my research theme. At the time, I was interested in exploring several themes, such as struggles for recognition, power relations, and commitment to different values, and found it difficult to limit myself to one theme. Other group members suggested other themes, which they thought might be interesting for me to explore. I had earlier told the group about key patterns and events in my life, both from my traditional upbringing and from my involvement in international development work, and their proposed research themes were based on our discussions of what seemed important for me. We had potential research themes 'on the agenda' for several group meetings, and I felt under increasing pressure for us to reach an agreement. This feeling of pressure became even more intense for me – and perhaps also for other group members – in a meeting, where one of the founders of the research programme participated. Before the meeting, I had outlined a research theme around struggles for recognition of my views and those of others, while the other participants in the meeting questioned whether this was the most relevant theme considering my explorations so far. They again brought up other potential research themes including, among others, trust. We also discussed the theme of compromise and what this might entail. After further deliberations, compromise was the research theme we all agreed would be relevant and interesting for me to explore – and importantly it seemed to cover aspects of other themes we had discussed earlier. In hindsight, I sensed that the discussions and the agreement on my research theme involved a process of compromise, with negotiations and adaptations of our views to those of others in the group. At first, I experienced it as a loss that I could not explore in depth all the other themes in which I was interested. Mutual recognition is a key value for me, and my sense of loss became even more intense when I imagined what I would have been able to explore if my agreed research theme had been recognition and struggles to achieve this. Later, this sense of loss evaporated (the narrative is a further elaboration of text in Stoltz, 2020, p135).

In the following sections, I will refer to the above example when I present my perspective on processes of compromise and the theoretical background to this. Further examples of compromising and how this might be experienced are also included below. I begin with setting out key principles and aspects that are important in my understanding of compromise.

Compromise: key principles and aspects

Opportunities for compromising are ever-present in conflictual situations within organisations, at different stages of research, and generally within our lives.

Based on organisational consultant Iver Drabæk's research (2007, 2008) and my own research (Stoltz, 2020), I argue that compromise is a social process emerging in conflictual situations in our interactions with others. It is a process requiring all parties to adapt their views to those of others who are part of the process. These mutual adaptations are processes that increase the capacity for people to stay in generative relation with each other, rather than ending up in a stalemate or, ultimately, ending relationships when those involved prefer not to. As I will explain, compromising therefore involves power relations, ethics, and emotions, the experience of which can change over time. A sense of loss when we give up part of our views or interests might, for example, shift to primarily an experience of change and novelty, as I explain at the end of the chapter.

Compromising: a social process of anticipation and adaptation

Based on the social psychologist and pragmatist philosopher George Herbert Mead's theory of communication (Mead, 1934), compromise, like all human interaction, can be understood as a process. Mead explains communication as chains of gestures and responses, which is an iterative process in which one person's gestures elicit responses in others, which then elicit a response in the first person, a new response in others, and so on.

He posits that meaning emerges in this sequence of gestures and responses. According to Mead, as human beings, we have an experiential awareness or anticipation of how others will react to our gestures and are able to take these anticipations into account in our chains of communication.

These anticipations concern not just how particular others will react, but also how an entire group of colleagues – or others in society more generally – would react. In conflict situations, we might anticipate how others would react if the conflict reached a complete stalemate, for example: Would our colleagues blame us if there were delays to a project or other negative consequences due to a conflict? Or would they see it as a fight we should abandon?

Mead explains this social regulation from our surroundings by using the term *the generalised other* to refer to the group, discourse, or society in which we imagine and consider the general view of the group or society (1934, p261) on, for example, a conflict. In other words, as human beings, we can imagine how particular others as well as a group will react to what we are about to say or do (Stacey and Griffin, 2008, p8). In our conversions with others and with ourselves, we are influenced by this social regulation but also by our more spontaneous sense of self, which Mead alludes to as a dialectic of our 'I' and 'me' (1934, pp174–175). For further explication of the I/me dialectic of Mead's theory, see Chauhan in this volume.

The anticipations of the reactions of others influence our communication, including our possible compromising in a conflictual situation. The way in which I and my research colleagues arrived at my research theme through many discussions and negotiations illustrates how compromising is a social process. None of the themes that I and other group members suggested at the start of our discussions ended up as my research theme. Instead, we all adapted our views to those of others in the group until we found a theme that included aspects that made sense to us all, although it was not our first preference at the time. In this process of adaptations, I anticipated how my more senior fellow researchers, my supervisor, and the founder of the research programme would react if, in the meeting, I had insisted on my preferred theme around struggles for recognition and had been unwilling to compromise. I feared they would consider me a stubborn newcomer who did not want to find a way to move forward with my research proposal. Most likely other group members also had anticipations of how other participants in the meeting would react to what they were about to suggest or say.

However, anticipations of the reactions of others cannot be used as part of a compromise tool to resolve organisational conflicts, as Rahim, Thomas, and Kilmann might have suggested. Rather, there is no guarantee that our anticipations of the reactions of others are correct, and furthermore we might surprise ourselves in what we say or do, as compromising emerges in our interactions with each other.

It is also important to highlight that our views and goals do not remain unchanged in our compromising; rather, it is a process of movement as we adapt to each other.

Compromising and power relations

I find the process sociologist Norbert Elias' perspective on power helpful in understanding the role of power in compromising. Elias explains that power should not be understood as something a leader or a group possesses, but rather as an integral part of all human relations, where we are dependent on each other to varying degrees and in different ways (Elias, 1978). Elias uses the metaphor of a game, such as chess or football (Elias, 1978, pp71–103), to explain how people are interdependent as they have functions for each other and are, therefore, in positions to constrain – and enable – each other. Importantly, the relative strength of each player or person varies:

> In so far as we are more dependent on others than they are on us, more directed by others than they are by us, they have power over us, whether we have become dependent on them by their use of naked force or by our need to be loved, our need for money, healing, status, a career, or simply for excitement.
>
> (Elias, 1978, p93)

This means that power relations are about who wants or needs what from whom, which is important in understanding what might be at stake in processes of compromise. My earlier example about agreeing on my research theme involved power differentials within the group. Here I was very aware that the other students in my research group were all far advanced in their research, while my supervisor and the founder of the programme had many years of research experience. Although they all listened carefully to my views and suggestions, I felt – as a newcomer to the programme – that their comments and suggestions carried higher weight in our discussions than did mine. Furthermore, I was dependent on all of them to obtain approval of my research proposal, and I felt under increasing pressure for us to agree on a research theme, enabling me to move on with my research proposal. I also had an underlying fear that my progress might be too slow and that I would not be able to continue my research studies, as had been the case for some other students.

This draws attention to how power relations can involve processes of inclusion in and exclusion from group(s) when we interact with each other (Scott, 1990; Elias and Scotson, 1994). This does not mean that we are either fully included in or fully excluded from a group; rather, the level of exclusion might differ depending on whether we are able to gain some influence through hidden transcripts or conversations. Instead of referring to exclusion from a group, I use therefore mainly the terms *marginalisation* and *being in a weaker position* in the following. In my example, I did not experience myself as excluded from the small research group; rather, I sensed that I was in a weaker position compared to my senior fellow researchers, my supervisor, and the founder of the programme. I might therefore have adapted my views more than the senior members of the group, although this is difficult to measure. Analogously in organisations, less experienced members of teams might be cautious of challenging more established colleagues through fear of becoming marginalised or dismissed, and so adapt their views more than their colleagues in processes of compromise.

Age and seniority are not the only examples of factors that can make researchers and employees in various organisations feel they are in weaker positions than others when in a conflictual situation and in processes of compromise. Other important factors, though not the only ones, that can make people experience themselves marginalised or in weaker positions in a group are area of expertise, gender, sexuality, race, and religious affiliation. I do not have the space here to describe all the mentioned factors and will limit myself to elaborate on how the area of expertise compared to those of others in the group and gendered expectations might influence our interactions in groups, as I sense they have for me in an interwoven way.

In my work as a sociologist – and woman – in international technically oriented projects, I have in several situations had the experience of having to fight to get others to listen to my views and suggestions about social aspects, to a greater extent than has been the case for my mostly male engineering colleagues and client representatives and their technical views. Compromise has been important to me in such situations, where my experience is that I have often adapted my views more than others to gain some influence – and, in some instances, to avoid being excluded from or marginalised in discussions in the group. In my efforts to be heard in a group, I have often resorted to private conversations with a few group members or other colleagues, which in some situations resulted in others speaking up in support of my views or even on my behalf, while in other situations, hidden conversations gave me sufficient confidence to speak up myself.

I find it helpful here to draw on the political scientist and anthropologist James Scott and his exploration of hidden transcripts in situations of dominance and resistance (1990). He uses the expression 'hidden transcript' about what particularly the less powerful say among themselves, behind the backs of the more powerful. The more powerful might, however, also have their hidden transcripts. The term indicates that the transcript is hidden from certain other people. It might, however, be made public, either intentionally or unintentionally. As Scott highlights, the frontier between public and hidden transcripts is not a solid wall, but rather a zone of constant struggle between different groups (1990, p14). The two scholars Ralph Stacey and Chris Mowles reach a similar conclusion about the interplay between shadow and legitimate themes in organisations (Stacey and Mowles, 2016, pp422–427), with many similarities between their reference to legitimate and shadow themes and Scott's distinction between public and hidden transcripts. Stacey and Mowles posit that there is often a complex interplay between shadow and legitimate themes in organisations and that new themes, new meanings, can emerge in this interplay and, with them, the pattern of power relations might change.

In my example above, I was in a minority situation both as a sociologist and a woman among mostly male engineering colleagues and client representatives. At first, I considered being in the clear minority as a sociologist (area of expertise) to be the main reason why I experienced myself in a weaker position than others. However, gradually, I came to realise this situation was also influenced by gendered expectations, which the organisational scholar Sara L. Muhr explains convincingly through her research (2019). She illuminates how different norms and expectations of women's and men's behaviour, as well as the habits we build based on these expectations, can play a role in our interactions with each other. As part of her research in leadership and gender, Muhr interviewed 150 Danish middle- and top-level leaders (both women and men). Most of the interviewees had an expectation that women are empathetic, quiet, and caring. In contrast, the expectation was that men are strong, aggressive, and focused on results (Muhr, 2019, pp114–121). I largely recognise these gendered expectations from my own upbringing and work life and see them reflected in the habits I have developed of being restrained and quiet, especially in large groups. Of course, women are not a homogeneous group – nor are men – and women and men react differently to the expectations they face. However, gendered expectations put pressure on women to behave in so-called feminine and men in so-called masculine ways (Sullivan, 2000; Muhr, 2019), both when in leadership positions and in other positions. Our habits are not static, however. Instead, they are continuously influenced by our other habits and by the customs and norms of the different groups and contexts we are part of. Thus, women – and men – are not passive victims based on gendered expectations. On the contrary, individual women and men help to shape, and in some cases challenge and change, existing gendered expectations and to create new expectations (Sullivan, 2000).

Gendered expectations might thus influence whether and how much women and men speak up in conflictual situations within research groups, and in other work situations, and whether they might adapt their views more than others in processes of compromise. The general expectation that women are emphatic, quiet, and caring might thus make many women adapt their views more than men in processes of compromise. They might, however, simultaneously be influenced by other factors such as, e.g., their age, seniority, and race.

These factors all influence the extent to which those involved in compromising are prepared or able to express their needs and hear others and will be reflected in whether someone speaks up for themselves, forms alliances with others, or seeks the support of formal or informal leaders.

Compromising and ethics

Adapting to each other's views is a reciprocal process, which involves ethics. To explain this further, I draw in the following on the philosopher Georg W.F. Hegel's explication of an individual's 'general free will', as interpreted by the philosopher Axel Honneth (2000). In his exposition of an individual's 'general free will', Hegel uses friendship and love as the paradigm for describing this freedom:

> Here, we are not one-sidedly within ourselves, but willingly limit ourselves with reference to an other, even while knowing ourselves in this limitation as ourselves. In this determinacy, the human being should not feel determined; on the contrary, he attains his self-awareness only by regarding the other as other. Thus, freedom lies neither in indeterminacy nor in determinacy, but is both at once. (…) (T)he will is not tied to something limited; on the contrary, it must proceed further, for the nature of the will is not this one-sidedness and restriction. Freedom is to will something determinate, yet to be with oneself in this determinacy and to return once more to the universal.
>
> Hegel: Philosophy of Right, 1820, quoted in Honneth (2000, p26)

I understand this to mean that we have, or achieve, this freedom when we recognise the views, needs, and interests of others and are willing to limit ourselves in this process. At the same time, such freedom requires that we recognise – and do not sacrifice – what is important to us. Paradoxically, in this freedom we are thus, at the same time, both limiting ourselves and not (fully) sacrificing our interests, in a state of indeterminate determinacy, the former referring to recognition of others and the latter to what is important for ourselves. Hegel uses the persuasive expression 'being with oneself in another' to explain this experience of simultaneous determinacy and indeterminacy (Honneth, 2000, p29).

I consider 'being with oneself in another' an inherent part of compromising, which involves our adaptations to the views and interests of others without fully giving up – or sacrificing – our own views or goals. Compromising is thus not a one-sided gesture, but rather a reciprocal process.

Returning to the example of agreeing my research theme, while there were power differentials involved – not least because I was a newcomer to the research programme and assumed that the comments and suggestions of other group members carried higher weight in our discussions than did mine – it was, however, still a reciprocal process. We listened carefully to each other, recognised each other's views and suggestions, and in the end found a way to move on through mutual adaptations. In my understanding, such a process of listening to each other, mutual recognition, and adaptations involves ethical considerations. The question is, however, whether compromise always involves ethical or moral aspects. I find it helpful here to bring in the philosopher Martin Benjamin's understanding of compromise and particularly his distinction between compromise concerning non-moral interests and compromise involving moral principles (1990).

Benjamin explains compromise related to non-moral equally legitimate interests with an example of two friends who want to spend a day together. One person wants to visit museums and a Spanish restaurant, while the other prefers to go to bookstores and a Korean restaurant. In their compromising, they might, e.g., combine a visit to museums with the Korean restaurant or visit both museums and bookstores and flip a coin for the restaurant (Benjamin, 1990, pp12–13).

The main example Benjamin uses to illustrate compromise involving moral principles is a strong disagreement among nursing and medical staff about the continued treatment of a young patient suffering from severe brain damage. Some staff argue that there is little hope for the patient to recover and that aggressive treatment should be reduced, while other staff argue that the aggressive treatment should continue, among others, referring to their dedication to the preservation and prolongation of life. In their compromising, the staff agree to continue the aggressive treatment for a specified period and then review the patient's condition again. If her condition has improved in specified ways, her treatment is to remain aggressive. If her condition has remained the same or deteriorated, she is to be treated less aggressively (Benjamin, 1990, pp24–38).

The process of compromise among the nursing and medical staff involves questions of life and death and thereby clear ethical or moral aspects. The question is whether this is also the case for the compromising taking place between the two friends who want to do different things together. I argue that it does involve ethical aspects, as their compromising indicates that each of them wants to make the other happy and avoid damaging their long friendship. They express this by listening to each other and thereby respecting and recognising each other's preferences in their process of mutual adaptations, which allows them to do something together instead of ending in a stalemate.

Ethical considerations are important in connection with research. When writing about others, as we do in the research programme I attended, this might involve harm to them. Ethics thus obviously needs much attention when choosing a research topic, a narrative, and how to describe the role of others (for further details, see the chapter on ethics in research in this volume). Ethics were also involved, as I mentioned earlier, in the compromising that took place when agreeing on my research theme, as this was a reciprocal process of listening to, recognising, and adapting to each other's views, without losing our integrity and what we consider important.

Compromising always entails acknowledgement and attempts to understand the other as well as negotiation (Nachi, 2004, pp293–294), which in my view means that compromising always involves moral or ethical aspects in its focus on reciprocal recognition with simultaneous adaptations to each other, where we are accountable to those either directly or indirectly participating in or affected by a process of compromise. In compromise, we must move away from what Mead calls the *narrow self* and instead develop a *larger self* where we identify with the interests of others and which thereby:

> ...transforms the basis for what we call compromise from the self to the relation between the self and the others.
>
> (Drabæk, 2007, p34)

I understand the development of a larger self to mean that we must consider the interests of others either directly or indirectly participating in or affected by a process of compromise. In a research context, those who are indirectly participating or affected could, e.g., be the wider research community or persons appearing in a narrative or participating in an interview that is used for the research. In a work context, they could, e.g., be work colleagues and clients.

Compromising, values, and emotions

Benjamin aptly describes compromise as both necessary and dangerous:

> Like fire, compromise is both necessary and dangerous to human life. Were we never to accept political compromise on matters of ethical

> conviction, we would cut ourselves off from large numbers of our fellow humans; were we always to accept it, we would become alienated from ourselves.
>
> (1990, p3)

Compromise is clearly necessary in many situations, as was the case when compromising evolved in the discussions of my potential research themes. As Benjamin highlights in the above quote, if we are not willing to participate in processes of compromise, we risk putting ourselves outside influence and isolating ourselves from many of our fellow human beings. Benjamin also indicates in the last sentence above that we would become alienated from ourselves – and implicitly the values we are committed to and generally what is important to us – if we were always to accept compromising. So, when might we consider it most ethical to not adapt our views to those of others? Perhaps to not harm others and/or preserve our own integrity by holding on to what is important to us.

Let's imagine a situation where an autoethnographic research group encourages one of its members, Y, to write about the gender bias and inequality that she and many of her female colleagues have experienced at her workplace, as Y had described to them earlier. Y agrees that gender bias and inequality is an important research topic but is concerned about how writing about this – especially when this would be in an autoethnographic way – might negatively influence her and her female colleagues' standing at her current workplace and with potential future employers. She is particularly concerned about the harm this could cause to her colleagues, as she feels she would have to include them, in an anonymised way, in her autoethnographic narratives. The research group acknowledges the concerns expressed by Y and suggests that they together explore how this risk of doing harm to Y's colleagues can be dealt with. After further discussions, the group suggests, as a way of compromising, to not include the colleagues who might be significantly harmed if included in Y's narrative accounts. Y's response is that such compromising would mean that she could not explore gender bias and inequality in depth, which she finds important if she were to take up such research. She cannot see other ways to avoid doing (significant) harm to her colleagues and is therefore not willing to involve herself in further discussions of compromising, although addressing gender bias and inequality is important to her. Y is torn between two principles or values that are both important to her: doing no harm to others and gender equality, which involves fighting gender bias and stereotypes. She chooses to give the highest priority to the principle of doing no harm to others and is not willing to compromise. She feels that compromising on this principle – or value commitment – would affect her integrity as a colleague, researcher, and as a human being. At the same time, she has a nagging feeling that she has sacrificed an opportunity to explore – and fight – gender bias and inequality, which leaves her with a sense of loss. She is convinced, however, that her experience of loss would have been even more intense, if she had compromised on the principle of not doing harm to others.

My research indicates that compromising might – perhaps often – involve some sense of loss for those involved. While many factors might influence the intensity of the feeling of loss – for example, whether in our experience we have adapted our views more than others, or whether we fear that others will condemn us for abandoning parts of our goals or value commitments – I find it particularly influenced by whether our compromising entails commitments to particular values or persons (Stoltz, 2020, p158). Values are ideals, which attract us and give our life meaning (Joas, 2000, p125), as also persuasively explained by the pragmatist John Dewey:

> The idealizing imagination seizes upon the most precious things found in the climacteric moments of experience and projects them. We need no external criterion and guarantee for their goodness. They are had, they exist as good, and out of them we frame our ideal ends.
>
> (1934, pp44–45)

I understand this to mean that we need no external criteria or guarantee for the goodness of the things that are most precious to us. These things or values simply exist as good, and we are therefore committed to them. It should therefore not come as a surprise to us that the feeling of loss in a process of compromise can be intense when it involves values that are important to us. As the sociologist Hans Joas explains:

> When we talk about values, a strong affectual dimension comes in …our commitment to these is different from our commitment to purely cognitive validity claims. We have to take seriously the fact that we cannot simply 'have' values as we may have opinions, but that we

> have to feel strongly committed to them if the word 'value commitment' is to make any sense.
>
> (2008, p90)

In the discussions of my potential research themes, I had – before an important meeting in our research group – outlined a research theme around mutual recognition, which is a key value to which I have been strongly committed for many years. When, in our compromising, we agreed on compromise as my research theme, it provoked initially rather intense feelings of loss that I would not be able to explore a key theme and value in my life, namely, recognition and struggles to achieve this.

However, irrespective of its intensity, the experience of loss might change after some time, as I explain in the next section.

Compromise and the emergence of novelty

I have so far described different aspects of understanding compromising as a complex and emergent phenomenon embedded in relations between interdependent people. As such, the experience of compromise – for example as loss – is not static. Rather, it can change over time, as our understanding of the past is continually revised in the 'living present', influenced by our anticipations of, or intentions for, the future (Stacey et al., 2000, p35, building on Hegel and Mead). Similarly, the values to which we are committed are not fixed either but can change over time.

The two examples below illustrate how our experience of compromising can change.

Examples of compromising involving new insights and cooperation

The first example is from my interactions within a research group. Here, my initial experience of our compromising as one of loss changed over time to a sense of emerging novelty – in the form of a new insight. A recurrent theme of discussion in our group – and in my wider research community – was my hesitance to speak up, particularly in large groups, both in research settings and in my work as a sociologist – and woman – in international projects. One of my fellow researchers pointed out in several of our group meetings that we all have a moral obligation to speak up in public. I disagreed, or at least was unsure, and referred to the influence I had gained from putting forward my views in smaller groups, which in turn had influenced the wider discussions (see also earlier in this chapter about Scott's explanations of 'hidden transcripts' and Stacey and Mowles' conclusions on the interplay between shadow and legitimate themes). I was a little annoyed with my research colleague's insistence that speaking up in public is a moral obligation for all of us. To me, he did not consider that some persons and groups are more powerful than others and that we all have different histories that influence our behaviour. In other words, I did not believe that speaking up in public was necessarily the best, or safest, way to gain influence in all situations. Our deliberations became more specific in a research group meeting after, as part of my research, I had explored what speaking up entails. This exploration made me realise that my experience of being marginalised as a sociologist – and woman – working in international technically oriented and male-dominated projects was not the only reason for my frequent silence in large groups. Another related reason was that rather than 'being with myself in another', I have often been lost in my recognition of the views of others and their anticipated reactions, if I did speak up. My experience was that the deliberations with my research colleague in this meeting involved compromising, entailing adaptations to each other's views. Initially, I experienced the adaptations of my views as a loss. However, as we continued our discussions and adaptations to each other, a new understanding evolved that the obligation to speak up in public is related to the purpose of speaking up being larger than one's own interests. This means, in other words, that the purpose of speaking up is experienced as important for others as well as oneself (the narrative is a further elaboration of text in Stoltz, 2020, p119).

In the last-mentioned meeting, my research colleague and I were both influenced by my exploration of speaking up and reasons for my frequent silence in large groups. This had not made us change our original views, but it made it easier for us to adapt our views and find a way to move on in our further discussions of my research. Our compromising also led to a new insight related the obligation to speak up.

I want to bring in another example, which differs from the first in that our compromising took place in a highly conflictual situation. Here, my initial sense of loss gradually evaporated as we adapted to each other and in this way avoided the revival of a previous conflictual situation, with my primary experience of our compromising being of a process that created or contributed to a new situation with constructive cooperation. As an external consultant, I had previously had a conflictual meeting with a senior employee Brian and two of his colleagues, all from one of my company's most important clients. It was a meeting where, in my experience, my colleagues and I had been unfairly treated, and I had therefore initiated a new meeting with the aim to establish constructive cooperation for the remaining part of the assignment but also to explain my views in relation to the strong criticism raised at the previous meeting. To ensure there was sufficient time for me to explain all my views, I interrupted Brian in his introduction to the meeting, thanked him and his colleagues for attending the meeting with short notice and went on to explain my views in relation to the strong criticism received earlier. Brian's facial expressions indicated that he was on the verge of interrupting me, but he did not. Just as I was completing my clarifications, another of Brian's colleagues managed to join the meeting on a telephone line. Brian quickly summarised the meeting so far, saying that our discussions indicated a need to improve our communication. I clearly did not feel that this adequately summarised the viewpoints I had just explained, but I did not say anything, although this initially left me with a sense of loss. The latter gradually evaporated as the meeting moved on in an atmosphere of open discussion and constructive cooperation where the focus was on our findings and future activities (the narrative is a summary of text in Stoltz, 2020, pp83–88).

In this meeting, Brian and I were both adapting to each other and in this way avoiding a revival of the conflictual situation from the previous meeting. This was especially the case, when Brian's facial expressions indicated that he was tempted to interrupt and counter my explanations, but he did not. Similarly, I did not object to Brian's summary of my explanations despite my disagreement. This process of compromise with mutual adaptations to each other not only led to a new situation, which any interaction between human beings does, but to a new situation that involved a change in the relationship between Brian and me.

Being in and between several frames of reference at the same time

Mead has a plausible explanation for how such new and changed situations, as I describe in the two examples above, might arise. He uses the term *sociality* to describe our capacity to be in – and consider – several frames of reference at the same time, with these frames of reference involving both past relationships and future intentions:

> The social character of the universe we find in the situation in which the novel event is in both the old order and the new which its advent heralds. Sociality is the capacity of being several things at once.
>
> (1932, p75)

Mead also refers to a process of adjustment or readjustment when we are *betwixt and between the old system and the new*, which leads to the emergence of novelty. Building on Mead's explications, Carroll and Simpson write:

> This 'in limbo' phase of action is the temporal dimension of framing movements that arise when two or more frames are in play.... In effect, sociality is the process of readjustment or reconstrual of meanings that is necessitated by movement from one frame to another.... It is in this transitional phase of readjustment, where emergent objects belong to different frames of meaning simultaneously, that shared meanings are re-cognized, selves and situations are reconstructed, and directions for further action are re-negotiated; in other words, sociality is generative of novelty and change. Being 'betwixt and between' is key to understanding those dynamic movements, such as problem-solving, interpersonal interactions and direction setting.
>
> (2012, p1289)

The above elucidation of the process of readjustment has similarities to my understanding of compromise: it is when we are in and between two or several frames of reference and adapt to both or several that something new and changed arises. For example, if I had objected to Brian's summary of my explanations, without considering the conflictual situation of the previous meeting and my desire to create a future cooperative atmosphere, we would probably not have moved into such cooperation. In the example with my research colleague, a new understanding of the obligation to speak up evolved when we considered our original viewpoints from earlier meetings (our past frame of reference) and the new knowledge obtained about speaking up and reasons for my frequent silence in large groups (our present frame of reference). It was when we were in both frames of reference, at the same time, that a new understanding evolved in our compromising.

My argument is thus that something new and changed can arise in processes of compromise when they involve reflection on, and consideration of, different frames of reference, both in the past and in the present or as intended for the future. Although compromising might entail some sense of loss, as explained earlier, this experience might be temporary and, at some stage of the process, be overshadowed by another experience, e.g., one of change and novelty. The change and novelty emerging from processes of compromise might thus take different forms, e.g., a new insight, and/or a more cooperative atmosphere when doing research or other types of work.

I suggest that compromising has some similarity with the, often, complex interplay between shadow and legitimate themes where new themes or meanings might emerge and the pattern of power relations might change (Stacey and Mowles, 2016, pp422–427). In compromising, there is a complex interplay of different viewpoints when we negotiate and adapt to each other. This might involve negotiations of power relations, value commitments, and what else is important to us. It is not possible to predict the outcomes of processes of compromise. Sometimes compromising involves emergence of new situations and meanings, possibly including some change in the pattern of power relations, at other times the situation and power relations seem to stay the same. Despite this uncertainty, I argue that willingness to engage with conflicts and participate in processes of compromise play an important part in opening potential spaces for new insights and increased cooperation to emerge in research and other work settings, and generally in the world.

Conclusion

If researchers are willing to engage with conflict and explore opportunities for compromising – and, if needed, support others in this process – it might lead to more views, and more people, being heard and to those perceiving themselves in a marginalised or weaker position gaining some influence. The same applies to other work situations. Important to mention is that power relations play an important part in compromising and persons or groups finding themselves in weaker positions – due to, for example, age, seniority, gendered expectations, race, or area of work – might be inclined to adapt their views more, in attempts to gain at least some influence, than is the case for others involved in the same processes of compromise.

The experience of compromise, for example as loss, can change over time, as our understanding of the past is revised. Our initial sense of loss might thus change to be (primarily) one of novelty. Compromising can create new insights within research and other fields, as researchers, managers, and/or employees recognise and adapt to the views of others without (fully) sacrificing their own views. Furthermore, compromising might contribute to strengthened cooperation between colleagues, within a group, or in a larger community. I consider leaders – whether in a formal leadership position or taking an informal leadership role – to have a particular responsibility for attempting to create or strengthen cooperative relationships, which includes willingness to participate in processes of compromise and supporting others in doing the same. Willingness to compromise might thus open spaces for new insights and increased cooperation to emerge, which is needed in research, other work settings, and generally in a world full of conflicts.

Note

1 The Thomas-Kilmann Conflict Mode Instrument includes the following strategies for managing organisational conflicts: avoiding, accommodating, competing, collaborating, and compromising. Further information can be found here: https://kilmanndiagnostics.com/a-brief-history-of-the-thomas-kilmann-conflict-mode-instrument (website accessed on 24 November, 2023).

References

Benjamin, M. (1990) *Splitting the Difference. Compromise and Integrity in Ethics and Politics*. Lawrence, KS: University Press of Kansas.

Carroll, B. and Simpson, B. (2012) Capturing sociality in the movement between frames: An illustration from leadership development. *Human Relations*, 65(10), pp. 1283–1309. doi: 10.1177/0018726712451185.

Dewey, J. (1934) *A Common Faith*. Publ. 2013. New Haven, CT: Yale University Press.

Drabæk, I. (2007) *From Compromise to Trust and Relationality: Dealing with Ethical Dilemmas and Paradoxes in Assurance Practice (Doctor of Management Thesis)*. University of Hertfordshire.

Drabæk, I. (2008) Compromises as processes of moving forward. In Stacey, R. and Griffin, D. (eds) *Complexity and the Experience of Values, Conflict and Compromise in Organizations*. London: Routledge, pp. 72–93.

Elias, N. (1978) *What Is Sociology*. New York: Columbia University Press.

Elias, N. and Scotson, J. L. (1994) *The Established and the Outsiders*. London: Sage Publications.

Honneth, A. (2000) *Suffering from Indeterminacy. An Attempt at a Reactualization of Hegel's Philosophy of Right*. Assen: Var Gorcum & Comp.

Joas, H. (2000) *The Genesis of Values*. Chicago, IL: The University of Chicago Press.

Joas, H. (2008) Value generalization. *Zfwu*, 9(1), pp. 88–97.

Mead, G. H. (1932) *The Philosophy of the Present*. New York: Prometheus Books, 2002.

Mead, G.H. (1934) *Mind, Self and Society: from the Standpoint of a Social Behaviorist*. Chicago, IL: The University of Chicago Press, 2015.

Mowles, C. (2022) *Complexity. A Key Idea for Business and Society*. London: Routledge.

Muhr, S. L. (2019) *Ledelse af køn. Hvordan kønsstereotyper former kvinders og mænds karrierer. En bog om barrierer og nye strategier (own translation: Gender Leadership. How Gender Stereotypes form the Careers of Women and Men. A Book about Barriers and New Strategies)*. Copenhagen: Djøf Forlag.

Nachi, M. (2004) The morality in/of compromise: Some theoretical reflections. *Social Science Information*, 43(2), pp. 291–305.

Rahim, M. A. (2002) Toward a theory of managing organizational conflict. *International Journal of Conflict Management*, 13(3), pp. 206–235.

Scott, J. C. (1990) *Domination and the Arts of Resistance. Hidden Transcripts*. New Haven, CT and London: Yale University Press.

Solsø, K. and Thorup, P. (2015) *Ledelse i Kompleksitet. En introduktion til Ralph Staceys teori om organisation og ledelse*. Copenhagen: Dansk Psykologisk Forlag.

Stacey, R. and Griffin, D. (eds) (2008) *Complexity and the Experience of Values, Conflict and Compromise in Organizations*. London: Routledge.

Stacey, R. D., Griffin, D. and Shaw, P. (2000) *Complexity and Management. Fad or Radical Challenge to Systems Thinking?* London: Routledge.

Stacey, R. D. and Mowles, C. (2016) *Strategic Management and Organisational Dynamics*. 7th ed. Harlow: Pearson Education Limited.

Stoltz, H. T. (2020) *Processes of Compromise in International Development Consultancies – Getting Heard as a Social Scientist (Doctor of Management Thesis)*. University of Hertfordshire.

Sullivan, S. (2000) Reconfiguring gender with John Dewey: Habit, bodies, and cultural change. *Hypatia*, 15(1), pp. 23–42.

Websites accessed:

https://kilmanndiagnostics.com/a-brief-history-of-the-thomas-kilmann-conflict-mode-instrument, accessed on 24 November 2023.

Part III

GOOD ENOUGH ENDINGS

9

THE POLITICS OF ENDINGS

Dilemmas of Making Contributions in Organisation and Management Studies

JANNIE RASMUSSEN

Introduction – on endings and contributions

What are good endings in research and in organisational life? Or, more broadly, what are endings and how are they linked to making contributions?

This book takes a non-essentialist, processual perspective on human life where social phenomena are understood to emerge from the interaction of interdependent heterogenous individuals. From this perspective, which I share, endings have no ontological existence apart from human interaction.[1] Endings can be understood as negotiated punctuations in the ongoing stream of experience, punctuations which mark a transition from one thing to another, the completion of something or an agreement on how to go on together. In this view, the social phenomena of endings are ubiquitous and are defined by societal norms as well as by micro-negotiations between agents. Making a contribution can be understood as one category

DOI: 10.4324/9781003410522-12

of endings that mark an agreement on the quality of some piece of work, be it a doctoral thesis, a journal article or a consulting job.

For instance, when completing my doctoral thesis, I experienced and negotiated many endings. During my three years on the programme, I negotiated endings of each project with my learning set and supervisors trying to find common ground on when the project was good enough for me to move on to the next stage in the process. In my final viva voce examination, I negotiated with my examiners about whether the thesis fulfilled the criteria for them to grant me the award of Doctor of Management. Did the thesis in fact contribute to both practice and the existing body of research?

In my daily work as a management consultant, I negotiate endings with my clients when we transition from the initial phase of exploring the possibilities of working together, marked by signing a contract, to doing work with the organisation. We negotiate continuously about whether the work we do contributes in a relevant way and delivers the desired results. Some of the criteria for judging this may be specified in the contract, some may be unspoken and implied in social expectations about what management consultants do.

Why do I care about endings and contributions? I care because I have something at stake. In my own radically social understanding of human life, we negotiate both our identities and the socio-moral order in each moment of interaction and each of us brings our own values and beliefs to the negotiation. In my final viva, I was keenly aware that while being granted the Doctoral title was important to me, it should not be at any price. I wanted to stay true to my own values and beliefs and hence a good enough ending for me would meet both these wishes.

In an organisation that a colleague and I have been working with for a while, we currently feel like we are constantly negotiating our contribution to the organisation. The organisation has not changed as fast as top management would like and we worry that they will evaluate our contribution as lacking and place the responsibility for the lack of desired change with us, conveniently forgetting that during the year-long contract they have cancelled several workshops, refrained from participating themselves (contrary to our recommendations) and fired most of the middle managers who were an essential part of the work. The judges are still out on what will be 'the ending' here, but the stakes feel particularly high since it is a large and influential client. We want the 'end' to be in our favour as it affects both our identities as consultants and the reputation of our company.

I hope these examples make clear how I see endings and contributions are connected. The question still left unanswered is why I care about making contributions in organisation and management studies.

I care because I would love to make a difference to consulting and to research – a difference that entails leaving more space for the uncertain, for recognising and accepting difference and a move towards less abstracting with more room for actual experience. For me, to make a difference to research requires that I engage with other researchers – also with those outside my own community. Lately, I have been trying to do just this, expand my circle of academic connections. However, these engagements with other researchers have proved not to be as straightforward as I (naïvely) believed they would be. This has confronted me with a familiar habitual pattern of mine where I tend to comply to be included; a pattern I have lately worked hard to change. It has also gotten me thinking about my own values and beliefs and how I may find ways to contribute that align with these.

A small vignette accounting a recent experience of talking to another researcher illustrates some of this.

> *I am in one of the offices in the consulting company where I have recently been employed. The sun is shining through the window and into my face as I am conversing on the screen with a researcher from a Danish University. She is part of a group of researchers that work closely with the consulting company I have recently joined so I am keen to make a good impression. It also seems a good opportunity for me to expand my academic circle in Denmark. She seems politely interested in my work but also somewhat sceptical about the community I have been part of. At a point in the conversation, she remarks that she has not seen many publications in journals from D-Man students and she asks what we are doing if not publishing. I struggle to find an answer and notice a sense of unease with myself as I shift in my chair. I have no doubt that what I and my fellow students are researching has value for others in our respective fields. But his question gets me thinking about the norms for academia and what it means to make a contribution in academic circles. I feel caught between competing goods. On the one hand I want to stay true to my beliefs and answer that we do not publish in journals since it seems to be just a game of academics communicating with other academics. On the other hand, I am keenly aware of*

> *my dependence on getting on well with this other researcher. I find myself thinking, that it seems there are certain implicit standards for making a contribution (that counts) in academic life and my work seems not to live up to those. In the end I offer a slight defence by saying how we publish elsewhere but I also sense something of a loss of interest with my counterpart. Why, I wonder, does publishing in the right journals seem so important to academics and will I have to go down that road to be accepted by a wider community of academics? If so, what compromises will it entail and am I willing to make them?*

To me, the example above can be seen as an implicit conversation about making contributions in science and what counts as a good enough contribution. I entered the meeting feeling quite satisfied with the work I had done on the D-Man, yet during the conversation I began to question the value of my own work and the ending that had already been negotiated around my work – namely that I had made something of value which marked a transition from student to Doctor of Management. Why did I suddenly question this already negotiated end – and my identity as a researcher? Possibly because I encountered a different set of values and a different conception of what it means to contribute as an academic in which contributing is strongly linked to publishing in the right journals. Furthermore, this happened in a relation in which I was more dependent on the other that she was on me since I wished to be accepted by her and the group she belonged to, and I wanted to represent my company well.

This experience has piqued my interest in understanding more about the academic community and the norms and values it rests on since in my understanding to navigate and negotiate my way into a wider academic circle I must understand the rules of the game.

Thinking about these rules of the game and what it means to make a contribution and negotiate 'good enough endings,' I am reminded of French sociologist and philosopher Pierre Bourdieu's notions of field, habitus and capital. In the following, I draw on his ideas to understand the power dynamics of academia and higher education as I have encountered them. I identify different rationalities at work in organisation and management research and explore how these may affect and be affected by researchers. I explore what it means to make a contribution to science from the perspective of each rationality, and I use my own experience of trying to find my new identity as a researcher to illustrate and highlight some possible dilemmas for researchers and practitioners. Finally, I conclude with some implications for practice, particularly implications for organisational life and management.

Bourdieu's theory of power

French sociologist, Pierre Bourdieu, presents an elaborate theory of how power, positions and identity are continuously preserved and changed through ongoing negotiations or battles between social actors. Bourdieu's theory captures the paradoxical nature of the social world and offers an analytical framework from which to understand social phenomena and experience. Bourdieu tries to describe, for analytical purposes, how the social world is at the same time enabling and constraining, as well as ordered by and ordering individual behaviour and social interactions.

I will not endeavour to describe the totality of Bourdieu's complex theory. Rather I will briefly present his three central and inter-related concepts and use these as a theoretical framework from which to understand the power dynamics in organisation and management research and my own struggles to find my way as a researcher-consultant, learning to play what Bourdieu calls 'the game'.

Bourdieu's notion of habitus

Bourdieu uses the concept *habitus* to explain the tendency for patterns in society to be repeated and be recognisable over time through the actions of individuals who are simultaneously same and different.

Habitus can be understood as the incorporated social (Bourdieu, 2020 p29), '…an open system of dispositions that is constantly subjected to experiences…' (Bourdieu and Wacquant, 2007, p133). Habitus is thus an individual's embodied, practical knowledge about how to act in social situations which is acquired through experience and upbringing, and which is constantly evolving throughout life if only with slight changes. Habitus is what enables us to respond appropriately in social interaction. At the same time, habitus is also what sometimes keeps us from moving on. My preference for compliance can be understood as part of my habitus. It influences how I approach others and position myself when negotiating my way into new groups. In the vignette, I suspect my preference of initial compliance played a part in my finding it difficult to respond to the other researcher's questions about the D-Man community.

In an organisational context such as my own (consultancy) my habitus plays out as those ways of consulting that feel 'natural' to me. Ways that are almost automatic (or at least unreflexive) that do not require much mental energy from me.

Any individual's habitus is at the same time unique and similar since, according to Bourdieu, there are classes of habitus (linked to positions in fields). But no two individuals have exactly the same historical trajectory and hence there will be both similarities and differences between them (Bourdieu, 2020, p29f).

Bourdieu's notion of habitus bears some resemblance to John Dewey's notion of habit as described by Solsø in Chapter 6. As I see it, the concept also bears some resemblance to G.H. Mead's idea of the generalised other and the I/me dialectic although Mead's concept is more directly sensitive to the improvisational aspects of an individual's actions and hence can better account for change (see for instance Holdsworth and Morgan, 2007). Still, keeping this in mind and noticing that Bourdieu himself does not consider habitus to be as deterministic as some of his critics have implied (Bourdieu and Wacquant, 2007, p133), I will still lean on Bourdieu's notion in this chapter.

Bourdieu's notion of capital

According to Bourdieu, all individuals struggle for recognition and position. An important element in these struggles is *capital*. Capital can be understood as anything that can be exchanged which affects the distribution of legitimacy and power (Nicolini, 2012, p59). In this sense, capital is the key power-concept in Bourdieu's theory.

Bourdieu describes capital as a kind of social energy linked to particular social fields and a structuring principle for those fields. Capital and field are interdependent. Capital is what structures the field and hence only has value within the field as well as what motivates people's actions in the field (Bourdieu, 2020, p225). On the other hand, the field determines which kinds of capital have value. Hence, capital both defines and is defined by the field. With capital comes position within a field and with position comes differing degrees of opportunity to influence the game that is played and to appropriate the products that are at stake in the game (Bourdieu and Wacquant, 2007, p102).

For instance, in my work as a consultant, I have experienced that expertise about organisations and the ability to facilitate interaction in many situations tend to increase my capital and hence my position in the field of organisational consulting. Of course, this is not a simple cause and effect relation since each time I 'flash' my expertise in consulting jobs or present clients with a plan for how I will facilitate interaction, I also contribute to confirming and maybe even enhancing the importance of expertise as capital in the field. Returning to my initial vignette, I think one of the things that contribute to my unease in the situation is my sense that I may not hold the capital required to succeed in the field. If the important source of capital is publications in journals, then I have none of that – leaving me with very little leverage in the field in Bourdieu's perspective.

Bourdieu's notion of field

Field is the final element in Bourdieu's complex theory. Field is a concept that seeks to capture forces in society which are organised around objects and patterns of relating. Fields are structured by positions (and capital) and governed by 'rules of interaction'. Society at large can be understood as a sort of meta-field which is comprised of various specific fields such as economics, religion, arts, academia and consultancy. Fields are in turn divided into subfields. For instance, the arts-field is divided in a theatre-field, a literature-field and so forth.

Bourdieu distinguishes between the field of forces and the field of struggles (Bourdieu and Wacquant, 2007; Bourdieu, 2020). The field of forces is the distribution of capital and the positions that follow from each individual's assumed capital – including the constraints and opportunities that follow. The field of struggles is the ongoing negotiations between agents who are all trying to accumulate capital and earn a position in the field – or trying to change the rules that govern the field to change the distribution of power and positions.

If we take the term field at face value, it may be misleading since it implies a spatial existence. This, however, is not what Bourdieu means. Rather, a field is:

> … the locus of relations of force – and not only of meaning – and of struggles aimed at transforming it, and therefore of endless change.
>
> (Bourdieu and Wacquant, 2007, p103)

In another place, Bourdieu describes the field as:

> … 1) a space of positions whose structure matches the distribution of specific capital and as 2) a field of struggles to transform this space.
> (Bourdieu, 2020, p337)

From these two quotes, it may be clearer how, despite Bourdieu's own use of spatial terms, the field can be understood as the constantly evolving relations of a group of people interacting who are at the same time constrained in their interactions by the ordering of positions and changing those orderings by their interactions.

Returning to the example of organisational consulting, this too can be considered a field. This field is comprised of consultants in different consulting companies, managers in different companies and academics from business schools. As a consultant, I am constantly negotiating implicitly in my interactions with managers and other consultants what consultants can and cannot be expected to do (the rules of interaction) and as indicated in one of my earlier examples, what counts as good enough endings. These negotiations are affected by what both managers and consultants are taught in business schools and what we read in journals and pick up from other academic channels. My initial vignette can also be seen as a negotiation in the field of academia. What is valued as capital by the other researcher is inevitably influenced by the wider field of academia but also by the particular dynamics between the individuals in the research communities that we both belong to. Hence, I was preoccupied with the values that I share with people in the DMan community and wondering if I would have to deviate too far from those to be accepted by the other community. I tried to push this understanding a little with my response, but I doubt it had much effect since I had little leverage in the field as indicated above.

Moving on from this brief description of Bourdieu's theory of power, I will now try to understand the field of management and organisation research and – returning to my subject – what it means and entails to make a contribution in this field. When aiming to understand the field, relevant questions are: what sorts of capital and habitus define the structure of the field? What struggles appear to be going on in the field? Which interests dominate the field (and hence define the relevant capitals and habitus) and which are dominated? How do these interests serve to preserve and change the field as well as the capitals and habitus of the field? How do these interests influence what counts as 'good enough endings' and hence what counts as valid contributions? These questions are equally relevant to understanding any other field and hence managers and consultants trying to understand what it means to make a contribution in an organisation (and in their particular organisation) may benefit from asking the same questions as a way to understand the particularities of their field.

Understanding the field of management and organisation research

In trying to understand the field of management and organisation research, I draw primarily on authors writing in the critical management tradition.

I am particularly reminded of a 2011 article in the Academy of Management review, where management researchers, Jörgen Sandberg and Haridimos Tsoukas, theorise about different kinds of theorising in organisation and management studies. They make the distinction between scientific rationality and practical rationality. In the following I will describe the two rationalities and what it means to make a contribution from each perspective.

Scientific rationality

Sandberg and Tsoukas argue that scientific rationality rests on three interconnected core assumptions (2011, p340):

1. That the physical and the social world exists independent of our interaction with it but that it can be captured by the human mind.
2. That knowing is about subjects appropriating objects (out there) by use of their intellectual capacity.
3. That improvement of practice depends on the development of increasingly more accurate representations of the world of discrete objects. This entails overcoming individual biases and hence scientists should strive to become as objective as possible.

British Professor of Organisation Studies, Ann Cunliffe, supplements this perspective by arguing that much of the knowledge produced in organisation and management theory is rooted in what she calls *masculinised rationality* (Cunliffe, 2022). Masculine rationality, she argues, sees good theories as:

> ... an abstraction of essential commonalities that can be generalized across contexts.
>
> (Cunliffe, 2022, p3)

Cunliffe presents how within masculinised rationality, theories are ranged from weak to strong according to the degree to which they answer questions of why events, actions and structures occur, and identify causal relationships and systematic reasons. Weak theories are descriptive with no abstractions. I find it curious how using terms such as weak and strong for me introduces an implicit valuation with strong being better than weak. This immediate response on my part is of course influenced by my habits but I suspect that others may share these habits. Hence, by using these words a relation of dominance and hierarchy between discrete approaches is introduced – rather than a continuum or different knowledge problematics that are conceived as overlapping as suggested by Cunliffe (2011, p653).

From the perspective of scientific rationality, making a contribution means abstracting from reality (Cunliffe, 2022) and producing general and universal knowledge about phenomena in the world the value of which can be *decided objectively by some universal standard* (Thomas, 2011). Most often, criteria for judging contributions within this rationality are objectivity and generalisability – the latter understood as the uncovering of universal patterns which increase our ability to predict effects of our actions. The ideal is epistemic knowledge which is produced by the objective scientist who observes the system from outside (Elias, 1970; Stacey and Mowles, 2016).

I recognise these ideals from my initial training at university as well as from my conversations with other researchers who ask me about autoethnography as my chosen method. The questions I am asked mainly focus on the validity of my research with this as my chosen method. How, they ask, can I generalise my results? How may others benefit from what I have been exploring if I primarily focus on unique cases? To me these questions indicate a scientific rationality perspective on science, and I think my difficulties in answering their questions relate to my answers being located in a different onto-epistemological approach, namely practical rationality (Sandberg and Tsoukas, 2011).

Practical rationality

Sandberg and Tsoukas describe practical rationality as an onto-epistemological premise that takes seriously the meaningful totality, temporal flow and irreducibly situational nature of practitioners' experiences (2011, p341f.). This leads to research that:

> ... enables management researchers to both stay close to the logic of practice and generate practical rationality theories – theories that capture essential aspects of the logic of practice.
>
> (Sandberg and Tsoukas, 2011, p350)

Cunliffe supplements this perspective by pointing to the need in organisation and management research for more human ways of theorising (Cunliffe, 2022). These are ways of theorising, which recognise the researcher's embeddedness in the world and their responsibilities to others (Cunliffe, 2022, p22). While she argues that such theorising is more human, she is not hereby implying 'better'. She recognises the need for different orientations to research where no orientations are privileged. Rather, focus is on 'crafting research' and paying attention to the alignment of scientific orientation and the chosen method (Cunliffe, 2011).

It should be clear from the description that practical rationality rests on quite different assumptions than scientific rationality:

1. That the physical and the social world emerges from our interaction with it and hence cannot be understood outside this interaction.
2. That knowing is about understanding more about this interaction and hence enabling action.
3. That improvement of practice comes from this deepened understanding and entails continuous individual and collective inquiry and reflexivity.

In contrast to scientific rationality, practical rationality is bound up with a non-epistemic knowledge ideal, identified by Aristotle in his *Nicomachean*

Ethics as *phronesis* or practical wisdom (2014, p101ff.). Research from a practical rationality perspective is concerned with enabling individuals and collectives to make *practical decisions* about what actions to proceed with (Aristotle, 2014, p104). One example of this is described in Chapter 6 where Solsø writes about John Dewey's conception of science. Building on Dewey, Solsø emphasises *inquiry with a scientific attitude.* This form of inquiry rests on Dewey's understanding of action as driven by habits and beliefs and focuses on systematic and rigorous inquiry into breakdowns, i.e. situations in which our current habits bring us in a non-satisfactory relationship to the situation at hand. By inquiring with an open mind, suspending judgement for a while, we can find new ways to go on.

The aim of social science resting on a phronetic knowledge ideal is to provide specific knowledge of particular cases, the value of which will lie in the degree to which they are recognised, accepted and appropriated by others as part of a wider dialogue around the themes being researched (Flyvbjerg, 2006).

This resonates with Danish professor of Psychology Svend Brinkmann's criterion of 'goodness' or moral criteria as a way of judging qualitative research (Brinkmann, 2012, p182). Judging research by the moral criterion in Brinkmann's terminology means judging the research by whether it has enabled the researcher and others to act well, whether it has enabled a deeper understanding of a problem or perhaps brought the researcher and others in a different relationship with the problem (Brinkmann, 2012, p182f.).

Reframing the three transcendentals of Scholasticism, Brinkmann introduces two other criteria as well: truth with a lower case 't'(epistemic criteria), and beauty (aesthetic criteria). The epistemic criterion refers to what Brinkmann's calls a *situated truth* and is concerned with the plausibility of the research. It is about telling authentic and plausible stories (Cunliffe, 2011, p667). Truth with a lower case 't' can be attained by researchers being transparent about their own position from which they make their descriptions (including theoretical and onto-epistemological perspective), by carefully situating the persons, episodes and objects of the research and by presenting coherence only when it is actually experienced and fragmentation when this is experienced (see also Larsen, Chapter 3 this volume). Hence, research from this perspective is descriptive rather than abstract.

Brinkmann's final criterion: beauty or the aesthetics of the work is concerned with how the reader is moved by the research. This criterion concerns the way of writing and presenting the research so that readers can empathise and resonate with what they encounter. Aesthetic qualities can be improved by researchers paying attention to relevant details. This involves what Anthropologist Clifford Geertz has called *thick description* which enables the reader to enter the world as the author experiences it. These thick descriptions are detailed descriptions of interaction that include not only the observable physical behaviours of actors but also their emotional reactions and thoughts, their contexts and their ideas and *interpretations* of the events in context. Finally, ethical self-consciousness, knowing one's own position and paying attention to others' positions are important (Geertz, 1973, p181) as is accepting that aspects of ourselves will be opaque to us, evading our immediate consciousness (Elias, 1970; Butler, 2005).

Importantly, the criteria should not be understood as pre-given absolutes or 'boxes to tick'. Rather, they are guidelines for crafting and judging qualitative research, and the judging is retrospective. In the end, quality in this perspective emerges as a result of interactions between the people involved: researchers, reviewers, the people involved in the research and any others somehow coming in touch with the research. It should also be clear from my description of the criteria, that they are not discrete categories since they overlap. Other chapters in this book describe in more detail how the research may strive to fulfil these criteria.

The onto-epistemological premises underlying practical rationality aligns well with the complex responsive processes of relating perspective that informs the chapters in this book, and with my understanding of the world. In this perspective, we are always involved as researchers (Stacey and Griffin, 2005) – and as consultants or managers. There is no view from nowhere, and organisations and organisational life must be understood from the perspectives of engagement by active participants who form and are formed by those same patterns, which constitute both the organisation and the individuals at the same time. The insights produced in research will come from the researcher's reflections on his/her own experience of these patterns, emerging in micro-interactions which are inevitably influenced by shared global patterns as well as reproducing and changing these patterns (Stacey and Griffin, 2005, p24). Put differently, the researcher's ability to be simultaneously involved and detached and to reflect on their own involvement will be important (Stacey and Griffin, 2005).

Thinking about the academic field in the light of the writings of Sandberg and Tsoukas, Cunliffe and Brinkmann as well as my own experiences of interactions with other researchers brings me to assume that the field is structured partly by the simultaneous existence of these different rationalities and what seems to be a negotiation between them regarding what organisation and management research should focus on and how it should be carried out – and as a result also what counts as a good enough ending/ what it means to make a contribution.

That practical rationality aligns with the way I view the world does not make it truer or better than scientific rationality in any absolute sense. It just offers a different kind of insight. Yet, as my vignette at the beginning of this chapter and my analysis above indicates, the different rationalities at work in the academic field battle for power (and recognition) in social and organisational research. Hence, what counts as a 'good enough ending' depends only partly on the onto-epistemological premise from which one judges, since the relations between the different conceptions as it is expressed in interactions in the field matter. Returning to the notion of the field, the two opposing conceptions of the good with their roots in scientific and practical rationality respectively seem to structure the field.[2] One relevant question that follows from this is how these different understandings are positioned within the field. Which understanding dominates and how are they linked to the kinds of capital at work in the field?

Dominance and capital at work in the field

Thinking about capital and positions within the field I am once again drawn to Ann Cunliffe's work. She offers some indication of how the different understandings are positioned within the field (Cunliffe, 2022). She writes that:

> … particular definitions of "good theory" and ways of theorizing continue to be privileged and to perpetuate the silencing of alternative and more diverse voices.
>
> (Cunliffe, 2022, p2)

She further argues that the definitions that are privileged and which seem imperative to getting published (and promoted) are those that fit her concept of masculinised theorising, which I have categorised above along with scientific rationality. She indicates that publishers, editors and reviewers of high-ranking journals act as gatekeepers who work to retain the privilege of scientific rationality.

I recognise from my own experience that scientific rationality dominates the field of organisation and management research. My sense of unease when asked about my own research is to me both a sign of the dominance of scientific rationality and my own habitual orientation to this way of thinking since scientific rationality was dominant at university both when I studied psychology and later my master's in business administration.

The dominance of scientific rationality spills into organisational life. On numerous occasions, I have been asked to conceptualise the essence of my doctoral thesis so that it will be more communicable to others. Furthermore, a lot of the publication sites that practitioner researchers may use to communicate their research insights have quite strict rules about how things may be communicated. On one occasion I was given a two-page maximum and a constriction saying I would have to make recommendations based on my insights. Making recommendations for me equates to reducing the complexity of things, something I try to avoid. In this case, I tried to keep some complexity in my writing only to find that the editor of the site returned my article in a quite different form where my open reflections had changed into sharp recommendations. In this case, I struggled for a while but eventually accepted publication in a less-preferred form thinking that someone reading it and maybe reflecting slightly was better than no one reading it at all.

I wonder why this dominance prevails. To my knowledge, there are plenty of researchers who think differently about their work and also plenty of journals and other publication opportunities where we as researchers might publish (Brinkmann, 2012, p183). Professors of organisational studies and behaviour, Mats Alvesson and André Spicer, offer some indications of what might be at work to keep the dominance of scientific rationality alive apart from the obvious observation that science grounded in scientific rationality is still what is primarily taught in universities and master's programmes (see for instance Simpson and Revsbæk, 2022, p233f.). Exploring why (academic) professionals seem to willingly comply with managerialism, Alvesson and Spicer point out that it has become increasingly important for researchers to publish in high-ranking journals and doing so is experienced by academics as an indicator of their excellence (Alvesson and Spicer, 2016, p32f.). They argue that the rise of managerialism in higher education has led to an increasing focus on performance where academics are measured by a '4 by 4' formula: publishing at least four articles in journals ranked as 4-star (Alvesson and Spicer, 2016, p33). According to Alvesson and Spicer, many academics seem to have surrendered to this practice, committing themselves (albeit with some cynicism) to the standards of measurement and position that dominate. This means they are able to keep their jobs in universities, whereas non-compliance may endanger their employment. Ann Cunliffe points to the same pattern when she worries that early career researchers may feel pressured to research, theorise and write in particular ways (Cunliffe, 2022, p2).

Returning to Bourdieu's concept of capital, this indicates that one of the ways capital in the field of academia is won is by publishing in high-ranking journals. Publishing in high-ranking journals is an important currency in the battle for positions and those who are able to comply with the standards of scientific rationality earn this capital more easily. I might even speculate that those whose habits fit this pattern will find it easier to enhance their position and win capital, whereas those whose habits fit less well will struggle more. Capital is linked to ability influence the field and the game and hence the accumulation of capital is important if one has this ambition.

That capital may be won by publishing in high-ranking journals also resonates with the conversation with the Danish researcher, recounted at the start of the chapter, who asked what we were doing in the D-Man community if not publishing – and my own difficulty in finding an adequate response. As a consultant I am trained to notice what is going on and to quickly try to discern the 'rules of the game' that is being played in the organisations I work with. In this case, I heard a 'question behind the question' which read something like: Why are you not playing the game like the rest of us? I felt very far from influential. I felt marginal – not marginalised because I do not think there was any intention to marginalise. Rather, I felt my own marginal position as a new researcher working within a non-dominant onto-epistemological framework. I even felt how this somewhat collided with my early training.

It would be easy to locate the problem only with me, but building on Bourdieu's idea that individual behaviour and thinking reflects larger societal patterns, it seems plausible that my inner struggles reflected the larger struggle in the academic community between proponents of scientific rationality and practical rationality.

As an upcoming researcher, I was preoccupied with being accepted by the larger academic community and to negotiate my position within this community. Having just finished the D-Man, I was further preoccupied with expanding my academic relations beyond the D-Man community. This would require that I was accepted by others. The question I am left with is whether it also required that I conform to different norms of good research? My guess would be that other upcoming researchers may also share this preoccupation as is suggested by Alvesson and Szkudlarek when they write:

> The career-oriented academic can be highly sensitive to not only the power associated with the academic peer community but also, and increasingly, in relationship to managerial ends.
>
> (2020, p2)

In summary, by reading other texts and my own experiences through Bourdieu's lens, it seems to me that the field of management and organisation research is structured (partly) by a battle between scientific rationality and practical rationality of which the former dominates and is linked to position within the field. An important capital at work in the field is publications in high-ranking journals and hence the ability to excel in this discipline leads to position within the field. Those whose habits and philosophical commitments (Cunliffe, 2011) match these requirements may find it easier to navigate and play the game in the field. However, there are indications that a number of 'players' in the field hold different ideas about the good yet find themselves playing the game after all (see for instance Alvesson and Spicer, 2016, Alvesson and Szkudlarek, 2020, Cunliffe, 2022). Indeed, in thinking about how I may expand my development as a researcher – and hence my ability to influence the game, I have thought about whether to apply for a position within a more scientifically oriented research community to enhance my position within the field. However, this poses a different set of problems for me, as I will elaborate on below.

Alvesson and Spicer (2016) suggest that playing the scientific rationality game despite a different onto-epistemological orientation may lead to cynicism or in my own case to disillusion. In this sense, the structure of the field may cause dilemmas for researchers who lean more towards practical rationality than towards scientific rationality. Below I will try to outline some of these dilemmas.

Dilemmas of becoming an academic scholar

Thinking with Bourdieu's theory, it seems position as well as acceptance and jobs within the field of management and organisation research are won by complying with the norms of scientific rationality and publishing in high-ranking journals. This may be more prevalent for upcoming researchers, such as myself, since players with more capital and higher positions have greater degrees of freedom from the constraints of the field (Bourdieu, 2020, p76). Hence, the ability to challenge the rules of the game increases with one's position, yet position is won by playing the game.

To me this has posed a dilemma since I have come to hold values about research which fall closer to the practical rationality perspective. Hence, I have at times felt caught between whether to comply with the requirements of scientific rationality or stick with my beliefs. If I were not trying to influence the academic community towards a greater inclusion of more experiential research, then the dilemma may be less hard felt since I would depend less on earning capital within the field. When, however, I do wish to change things and would like to keep doing research along with my work as a consultant – I feel the dilemma in a stronger way. Furthermore, my experience so far as a new researcher indicates to me that acceptance in academic circles comes easier if one has published in the right journals. Although I find it more important that the work I do makes a difference to practitioners, I would also like to be included into a wider academic community since I need the inspiration and challenge I get from thinking together with other academics.

Since I believe that both position and identity are negotiated in everyday micro-interactions and is also related to group membership, it is inevitable that my identity will be affected by what I do as has indeed been argued by Alvesson and Szkudlarek (2020) and Alvesson and Spicer (2016). Hence, the dilemma feels like a choice between my integrity and identity as a social researcher and my position within the community of researchers.

It may even be a question of publishing or not publishing. Only, if I do not publish then can I be said to make a contribution? If no one reads it and there is no resonance, then one could argue that there is no contribution since meaning emerges in interaction. Of course, this depends on whom I define as my audience. I may indeed be able to make a practical contribution to my clients by using my findings in my work and by approaching consultancy with a Deweyan mindset. I may also share my thoughts with others in non-academic ways which could also offer opportunities for resonance. The practical rationality perspective offers alternatives for making a contribution other than publishing in journals since the criterion of enabling better action may indeed not involve publishing in some journal that few people read. However, influencing the field of academia requires that I do publish in journals. Increasing my capital may require that these be high ranking. Only, as Alvesson and Spicer point out, by going down this road, my contributions may fail to say very much which is novel or has any impact (2016, p33) and it may lead to cynicism (2016, p33). From a practical rationality perspective, this would mean failure to contribute since there would probably be less resonance and less enablement of action.

Speculating about the wider relevance of my own experiences, it seems that researchers who adhere to the onto-epistemological premises of practical rationality and wish to be accepted by the wider academic community may find themselves in dilemmas of whether to comply with the dominant norms or whether to stick with their beliefs. Either way their choice depends on their own and others' values, their habits and their aspirations; any choice of action will have an impact on their identity and their position in the field.

From this perspective, good enough endings and what it means to make a contribution are not given in advance and may be hard to define, although as Askeland writes about in Chapter 11, dominant stage models of grief may lead us to believe that endings are identifiable and that they separate us from something previously held valuable. Rather, by understanding good enough endings through Bourdieu's theory and my own experiences as recounted at the beginning of the chapter, they emerge as a result of interconnected 'inner' negotiations between competing values and habits and 'outer' negotiations within the field which the researcher belongs to or aspires to be included in. In these negotiations, both the researcher and the other members of relevant communities have something at stake. The examiner who grants a degree or the editor who accepts a paper are not only concerned with the content of the paper but also with the effects of their decision on their own sense of self, their position in field and on the values and norms of the field – the 'rules of the game'. Good enough endings affect and are ongoing negotiations affected by participants' aspirations, current sense of self as well as association with and position within relevant fields.

I find similar dynamics at work in organisational life. Some of my clients are perfectly happy with an iterative and experiential approach in which we learn and explore together as we go along, whereas others ask for elaborate plans and detailed programmes for seminars – and judge the quality of the work not from a perspective of whether their understanding of things have changed but whether we have stuck with the plan and delivered the processes agreed on. Hence, what it means to make a contribution depends on whom I interact with – both in academia and in organisational life.

Writing this chapter has highlighted for me that rather than seeing academic inclusion as a question of compliance and loss of integrity or non-compliance and exclusion and marginal existence yet intact integrity, it is important not to get fixed on one way of understanding experience but rather to keep looking for more ways. It is important to keep the inquiry open. By doing so, I have come to understand the field as less a question of only two opposing rationalities but rather as constituted by multiple unique individuals who all try to navigate the complexities of the field.

Below, I will explore what this view on endings and making a contribution may imply for both academic practice and for managers preoccupied with making contributions in organisational life. I offer these not as universal conclusions but as inspiration to other researchers and to managers curious about making contributions in organisational life. Hence, the value of my implications for practice should be judged by Brinkmann's criteria of goodness, that is whether they resonate and whether others judge them transferable to their own practice and will bring them in a different relationship with the problems they are facing. During my process of writing, it has been helpful for me to engage reflexively with both my own and others' habitual patterns of thinking around science (and consultancy) as well as the different values and aspirations involved and how these were enabling and constraining our negotiations around good enough endings. Reflexivity is the ability to reflect on one's reflections, that is, on how one makes sense of experience (see also Mowles on reflexivity, Chapter 5 this volume). In Bourdieu's terms, reflexivity is the only way out of the social traps that characterises those aspects of human behaviour influenced by habitus (Bourdieu and Wacquant, 2007, p126). In this sense, he is aligned with Dewey (see Solsø, Chapter 6 this volume) who saw the ability to question one's assumptions as essential to developing our thinking.

Implications for practice

As I have been writing this chapter and thought about my own experiences of negotiating good enough endings, I have come to see these as ongoing processes, rather than as a series of unconnected events with discrete beginnings and endings. I am now clearer about seeing making contributions not as a search for objective truths but as historical-relational negotiations of power, position, identity and values which involve dilemmas. The negotiations are not over since meaning is an ongoing relational movement.

Reflecting on it now, the parallels to working life are striking. It seems to me onto-epistemological negotiations are ubiquitous. I recently experienced these differences in negotiating a contract with a client. My client wanted a full plan for activities over the next year that he could get approval of in the board and which would lead to success with his plans for the organisation. He believed I could deliver such a plan. Building on my understanding of the world as essentially unpredictable I wanted to keep things as open as possible and to be able to take one step at a time. Initially he couldn't understand why I could not just design a process leading to the desired end, and it took several meetings and some phone calls to arrive at an agreement of what would constitute a good enough contract (and a temporary end of the negotiation phase). The difficulty for me lay in my dependence on him for the job. This is further linked to my being part of an organisation where I am expected to contribute to the company's revenue. Hence, I cannot turn down every consulting job that does not immediately match my worldview. My client on his part had obligations to the board of directors who wanted a plan if they were to allow the funds for the process. In the end, we found an agreement where I sketched the steps in a process but did not specify exactly what each step entailed. Agreeing on a good enough contract in this case entailed a negotiation in which differing beliefs had to meet in some sense in the final contract for the job.

Writing this chapter has also further increased my awareness to the potentials and limitations of thinking with theory. Reading and understanding my experiences and other texts on academia through Bourdieu's theory has directed my attention to the dynamics of the field. Combining this with Sandberg and Tsoukas' distinction between two different rationalities (which is indeed an abstraction from reality) almost made me think of the field and the battle as a 'join them or beat them' game. Reading Cunliffe's 2011 text in which she speaks of different knowledge problematics and thinking about the complexity of various academic communities has called my attention to a different way of thinking – as multiple unique individuals all trying to navigate the complexities of the field rather than opposing beliefs. Neither of these perspectives is to be understood in a representational way. Each perspective comes with enabling constraints. My point is that thinking with theory is helpful since it pushes me out of my habitual patterns of thinking. Only, new patterns rapidly emerge and to me it is important to be equally irreverent to these and to keep challenging them since this will lead to new opportunities for action and help me avoid what Askeland in Chapter 11 calls an entrapment in theoretical confines.

The reflexive engagement with the process of becoming a researcher that this chapter represents has enabled me to move from non-reflexive compliance with (traditional) norms to reflexive engagement with the dilemmas, following from the ongoing debates around what constitutes good science within the field of organisation and management research. For me, it has made a tremendous difference to being able to understand good enough endings and contributions not as universal recipes that I must learn to decipher and deliver but as ongoing negotiations between political individuals. It has helped me to recognise my own part in a larger game and to make conscious decisions about how I might participate in the game. It has further helped me de-individualise my reactions.

The constraints have not been removed. The debate between onto-epistemological premises in organisation and management research as well as in organisational life is ongoing; from my perspective, the best we can do as researchers and practitioners is to reflexively engage with these debates and how they affect us, what we believe we must do to be included and whether we want to be included or will look for different communities.

Or – to use the words of pragmatist social psychologist G H. Mead: hold all the conflicting ends in view while also questioning my own assumptions and 'truths' (Mead, 1923, p236).

This way of thinking brings to mind a term from a recent book on doing process research in organisations edited by Barbara Simpson and Line Revsbæk (Simpson and Revsbæk, 2022). They talk about research as 'noticing differently' and the chapters in their book suggest various methods by which this ability can be advanced. Some of these methods are abduction (reflexive engagement with problematic situations as elaborated by Solsø in Chapter 7), thinking with theory as I have done in this chapter, paying attention to affective states and paying attention to detail and process.

As managers and researchers curious about understanding organisational life and expanding our ability to navigate the complexities, training our ability to notice differently and to challenge our fixed assumptions about good enough ends and what counts as a contribution may enable us to relate differently to current situations and hence fulfil Brinkmann's criterion of 'goodness'.

Notes

1 I acknowledge that there are endings in nature such as death and decay but the fact that we consider them endings is a human construction.
2 I am aware that this is a very crude distinction and division in only two opposing understandings and that one could make much more nuanced distinctions dividing research in a more sophisticated way.

References

Alvesson, M. and Spicer, A. (2016) (Un)conditional surrender? Why do professionals willingly comply with managerialism. *Journal of Organizational Change Management*, 29 (1), pp. 29–45

Alvesson, M. and Szkudlarek, B. (2020) Honorable surrender: On the erosion of resistance in a University Setting. *Journal of Management Inquiry*, 30 (4), pp. 1–14, Sage

Aristotle (2014) *Nicomachean Ethics*, Indianapolis, IN/Cambridge: Hackett Publishing Company

Bourdieu, P. (2020) *Habitus and Field: General Sociology, Volume 2*, Cambridge: Polity Press

Bourdieu, P. and Wacquant, L.D. (2007) *An Invitation to Reflexive Sociology*, Cambridge: Polity Press

Brinkmann, S. (2012) *Qualitative Inquiry in Everyday Life*, Los Angeles, CA/London/New Delhi/Singapore: Sage Publications

Butler, J. (2005) *Giving an Account of Oneself*, New York: Fordham University Press

Cunliffe, A.L. (2011) Crafting qualitative research: Morgan and Smircich 30 years on. *Organizational Research Methods*, 14 (4), pp. 647–673

Cunliffe, A.L. (2022) Must I grow a pair of balls to theorize about theory in organization and management studies? *Organization Theory*, 3, pp. 1–28, Sage

Elias, N. ([1970] 1978) *What Is Sociology*, New York: Columbia University Press

Flyvbjerg, B. (2006) Making organization research matter: Power, values and phronesis. In: Clegg, S.R., Hardy, C., Lawrence, T.B., and Nord, W.R. (eds) *The Sage Handbook of Organization Studies*, 2nd edition, pp. 370–387, London: Sage

Geertz, C. (1973) *The Interpretation of Cultures*; Selected Essays, New York: Basic Books

Holdsworth, C. and Morgan, D. (2007) Revisiting the generalized other: An exploration. *Sociology*, 41 (3), pp. 401–417, Sage Publications

Mead, G.H. (1923) Scientific method and the moral sciences. *International Journal of Ethics*, 33 (3), pp. 229–247, The University of Chicago Press

Mead, G.H. (1925) The genesis of the self and social control. *International Journal of Ethics*, 35 (3), 251–277

Mead, G.H. (1934) *Mind, Self and Society: from the Standpoint of a Social Behaviorist*. Chicago, IL: The University of Chicago Press, 2015

Nicolini, D. (2012) *Practice Theory, Work and Organization: An Introduction*, Oxford: Oxford University Press

Sandberg, J. and Tsoukas, H. (2011) Grasping the logic of practice: theorizing through practical rationality. *The Academy of Management Review*, 36 (2), pp. 338–360

Simpson, B. and Revsbæk, L. (2022) *Doing Process Research in Organizations: Noticing Differently*, Oxford: Oxford University Press

Stacey, R. and Griffin, D. (2005) *A Complexity Perspective on Researching Organizations: Taking Experience Seriously*, London and New York: Routledge

Stacey, R. and Mowles, C. (2016) *Strategic Management and Organisational Dynamics. The Challenge of Complexity to Ways of Thinking about Organizations*, 7th edition, Harlow: Pearson Education Limited

Thomas, G. (2011) The case: Generalisation, theory and phronesis in case study. *Oxford Review of Education*, 37 (1), pp. 21–35

10

THE ETHICS OF WRITING ABOUT EXPERIENCE

A Dialogue

TOBIT EMMENS, KIRAN CHAUHAN AND CHRIS MOWLES

Introduction

This chapter is the edited transcript of a conversation between Tobit Emmens (TE), Kiran Chauhan (KC) and Chris Mowles (CM) where we try to take the perspectives of recent student, supervisor, and programme director, respectively, on the ethics of writing about experience.[1] There has been a lot written about the ethics of using first-person accounts in research, mainly from scholars in the tradition of autoethnography, which students on the DMan also draw on. The question we became interested in is: what changes if uncertainty rather than risk is privileged, and we take the paradox of the individual and social seriously.

We have used the framework for considering qualitative research ethics suggested by the autoethnography scholar Heewon Chang (2022) to structure the chapter as follows:

- *anticipatory ethics* concern motivations, intents decisions and the ethics of consequence, i.e., the anticipated benefits and harms of planning to do a study in this way;

DOI: 10.4324/9781003410522-13

- *procedural ethics* deal with obtaining approvals from ethics committees or institutional research boards, devising protocols and following them, including processes for getting informed consent with the broad principle of not doing harm.
- *relational ethics* concern the obligations that arise between researchers and the communities they work with; so how do we go about trying not harm others, and ourselves in this case? And if we're considering ethics in pragmatist or situational way, what do we need to think about?
- *analytical ethics* are about how we interrogate and make sense of our data in ethical ways, being mindful of the potential to overlook and overgeneralise.
- *reporting ethics* cover considering the benefits and harms in the life of the material after presentation or publication.

Anticipatory ethics

KC: So, if we start with anticipatory ethics, often in research degrees, there are choices to be made about which kinds of methods will be used. So at that stage, there'll be deliberations about the potential for some of the topics we are going to cover in the chapter to arise. However, anyone coming to a programme like the DMan, which has inquiring into first-person experience at work as the primary method, is already making a choice about wanting to engage in this way. I wonder if people really know what they're getting into though. Tobit, as a relatively recent student, what was it like coming and how much did you think about what it would be like to write about yourself and others?

TE: It's nearly three and a half years since I joined the programme so I'm trying to remember some of the details of this process. I don't recall thinking about the ethics of what I would be doing other than this was a doctoral research programme and would require ethical approval. It wasn't until I was drawing to the end of my first project that I started to tackle the ethics of writing about my work. And I think initially I thought of it as a bureaucratic step I had to go through. I work in healthcare research, so the world of research ethics and the associated bureaucracy is one I know well and consider a normal part of the work I do. And that was it really – it just felt like a normal process to go through to proceed with my research.

Having secured ethics approval from the Ethics Committee, it wasn't until I was starting to dive into my second project, writing about experiences at work that were frustrating, surprising, strange, and made me angry, that the 'real' ethics started to rise to the fore. I say 'real' ethics because the research ethics approval felt procedural and theoretical, but in starting my second project it really dawned on me that this is about my life, this is about other people's lives. And here I am trying to make a narrative account plausible, evocative, full of tension or as Geertz (1973) calls it, a thick description. That's when the ethics of the research became really evident.

KC: So, Chris, you talk informally with everyone who's thinking about coming to the program, and you tell them about what they're going to be doing. And we reiterate it when we formally interview people too. It's interesting, then, that for some people joining the programme, it seems almost a surprise that these questions arise. What do you think is going on in those conversations?

CM: We always say to people: you know this is going to be critical and we will problematise things that you may have taken for granted about management and leadership? Some people don't seem quite sure what it is that I'm asking for, and think it will be no problem. I often hear: 'Oh yes, that's exactly what I want'. And to: you know, you're going have to write about your colleagues, don't you? 'Yes, that's fine, I've got very good relationship with my colleagues'. Other people go to the opposite extreme and think that they're going have to negotiate every single conversation. For example, one prospective student was quite disturbed by the idea of writing about his colleagues and asked me for examples of what permissions he should get and how I could help him secure them, especially from all the authority figures in the organisation. This could be a huge stumbling block for him.

KC: Yeah, I remember there was one student we interviewed who, when they thought they going be able to write about past experiences, we're quite comfortable. I think they were working in a small startup or something, and when they started thinking they actually have write about their colleagues' real time work, they decided they it wasn't the right program for them.

CM: Exactly that. They didn't want to destabilise relationships which speaks to our question about what happens if we take uncertainty rather than risk, and privilege and the individual and the social rather than just the individual. I think the third thing implied then is the huge emphasis that we put on reflexivity (see Chapter 5 in this volume): to hang on to uncertainty and in order to pay attention to the individual and the social, it does imply huge amount of reflexive ability. Maybe it's not so surprising that people don't fully appreciate what they're getting into at the beginning of their research journey as people like to call it – as Tobit describes. You need a substantial reflexive ability, because there's quite a lot of emphasis in first-person methods on the student and to notice what the ethical problems might be. If they're not very reflexive, they might be blundering around not realising the ethical challenges that face them. And I suppose as you get deeper into the research, you become more and more aware of the group dynamic process of the forming of the individual self in social interaction.

KC: I think it really relates to what Tobit was saying and the some of the literature, which suggests that any kind of writing about events is by its nature not an innocent practice (Denzin, 2000, p256) – we're enacting the world as we write it (Denzin, 2006), where the writer's voice is privileged (Adams, 2008). Of course, that points to other issues about who gets to write these accounts, and indeed who gets to hear them, which we probably don't have space to get into here. In any case, unless you can gain some distance to your own voice, then it's hard not just to keep telling the story that you want to hear rather than effectively – and this is what I think doing research is – trying to find the things that you haven't already thought, and neither have others.

TE: I think, Chris, what you're saying for me really draws out the 'practice-theory' divide and the DMan requires one to write in a way that in a way that keeps the dialectic of theory and practice alive; I think this is what Alvesson and Kärreman (2011) mean when they talk about empirical material being 'a potential dialogue partner, leading to questioning, doubting, and problematising existing/dominant expectations' (p119). So, I understood, in theory, that I was going be writing about colleagues, and that it could be challenging to problematise it. That made perfect sense. The doing of it? Well, it was fine until I had to start doing it. And the closer I got towards the end of the program, the more I had to start really thinking about the other people who might read what I'd written. What would they think of it? Had I revealed too much? That's when the ethical dilemmas really rose to the surface.

CM: I wonder if actually what we're talking about is experiential ethics. Because, in a sense that's exactly the same with some of the other concepts that we use, sometimes glibly on the program, like paradox, for example. People often say they understand in theory what paradox is, but actually it's only when you experience the push-pull of paradox that you know what it is we're talking about.

Procedural ethics

KC: We touched on dealings with the Ethics Committee earlier, let's dive into procedural ethics a bit further. Tobit, you mentioned your ethics forms, and applying to the committee; it feels like that all sits within a (broadly speaking) deontological paradigm, right? As if you can specify the consent requirements at the beginning – informing or obtaining permissions from organisational gatekeepers, sponsors, colleagues or clients (e.g. Barnes, 1979) – and then just follow them. This seem a bit at odds with the idea that first-person methods are embodied, contextual, contingent and relational (Tullis, 2022), or indeed as some have said that autoethnography is 'life itself' (Richardson, 2000). To your point, Tobit, about research being a critical dialogue partner to work – research is part of work, and work is part of research. So, there's also a pragmatist and situational way of thinking about ethics, which may be quite challenging to those kinds of protocol-based ways of thinking. That's not saying that the protocols aren't important; setting out what you're going to do so that somebody else can review it and confirm they are content that the proposal meets the Institution's ethical standards is important.

CM: I think so. And I feel that getting ethics approvals has got harder, but I'm told that the protocols haven't changed. Did you have any pushback in getting ethics approval, Tobit? I know they can be inconsistent, because ethics approvals are shared out: there is an Ethics Committee, but there are so many ethics approvals to do that they use a range of people, and what kind of response you get depends on how familiar they are with qualitative research in general and the particular kind of research that we're doing.

TE: The paperwork itself was relatively straightforward; especially compared to the extensive health research ethics applications I'm used to. So, a few pages seemed okay, and the protocol requirements were not too onerous. The main pushback I got was about what constitutes a participant, what rights a participant should have and what kind of consent procedures would be used. Initially, my position was: I'm writing about my own practice – so I'm the only 'participant'. However, the research Ethics Committee took a broader view. In the end, ethical approval was fairly quick, and the reviewers recognised it would be impractical to seek consent from those I might write about prior to writing, but people should be informed about my work. The Ethics Committee also stipulated that if I was to use direct quotes I would need appropriate consent, and I needed to offer colleagues a chance to opt out of being included in the narrative should they wish. This seemed reasonable.

KC: The argument that the researcher is the only participant is really problematic. First, and maybe it's a weaker argument, if we take the paradox of the individual and social seriously, then in writing about our 'own' experience, we are already reflecting the world of experience from which we have selected something to describe. Indeed, we would lose the 'ethno' bit of autoethnography (if that's what we're doing) if we weren't trying to describe our social world at the same time as events as we recall them. Probably a stronger argument is that it's really hard to write about events at work without writing about other people. But are they a participant or not?

There have been some attempts at criteria (e.g. Tullis, 2022) – are they alive? Are they identifiable? Are they materially depicted in the story or is it more of a passing reference? Those kinds of factors can lend themselves to some kind of assessment of whether someone can be regarded as a participant, but I think it's a really tricky one. On the one hand, you are writing about your perspective, and you could say 'well, this is my perspective and you don't have to agree with it', but that doesn't seem good enough to me.

TE: I agree that that position isn't really good enough, and that was the position I arrived at as I approached the final stages of writing up my research. But it was a pragmatic decision to make at the beginning in order to progress with my research. Otherwise, I might not have been able to get to the end of the second project where I started to write about and problematise my current experiences with others at work.

Whether anyone mentioned becomes a participant or not requires further thought; what changes if they're my ally in a narrative or an antagonist? I might think differently about the ethics of depicting someone who triggered a heated event – to the extent that it felt worth writing about – versus someone I think is on my side. Those kinds of decisions are very hard proceduralise in an ethics application or approval.

KC: So that comes back to this idea of narrative privilege (Adams, 2008) and that narrativistation is a site of moral responsibility (Richardson, 1990, p131). You've got the pen, and anytime you write something down, you're creating ethical dilemmas for yourself and for others who are depicted, whether they know about it or not. Chris, how do you imagine the Ethics Committee thinks about all of this?

CM: My experience is that there has been a huge shift in favour of what they think of as participants. It was suggested to me that writing about others is like taking photographs. So, if you think about the way, say, photography has changed, 20 years ago, you would take pictures of people in the street and you wouldn't ask their permission – they were just caught up in your photography. These days, you would probably ask people for permission probably before you took the photograph, or certainly after you've taken the photograph. My reply is that first-person writing may have some similarities to photography, but actually it's more like a kind of investigative journalism, if you like. Journalists do say to people 'we've written about this story about you, and do you want to comment, because we're going to publish tomorrow morning'. But they don't give the people they're writing about – unless there's a potential of libelling – permission to withdraw their consent from their writing about them. Otherwise, they'd never write about anything.

Of course, the world's a lot more litigious than it was 20 years ago, so some of it might be about concerns that the university might be sued.

KC: And I suppose that's an assessment of risk: it is still trying to protect the privacy and dignity of those depicted – people wouldn't be suing universities unless they thought they'd been harmed in some way. So, does it come back to the same kinds of issues? What kinds of harms are we concerned about?

Relational ethics

Doing no harm: to others

KC: Depicting others in this sort of work risks perceived or actual reputational damage or traumatising those or others who might read the account

(Roth, 2009). Perhaps especially if someone stumbles upon an account rather than being prewarned about it through processes of member-checking, or being given the opportunity to comment.

So where do we get to with consent? There's one version of that which is informed consent *in advance*, like the photography example you were talking about Chris. And, there's also informed consent *as soon as possible* (Tullis, 2022), which might be in advance, but it might be during, because suddenly you're realising there something happening, which might worth talking about. But it might also be afterwards and there is a view (Tolich, 2010) which says that retrospective consent might be coercive because it's likely to fall to the benefit of the researcher. I think the question of how much choice people actually do have in those stories is interesting.

TE: I think about how my mum reacted when she read my first project. Her first response was along the lines of 'hmm, well, I suppose so', but I could see she wasn't too happy with some of what I had written, so we had to negotiate the narrative, and I rewrote some of it. Other 'participants' might feel coerced to just accept what is written, I think it really depends on what is being written. In my research, I know I privileged certain narrative accounts. Here, I think retrospective consent is ethically and procedurally difficult – what if it is not given? – and this is where I ended up, when even after further anonymisation, a key character in one of my narratives wanted to opt out. I had to have a conversation about it in my final viva: my examiners could see that I'd done my project work and that it led to the contributions I had offered, but they weren't happy for some of the narrative material to be put in the public domain. In the end, the section was redacted.

KC: So, you're making an argument for informed consent, then? It's quite a dilemma though about the competing goods of the value of research insights that may be produced from describing things that are hard to write about – for you and for those represented – versus how you attend to the rights to privacy and dignity of those who feature in your accounts. There are of course a range of established methods of responding to these issues, especially if someone objects to your account. Changing demographic features, or using composite characters is one way (Ellis, 2007); fictionalising to disguise time and place is another (Ellis, 2004). On hearing the objections, you can review, reanalyse or account for the objections somehow (Tullis, 2022). I suppose, ultimately you might decide to withdraw the account, but that feels hard when you've spent six months to a year working up something that feels important.

In your case, Tobit, even though you'd done everything that your ethical protocol demanded, I suppose it comes back to pragmatist ethics, rather than deontological ethics: you can do everything on the protocol, but you can't predict the responses of other people.

TE: Yes, and I think the pertinent questions then becomes: how do we explain the nature of what we're doing in order to seek generalised permission to proceed and then consent where it is needed? We can say it's for academic purposes and that it's all anonymised. All these things are, on the one hand, good consent processes; on the other hand, they could equally be coercive. I think if I was going to do this kind of work again, I would try to be much more collaborative, much earlier on.

I think I have been coming at this from quite a narrow focus, talking as we have been, that ethics is centred on preventing harm to the people that that feature in our narratives. And Chris is drawing attention to wider harms: for example, the potential reputational harms to the organisation that's granted the permission; or the organisation where you're doing the research. It would be quite easy to take a really narrow view of 'do no harm' – in a deontological way – and think it's reasonable to say, 'well, I'm not causing the most vulnerable people any harm here, and organisational entities aren't really that vulnerable'. But actually, the wider you make the focus, the more complicated the ethical dilemmas become, to the point that Chris makes that you might not be able to write about anything at all.

CM: I think that that's where it strays into some of the differences between pragmatism versus idealism. So, if you take a radically idealist point of view, the world is the way I see it (e.g. Hacking, 1999). So, I can say I've been deeply harmed by what you've said in what you've written and you can't gainsay that because my view of the world is valid. Whereas the pragmatist approach is that we need to negotiate this. If we're in a community of inquirers (e.g. Shields, 2003), saying 'this is deeply harmful to me' invites a negotiation about what we think harm or violence is that's happening here.

TE: Which I suppose takes us into the nature of collaboration in these kinds of methods – how do we find ways to negotiate with the people that we're involved with in order to write something, something that's useful.

CM: It also problematises the 'auto' of the autoethnography in a way that goes beyond the perspective we were talking about earlier about the self being social – here, we're saying that what you recount it isn't *just* your point of view. This is Alistair McIntyre's argument about ethics and narrativisation: 'I can only answer the question "What am I to do?" If I can answer the prior question "Of what story or stories do I find myself part?"' (MacIntyre, 1985, p216). So for MacIntyre, we can never have a complete story of the self because we also figure in other people's stories about us. Mead says something similar when he talks about individual experience being a peculiar stratification of the common life (Mead, 1925) implying that experience is something that we're all participating in even if we have our own 'take' on it. Otherwise, it becomes navel gazing and irrefutable, doesn't it? Anything that I think is happening is happening.

KC: Navel gazing might be making it seem of no value. But people write memoirs and autobiographies, and those can be interesting and useful things to have around because they give you a sense of someone else's experience as they perceived it. But they're not the same thing as research. The 'ethno' bit of autoethnography means that we have to be using those accounts as a way to explore what happens in society, or organisations, or groups. So then by bringing other people into the conversation, I guess we get to round out some of the pet perspectives we have. We'll come back to this under analytical ethics.

TE: This is where reflexivity comes back in, not as an individual pursuit, but also as a social and collective pursuit. In the context of first-person research, of course I can be (or try to be) reflexive about what I've written, but the reflections of others – in our learning sets or the wider research group (see Solsø, this volume) –are really important.

CM: I think you're right, and it relates to what you were saying, Kiran, about autobiographies. I've been reading the reviews of the autobiographies of a number of politicians recently, and one of the key criticisms is the degree to which these autobiographies are self-serving. So, for example, in Theresa May and Matt Hancock's autobiographies, they portray themselves as the heroes in their stories; and yet, isn't it interesting that they can say this about compassion for immigrants, at the same time as having architecting the hostile environment for immigrants only a decade earlier? That kind of critique is exactly what we do, to a degree, in the learning sets. For example, when learning set members say about their colleagues' narratives, 'do you not think that this is a bit self serving?' or 'can you not see that there are other participants in this drama that you're writing about?'

TE: In a way though, a doctorate can be about creating something that you can use as a tool to progress what you want. Is it so different from someone writing an autobiography? A qualification can be a mechanism to make money, or further one's career, or standing.

KC: This goes back to anticipatory ethics for me because it relates to the motivation for doing this kind of research. I think it's a problem if you're main aim is to paint a great picture of yourself, or to stick the boot into people whom you're holding grudges against, or to elaborate a gripe you have about a particular aspect of society. These kinds of motivations I think hugely constrain the possibilities of first-person research because, coming back to the uncertainty question, I think researchers need to come with an openness to what they might find – what Hartmut Rosa calls an attitude of semi-controllability (Rosa, 2020) – rather than a defensive reliance on rehearsing of your own story as means to retaining control. That requires quite some tolerance for feeling disturbed, but for me seems important for finding new things to say about the world.

Doing no harm: to self

KC: I think the question of motivation is important to be asking at the beginning of these kinds of research processes, though as we talked about, researchers may not know all of their motivations at the outset and I think this takes us further into relational ethics: we've been talking about harms to others and harms to ourselves, and one harm to the self is having your version of the world put up for interrogation and critique (Wall, 2008). Some people may be fine with that, and some people are really not ready to hear this kind of critique, particularly if the versions of the stories that they are presenting are bound up with long held beliefs that, when challenged are actually quite identity-threatening.

CM: I've found that when you're dealing with somebody who has absolutely cast-iron certainties and charismatic beliefs about the world, they may also spill over into other aspects of personality structure as well. So to challenge one part would be to challenge all parts, and there are certain things that they're absolutely committed to, without doubt and without reservation.

TE: Yes, it's the pulling at a thread metaphor: if you start tugging, then things start to unravel. In my first project, I recounted how 'everything' unravelled and was woven into something new – I described coming to a different position in the way I thought. The things that I thought were certain, weren't certain; I guess I could have started furiously stitching to try and hold things together, but in doing that one might risk being left with some very uncomfortable seams. Sewing metaphors aside, I think I am saying that this relates to the anticipatory ethics when you join a programme such as the DMan, or when you start doing this type of inquiry. You might not necessarily be thinking (or willing to think) about any of this; but as the research unfolds, you have to make decisions about how you proceed, or whether you step back and retreat.

KC: I think this also raises an ethical dilemma for supervisors: how close to feeling destabilised do you encourage your supervisee to go so they can move into something that's really interesting from research perspective (rather than just rehearsing things they or other people have already said) versus exercising a duty of care as a pedagogue? It brings up a conflict, I think, in the role of the supervisor to, on the one hand, hold the task clear and be a keeper of standards; and on the other, we need to provide a containing enough environment for supervisees to be able to explore things that they may be not have ever been able to. The latter to me involves a kind of Rogerian unconditional positive regard but the two can be hard to balance. And it starts, as you were describing Tobit, with the first project where we're asking you to inquire quite deeply into your life history. I have the same kind of experience with doing professional lifeline or lifeline work with managers.

I think having the ability to draw on different roles for different purposes at different times – for example, other members of the supervisory team – becomes quite important because as supervisors we end up quite holding quite a lot too; it's another harm, which probably would rarely come up in an ethics protocol conversation, but it is one of the relational ethics issues because there's you in relation students, and researchers in relation to the people that they're writing about.

CM: I think there has to be that tension between critique and care, really. And I think over time – certainly since Ralph and Doug's[2] days – some would say our critical standards have relaxed a bit. I'm not sure what I think about that. It may reflect a wider pattern of universities becoming more customer-oriented – on other programmes, I would say that that the usual standard is to let people drift. I think there are ethical issues there too, though: if, as a supervisor, you're prepared for your student to go to a viva examination when you're not happy with their work, what does that say about you?

TE: Well, it might just seem easier to let people drift, especially if the research appears to be taking its toll on the researcher. I agree that the work that we produce reflects not just on the author but also on the learning set, the supervisor and the program as a whole. Someone passing their viva also reflects on the examiners, and the associated university.

KC: What about other harms to self? The literature about writing about experience highlights how, at the same time as being cathartic and a way to make sense of difficult experiences (Berry, 2022), recounting those experiences holds the potential for being re-traumatised, having to relive painful experiences (Ellis, 2004), and even rekindling illness (Chatham-Carpenter, 2010). I suppose these risks are heightened if, as you were saying at the beginning, Tobit, the invitation is to write evocatively about your experience. So, there's an immediate sort of sense of how you care for yourself in those processes, particularly when you're being encouraged to dive deeper all the time.

There are longer term issues too that arise from being de facto identifiable – even if no one else is – as the author of the work. What consequences might there be for my reputation, or future employability of having my habits and vulnerabilities (Dashper, 2015, Lapadat, 2017) available for anyone to scrutinise on the British Library research archive? A kind of double bind emerges where the reasons that you might write about something become the reasons why you wouldn't write about them. Add to that knowing that your stories are going to be interrogated by others which may also be disturbing means your question Tobit, of how much to reveal, how quickly and how deeply, become really important (Snyder-Young, 2011).

TE: Of course, we are talking about unintentional harms, but in preparing for this conversation, I found myself wondering whether people come to programmes like these to purposefully cause harm to themselves. Being so focussed on experience and reflection might inadvertently provide a platform to be really self-destructive. So in addition to the harms we've talked about, I think there are the ethical issues regarding people who choose the DMan as a path of self-destruction or revenge?

CM: We have had students like that – their focus seemed to be processing their trauma so the research group seemed to be primarily about therapy. It becomes very disturbing for other students who couldn't bear to listen to some students giving their accounts after a time. Because we are diving into psychodynamic processes, it would be easy to confuse what we're doing with therapy; being in a research group like the DMan can be therapeutic, but that's not the purpose of the group. The core purpose is academic research. Things get complicated because some people might be coming looking for therapy, and then end up staying for the research, or the other way around. So then there's a judgment about how quickly to curtail their enrolment that if they're not making the academic progress. In this way other researchers on the programme become 'participants' in the orthodox way of understanding research. If a particular student's travails begin to suck oxygen out of the group in a psychodynamic programme, then that becomes something to tackle too.

Analytical ethics

TE: I'd like to come back to the idea of collaboration. In the DMan context, the learning set and research community becomes the reference point for working collaboratively, perhaps in a way that minimises the need to think about the collaboration with colleagues and those who feature in our accounts from the outset. Of course, that might also affect what you end up writing about and how you write about things – by letting people know you may write about your interactions with them perhaps inevitably changes what might happen. I suppose it's the analogy of the butterfly effect from the complexity sciences.

CM: I think the kind of collaboration does seem to demarcate the difference between research and fiction in as much as it relates to how you account for different perspectives, what Anderson (2006) calls analytical reflexivity, and Elias might call being detached about one's involvement; it's a safeguard against the kind of self-absorption (Rosaldo, 1993) we've been talking about. I'm thinking about the Norwegian author, Karl Ove Knausgård, who's made a lot of money from writing six autobiographical novels, in a series called My Struggle (*Min Kamp* in Norwegian), which has got his family up in arms. He's saying, on the one hand, it's my experience and therefore he's clearly exposing the people represented; on the other hand, this is a novel implying it's a work of fiction.

So, first-person writing can blur the boundaries between truth and fiction. However, in pragmatic terms, we are trying to get at something, but we're not claiming it as truth; we are saying, in Elias' terms, that what we have written aims to be more or less reality convergent, but we are not prepared to say this is definitely what's going on. In that sense, unlike Knausgård, we're not going hide behind the idea that this is fiction and therefore you can't read any claims on truth.

Is there is a little bit of an evasion there to say, well, this is my account of it? Perhaps, but this does highlight the importance of the community of inquiry: that it's only through processing with other people that we can get a sense that there is some reality trying to be got at.

TE: I think what you're saying is interesting, Chris, but fictionalisation, or 'composite characters' as Kiran mentioned earlier, can communicate truths, can't they? I'm thinking of Ocean Vuong, the Vietnamese poet. I recall finishing his book thinking I had got to know his friend, Trevor, pretty well. But then I read the postscript which reveals that Trevor is not a real person; rather, he's a composite of many of the partners Vuong ever had – the composite character was a way of protecting individual identities. But it seemed authentic and plausible; it felt true and yet there is no such person as Trevor. Perhaps there is a place for 'truthful' composite characters that allow one to progress much more challenging areas of work.

CM: It's similar to what therapists do in constructing case studies. For example, a good friend of mine, Nick Luxmoore, who died prematurely a couple of years back was a school counsellor. He wrote a number of books (e.g. Luxmoore, 2017, 2019) about the therapeutic themes he dealt with, but using composite characters so that no-one could be identified.

KC: I'm wondering, when we think composite characters have gone too far? Put another way, how do we make sure that when we're interpreting our accounts, when we're interrogating them, we're doing that in good faith, having an awareness of our own agenda as we've talked about before, we're not trying to put the boot in, or further ourselves in some or other way? Being able to draw on other people to help you think about whether a composite, for example, brings up the same issues as if the story was presented more as it happened seems important. Learning sets are one forum in which this can happen. We also invite students to present their work to the whole research community; these are all processes of gaining psychological distance from the events that have happened to be able to see oneself as a character. And actually, some people recommend writing about yourself as a character in the story as a way of getting some distance from it (Wyatt, 2006); improvisations, role play and forum theatre might be other ways.

So analytical reflexivity feels like it's a really important part of being able to work through some of the dilemmas that we're talking about and doing that in groups gives us, I suppose, a lot more input into the extent to which we may be rehearsing our habitual stories, presenting ourselves and others as heroes (Bolen and Adams, 2017) and villains. In so doing, the intention is to become more able to understand how our local interactions relate to the global patterns they form and are formed by. From an ethical perspective, it helps researchers to take up Mead's position on ethics:

> The only rule that an ethics can present is that an individual should rationally deal with all the values that are found in a specific problem. ... But when the immediate interests come into conflict with others we had not recognised, we tend to ignore the others and take into account only those which are immediate. The difficulty is to make ourselves recognise the other and wider interests, and then to bring them into some sort of rational relationship with the more immediate ones.
>
> (Mead, 1934, pp388–389)

TE: I agree, but of course, even when we're engaged in analytical reflection we can still be choosing to present the work in a particular way. When it comes to students sharing their work with the wider community, Chris encourages students *not* to present their work '*to the good*', but rather present questions or dilemmas...

CM: ...with 'just the right amount of doubt'

TE: exactly, Chris, but I was always concerned with making sure I didn't look as if I didn't know what I was talking about, even if that's how I might have been feeling. So, I think the way that we present ourselves is always calculated – it's always a performance with an audience in mind (Goffman, 1959, pp114–117) and therefore politics and ethics are ever present in our work. As Hannah Arendt said: 'the political realm arises directly from acting together, "the sharing of words and deeds"' (Arendt, 1958, p198).

KC: I think this brings us back to Chris' point earlier about experiential ethics. Of course, there are deontological aspects to first person research, and there are the kind of situational concerns which are called out in terms of the actual writing – some autoethnography scholars have described this as a distinction between procedural and process ethics (Ellis, 2007). Moreover, I think the whole experience of having to engage with first-person research in the way that we do it on the DMan provides opportunities for exploring ethics. Be it exploring the politics of interdependence in the learning set, or the research community, or their professional groups or with other academics: I see one measure of a researcher's (or manager's) progress as being about the development of an increasingly sophisticated ethical sensitivity, in which they are able to take wider and wider circles of concern (Nussbaum, 2003) into account.

Reporting ethics

KC: One thing that's reasonably certain is that, if you gain your doctorate, what you've written will be published at least on the British Library's Thesis Repository. Anything published these days can take on a life of its own and we've talked about how we might safeguard identities and alert people to their inclusion in what's being published, but what other consequences are there to consider for the publication?

TE: When people read an anonymised account about themselves, they might recognise themselves in the text, and as such, it may not seem to be an anonymised account. For anyone else, it would read as an anonymised account. Of course, if the work is particularly intriguing, dramatic or sensational, a reader might do some digging, and it might be possible to reidentify what appeared to be a well-anonymised account.

I think we're back to informed consent – and the earlier the collaborative approach the better I think, including pre-publication conversations with the people that may be able to identify themselves in the research.

CM: I think we should come back to uncertainty. I appreciate what you're saying, Tobit, but the thing about uncertainty is that even when we've done everything we can to secure an outcome lacking in harm, there may be some harm. Equally, the opposite is true: when we think something might be harmful, in the end, it may prove not to be. The second thing about uncertainty is it depends when you judge it. So, we rushed to ask somebody's permission just before publication, which was 'as soon as possible' in the terms we're using. And they say, 'No, I couldn't possibly bear that'. Then you ask them again in a year's time and they say 'You know what? Things have shifted for me, and I don't feel so bad about it. Actually, now I look back on it, I would have preferred that you published it'. Taking uncertainty seriously does imply that we can never know about outcomes over time.

TE: Yes, what you're saying here, Chris, is really important. Perhaps in our ethical response to this uncertainty, we end up caught up in the procedural, relational and reporting ethics. I think navigating this complexity is what pragmatic and negotiated ethics are, and here we need to be careful we don't lose the provisional and fallible nature of the decisions we reach (Martela, 2015, Peirce, 1994).

KC: What you're saying, Chris, also accords with something Jillian Tullis says about the imperative to 'do no harm' as an imagined state and not a guarantee (Tullis, 2022, p107) as a way of drawing attention to the uncertainty you're highlighting.

CM: So who calls it? When? How do you know about the balance of goods and bads? I can think of an example where one student had gone as far as workshopping a contentious event they had written about concerning themselves and another person with the actual person they wrote about in their thesis; so it was already public and the 'respondent' had engaged creatively and generously to the initial narrative, but the student's final examiner was very concerned and suggested the account be redacted. Another student wrote about their role as a senior civil servant and was anxious throughout about everything they were writing about. And then by the time she finished, there was an election and a change of regime, and they and everybody they'd been working with lost their jobs. Now, you can say, well, that doesn't take away the ethical considerations just because they're no longer in post – taking uncertainty seriously doesn't mean that we shouldn't think carefully about what we write. We should. But nonetheless, it's also worth keeping in mind that circumstances can change very dramatically.

KC: Does this take us back to pragmatism? This kind of research can start to feel like everything to everyone, can't it? The first example you just gave perhaps illustrates how examiners might be impacted by the theses they pass; just as managers might feel the work of their juniors reflect on them. So, there must be some lines to draw, but they're not clear ones.

TE: I think to an extent, yes. The pragmatist position on ethics is that it needs to be constantly negotiated based on the context that that you're currently in. Which makes sense during the research process, but much harder once work is published.

Closing remarks

KC: Something that I'm still thinking about is the idea that reflexive inquiry using first-person material is not just the process of research; I think we can also see it as a process of moral development in as much as it can provoke the evolution of a more sophisticated ethical attitude, as I mentioned earlier. I'm thinking about the critique of contemporary Western business schools (described in the introduction to this book) that has led to calls for management development and education that promotes wisdom and pro-sociality rather than abstract knowledge or sidestepping our moral responsibilities towards each other.

But, I also feel that as a supervisor, I can do all the groundwork, but I still can never predict what it's going be like to work with a particular student as they go on their research journey. I feel that leaves us with quite some responsibility with us as pedagogues, Chris. I wonder what more we could be doing to guide prospective and new researchers through the ethical conundrums we have been discussion. Because if there's one thing that comes out clearly in our conversation, these kinds of approaches are rife with dilemmas for everyone concerned. I suppose having this chapter for people to read might help by demystifying some of the issues, if people remember they've read it. Tobit, how do you imagine it would have been to have had this chapter to read at the outset of your degree?

TE: I think it would have helped with the dilemma created by having to respond to the procedural nature of research ethics approval and the many subsequent relational and pragmatic ethical dilemmas I faced, and decisions I had to make in response to these, while doing narrative autoethnographic management research. For me, the conversation has emphasised the depth, breadth and ethical complexity of this type of research in contrast to a belief that the procedural or deontological ethical approval solves the ethical issues we face when researching and writing about our experiences of being in organisations.

CM: After 30 years of managerialism, I think organisations can be brutal places. Robert Jackall's book, *Moral Mazes*, was republished in 2009, 20 years after he first wrote it, and it remains full of accounts of internecine politics and the idea that the principle concern of most people in American organisations is to make your boss look good. When people in positions of power can impose forms of technically skilled surveillance and violence on employees – measuring keystrokes, and watching what people are doing on their computers at home, or deploying forms of what Schein et al. (1961) referred to as coercive persuasion – the idea of oppression at work, I think, is much more real and tangible than it perhaps ever has been.

Further, when I think about some of the politics I hear that students are involved in, and how badly people have behaved in their organisations, is not really surprising that those in positions of authority don't want that written about. If we're interested in the pro-sociality you talked just now about, Kiran, then who is served by keeping this violence in the shadows? Although our standards should be much higher than the people that we're writing about, I think sometimes we might worry too much about the ethics of writing about what's going on in organisations if we are only concerned about the harm to individuals. It matters who the individuals are, too, and how powerful in the hierarchy. Of course, our understanding of harms has become more sophisticated and nuanced, but at the same time processes of coercion have become more sophisticated too. We cannot remain silent about social processes of domination and how they work in practice.

Notes

1 We were interested to notice that even when talking about the ethics of writing autoethnographically, trying to ensure the discussion did not become overly abstract involved talking about consent and ethics with Tobit's examiners and with university officials.

2 Ralph Stacey and Doug Griffin, two of the original founders of the programme.

References

Adams, T. (2008). A review of narrative ethics. *Qualitative Inquiry, 14*(2), pp175–194.

Alvesson, M. and Kärreman, D. (2011). *Qualitative Research and Theory Development: Mystery as Method*. SAGE.

Anderson, L. (2006). Analytic autoethnography. *Journal of Contemporary Ethnography, 35*, pp373–395.

Arendt, H. (1958). *The Human Condition*, Second Edition 2018. University of Chicago Press.

Barnes, J.A. (1979). *Who Should Know What? Social Science, Privacy and Ethics.* Cambridge University Press.

Berry, K. (2022). Meditations on the story I cannot write. In T.E. Adams, S. Holman Jones and C. Ellis (Eds.) *Handbook of Autoethnography*, 2nd Edition (pp29–40). Routledge.

Bolen, D. and Adams, T. (2017). Narrative ethics. In I. Goodson, A. Antikainen, P. Sikes and M. Andrews (Eds.) *The Routledge Handbook on Narrative and Life History* (pp618–620). Routledge.

Chang, H. (2022). Individual and collaborative autoethnography. In T.E. Adams, S. Holman Jones and C. Ellis (Eds.) *Handbook of Autoethnography*, 2nd Edition (pp53–66). Routledge.

Chatham-Carpenter, A. (2010). 'Do thyself no harm': Protecting ourselves as autoethnographers. *Journal of Research Practice*, *6*(1): Article M1, pp1–13.

Dashper, K. (2015). Revise, resubmit and reveal? An autoethnographer's story of facing the challenges of revealing the self through publication. *Current Sociology*, *63*, pp511–527.

Denzin, N.K. (2000). Aesthetics and practices of qualitative inquiry. *Qualitative Inquiry*, *6*(2), pp256–265.

Denzin, N.K. (2006). Pedagogy, performance and autoethnography. *Text and Performance Quarterly*, *26*(4), pp333–338.

Ellis, C. (2004). *The Ethnographic I: A Methodological Novel about Autoethnography*. AltaMira Press.

Ellis, C. (2007). Telling secrets, revealing lies. Relational ethics in research with intimate others. *International Review of Qualitative Research*, 2, pp3–28.

Geertz, C. (1973). *The Interpretation of Cultures.* Basic Books.

Goffman, E. (1959). *The Presentation of Self in Everyday Life.* Doubleday.

Hacking, I. (1999). *The Social Construction of What?* Harvard University Press.

Lapadat, J.C. (2017). Ethics in autoethnography and collaborative autoethnography. *Qualitative Inquiry*, *23*(8), pp589–603.

Luxmoore, N. (2017). *Practical Supervision for Counsellors Who Work with Young People.* Jessica Kingsley Publishers.

Luxmoore, N. (2019). *The Art of Working with Anxious, Antagonistic Adolescents: Ways Forward for Frontline Professionals.* Jessica Kingsley Publishers.

MacIntyre, A. (1985). *After Virtue.* Duckworth.

Martela, F. (2015). Fallible inquiry with ethical ends-in-view: A pragmatist philosophy of science for organizational research. *Organization Studies*, 36(4), pp537–563.

Mead, G.H. (1925). The genesis of the self and social control. *International Journal of Ethics*, 35, pp251–277.

Mead, G.H. (1934). *Mind, Self, And Society: From the Standpoint of a Social Behaviorist*, Chicago, IL: University of Chicago Press, 2015.

Nussbaum, M. (2003). *Upheavals of Thought: The Intelligence of Emotions.* Cambridge University Press.

Peirce, C.S. (1994). *The Collected Papers of Charles Sanders Peirce*, Online edition, *John Deely 1931-1935*. Harvard University Press.

Richardson, L. (1990). Narrative and sociology. *Journal of Contemporary Ethnography*, 19(1), pp116–135.

Richardson, L. (2000). Evaluating ethnography. *Qualitative Inquiry*, 6(2), pp253–255.

Rosa, H. (2020). *The Uncontrollability of the World*. Polity Press.

Rosaldo, R. (1993). *Culture and Truth: The Remaking of Social Analysis*. Beacon.

Roth, W.-M. (2009). Auto/ethnography and the question of ethics. Paper presented at the Forum Qualitative Sozialforschung/Forum: *Qualitative Social Research*, 10(1).

Schein, E.H., Schneier, I., and Barker, C.H. (1961). *Coercive Persuasion.* W. W. Norton & Company.

Shields, P. (2003). The community of inquiry: Classical pragmatism and public administration. *Administration & Society*, 35(5), pp510–538.

Snyder-Young, D. (2011). 'Here to tell her story': Analysing the autoethnographic performances of others. *Qualitative Inquiry*, 17(10), pp943–951.

Tolich, M. (2010). A critique of current practice: Ten foundational guidelines for autoethnographers. *Qualitative Health Research*, 20, pp1599–1610.

Tullis, J.A. (2022). Self and others: Ethics in autoethnographic research. In T.E. Adams, S. Holman Jones and C. Ellis (Eds.) *Handbook of Autoethnography*, 2nd Edition (pp101–114). Routledge.

Wall, S. (2008). Easier said than done: Writing an autoethnography. *International Journal of Qualitative Methods*, 7, pp38–53

Wyatt, J. (2006). Psychic distance, consent and other ethical issues: Reflections on the writing of "A Gentle Going?" *Qualitative Inquiry*, 12(4), pp813–818.

11

IN THE BEGINNING IS ALREADY THE END

MAJ KARIN ASKELAND

The lived experience of endings

Natality
to begin again
not with blank slates
but with bruises and unhealed tissue
with open wounds and old scars

life,
painfully glorious

demanding from us always
the courage
to begin
again

DOI: 10.4324/9781003410522-14

All things must pass, it is said in common parlance. Sometimes coming to an end fills us with sadness of what has passed and no longer is, and sometimes an ending brings contentment, relief or joy. Frequently, the ending is bittersweet, with a taste of loss and gain at the same time. In the workplace, we tend to focus on the gain and leave the loss in the shadows (Askeland, 2019). We can idealise new beginnings, we face forward and move towards the future, with our backs turned to the past, afraid that it might catch up with us and cause us to lose momentum. It is as if 'forward' is a real direction, that 'the future' is a place we can actually move towards and that speed is an unquestionably good thing. I have spent some time researching where these ideas come from and what some of the consequences of being guided by them seem to be. I have also found alternative ways of making sense of endings. I will share this with you in this chapter. I invite you to allow your own experience of endings in your research or your leadership to take front stage as you read.

Ending a professional doctorate – a personal story of endings

The day of the viva carried sunshine, adrenalin and multiple layers of endings. It felt like I was approaching the finishing line after a very long and hard marathon. I was defending my research on the politics of change and endings in business. I had drawn on insights from bereavement studies. And one of my examiners had told us upfront that she had just recently lost a loved one. It was by no means a purely intellectual exercise, or a delivery of a neat package. It was a careful negotiation of what to say and not, filled with intense emotion. And it soon turned out that the finishing line was a temporary illusion.

A new consulting job was awaiting after the viva; a whole new and unfamiliar landscape. I missed my colleagues on the doctoral program. I had grown used to our ways of working together, the work was meaningful and we had become close through our shared struggles. I had also closed down my own consultancy business recently, a business I had invested a lot of effort and hours into and that had given both success and struggle in return. I had enjoyed the journey and appreciated the partnership and friendship with my colleagues there, but this was ending too. And in the middle of all of this, my father died from Alzheimer's disease, which triggered a stronger grief that I had anticipated. Happy with my new colleagues,

I was also filled with melancholy and sadness of what had passed and was no more. And all of this was entangled and by no means a straight forward experience to make sense of.

Having been granted the degree of Doctor of Management, people seemed to expect of me to be able to share profound insights with them, or at least this was my fantasy. As a bare minimum, I expected of myself to be able to explain what I had learned in a way that people could understand. But I seemed to have begun talking in some sort of strange language. I was met with wide eyes and tilted heads or raised eyebrows and didn't feel particularly like an expert at all. On the contrary, I was full of questions.

My new employer knew 'the old me'. My CV naturally also reflected what I had done in the past, but had begun moving away from. I had changed in ways I was just beginning to realise. I came to understand that the ending of my research programme was not the finishing line at all, but rather the beginning of something unfamiliar. I had to find myself anew.

Ways of making sense of endings

The ultimate ending is death. And as I will show in this section, as with death we also seem to fear endings in general.

> [The fear of death] is a mainspring of human activity, activity designed largely to avoid the fatality of death.
>
> (Becker, 1973, Preface)

In the ideology of change and social innovation, Schumpeter's (1942) work on the entrepreneur as a creative destructor of the old is often referred to, and creativity and innovation praised whilst routine and stability is stigmatised as resistance to change. This effectively glosses over the darker side of innovation; disruption and destruction, and silences political resistance, conflict, struggle and pain (Askeland, 2019). Every new beginning necessarily involves something coming to an end (Schumpeter, 1942) and all endings entail loss of some sort (Marris, 1974, Neimeyer and Klass, 2014), big or small, good or bad and everything in between.

In his books 'Loss and Change' and 'The Politics of Uncertainty', sociologist Peter Marris (1974, 1996) argues that theories of grief and individual bereavement can be applied to understand responses to change and loss in organisational life. In my research, I draw on the field of bereavement studies to explore the intensified struggle for meaning during periods of disruptive change and transition into something unfamiliar.

If we look at the field of organisational change, it is largely silent when it comes to the issues of loss and grief (Bell and Taylor, 2011). But organisational life is full of endings; projects end, people leave or are laid off, departments are reorganised, companies merge and old cultures end, just to give a few examples. If endings *are* addressed at all in literature, psychological stage models that promote *letting go and moving on* as a solution to loss still dominate (Bell and Taylor, 2011).

Endings and loss are also underexplored qualities of the research experience (Vince, 2020). A search of endings and research on Google scholar results in articles mainly in the field of psychoanalysis, where endings and terminations of the therapeutic alliance are well covered. In this field, it is argued for the importance of taking endings seriously from the very beginning. I find two of the constructs from this field particularly helpful when I explore the potential consequences of not dealing with endings in research and change processes and what an alternative might look like: 'unfinished business' and 'the principle of good enough'. I will draw on these later in the chapter.

How we make sense of our experience strongly influences our responses in our interactions which makes it important to pay attention to why we think as we do. The way we look at the world and make sense of our experiences is *one* way, not *the* way. It is one set of concepts and assumptions. In the following, I will explore where the idea of letting go and moving on comes from and what some of the implications of this way of thinking seem to be.

Letting go and moving on

In the context of theorising about endings, the idea of letting go and moving on originally stems from Freud's concept of grief work (1917). For Freud, mourning was a process whereby emotional bonds to the deceased are severed, let go of, so that the bereaved can become autonomous again and invest in new relationships. Freud defined mourning as 'the reaction to the loss of a loved person, or to the loss of some abstraction which has taken the place of one, such as one's country, liberty, an ideal, and so on'

(Freud, 1917, p242). Notice that Freud's definition of grief does not just entail the loss of a loved one but also the loss of something deeply valued.

Freud's concept of grief, promoting 'letting go', remained dominant for the most part in the psychoanalytic field until 1944, when Erich Lindemann (1979) began the contemporary discourse about grief (Klass and Steffen, 2018). Lindemann was a leader in the mental health movement in psychiatry, and he uncritically accepted the Freud's idea that the task of grief was to sever the bonds with the dead so as to free the survivor to form new bonds. 'Letting go' was popularised through Lindemann (1979) and has come to become a dominating 'worldview' when it comes to dealing with loss and grief.

Kübler-Ross (1969), a Swiss-American psychiatrist, introduced five stages of grief in her work with terminally ill patients; denial, anger, bargaining for more time, depression and finally acceptance. Stage models have been commonly used to 'assist' the bereaved to 'progress' through grief and suggest that the individual must ultimately resolve loss by letting go. It is assumed that recovery can only occur when the mourner is able to move on. In organisational studies, if endings are dealt with at all, stage models are predominantly used to handle change and endings (Bell and Taylor, 2011).

If I were being guided by the ideal that I should let go and move on, assisted by stage models, how might I have dealt with my own experiences of ending my research program? With my background as a scientist and engineer, strongly influenced by the protestant work ethic (Weber et al., 1930/2001) in my upbringing, this was in fact my worldview for a very long time. In his work, Weber argues that the protestant ethic – which attaches a religious importance to labouring at one's job – has been central to the effective growth of capitalism. One can see how this has become a fertile ground for the ideals of letting go and moving on to flourish, with not 'wasting time' and being active, effective and productive as central tenets.

For many years, I paid little or no attention to how I felt as I approached an ending. I simply gritted my teeth and pushed away the feeling of anxiety and unease or sadness and tried to be 'strong'. I would not have noticed the bittersweetness of coming to a close. I would have been less mindful of other people's emotional experiences. I would have been less deliberate in staying in touch with people and ideas and I would have been much more impatient with myself and others in 'selling my ideas' expecting them to be taken up and probably frustrated with what I might have called 'resistance to change'.

In the field of bereavement studies, the idea(l) of letting go and moving on was challenged in the 1980s with a different way of making sense of loss through the theory of continuing bonds (e.g. Klass et al., 1996). Today, the idea that relations continue after the ending is widely accepted in this field; however, in organisational studies, the ideal of letting go and moving on remains prevalent.

The problem of idealising 'letting go and moving on'

In their 2011 article in the *Scandinavian Journal of Management*, professors of Organisation and Leadership Emma Bell and Scott Taylor problematise this prevalence. They see the dominance of stage models of grief as partly due to a managerialist focus on grief as a problem (among all kinds of other problems) to be solved, to be handled effectively 'so as to minimise its impact on organisational and employee performance' (Bell and Taylor, 2011, p5). They argue that stage models of grief form part of 'a dominant psychological discourse that serves to discipline people into appropriate behaviours', to 'police the passionate emotions associated with loss through bereavement' (Bell and Taylor, 2011, p5).

Disciplining and policing sounds harsh and perhaps not something that most researchers or managers would deliberately engage in. But might we unconsciously do this, with the best of intentions to grow our ideas and our businesses? Perhaps the 'disciplining' can take shape of well-meaning encouragements to stop talking about the past. Or maybe we find ourselves participating in negative talk about employees who seem angry or depressed, impatiently expecting them to stop resisting change and get on with it. On several occasions, I have experienced managers talking with discontent about how their employees perform something we in Norwegian call 'kos med misnøye' – which roughly translates to 'wallowing in misery' – without noticing that they are doing the very same in their talk about the employees. And without being aware that they are feeding stories about the employees that create that very phenomenon they so much dislike. I have done the same myself in my frustration about other people's 'lack of willingness to change' or 'lack of initiative to make change happen'.

Bell and Taylor address three cultural beliefs and values that influence how we face loss in the Global North. The first one is how we tend to construct life and death (beginnings and endings) as a dualism, where the end is construed as an absolute and irreversible point. Stage models of grief become means of clearly separating what has been from what is coming. One consequence of this is that spending time reminiscing about the past is seen as counter-productive. And if we are driven to be productive and make sense of something as counter-productive, we will most likely try to influence a different behaviour, either by self-disciplining and not allowing ourselves to think about the past, or not listening to others who try to make sense of what has happened.

The second cultural assumption that influences the grieving process in western societies is conditioned by the Protestant ethic, which encourages stoicism, individualism and rationality (Charmaz and Milligan, 2008). It is the individual that carries the heavy load of grief and must live through it and should do so in a calm and collected way, without too much drama. I have already mentioned how this ethic has influenced my own way of moving through endings in the past by gritting my teeth and being 'strong', numbing down emotions.

The third cultural assumption that encourages reproduction of stage models of grief construes certain emotions as positive and others as negative. A preoccupation with positive emotions and avoidance of negative emotions as ineffective for business performance promotes letting go and moving on. This marginalises so called 'negative emotions' as sources of destruction or disruption without acknowledging that the very same emotions are fundamental to identity formation and can be a source of personal and social development (Fineman, 2006).

What seems to surface here, as far as I can see, is that the urge to let go and move on quickly is in the air we breathe in capitalist western societies and that we are largely unaware of how much this influences us. The price we pay affects our personal and social development and identity formation. Paradoxically, the ideal of letting go and moving on seems to both rush people to move quickly – and to keep them in their place at the same time.

In their work, Bell and Taylor call for further research to understand how discursive demands to let go and move on may be resisted and translate the theory of continuing bonds into management research as an alternative way to understand endings and loss.

Continuing bonds

As mentioned earlier, researchers in the 1980s started to problematise the idea of letting go and moving on in bereavement. Dennis Klass, who had been an assistant to Kübler-Ross' seminar on death and dying, argued that well-adjusted survivors did not sever their bonds with the dead. Instead, ongoing relationships with the deceased were argued to be normal, not pathological or a maladjustment, and that the idea of 'finishing' grief is irrelevant. In 1996, Klass, together with Phyllis Silverman and Steven Nickman, introduced the continuing bonds model as a new way of understanding grief.

> A bond is, in common parlance, love. Love is not a thing. It is not a feeling or emotional state within the self. Love is a relationship between two or more people.
>
> (Klass and Steffen, 2018, pxvii)

They contended that grief is *not* a problem to be solved, or something to get over as quickly as possible, but an 'ongoing process in which people reorganise their lives following a significant loss' (Klass and Steffen, 2018, p341). This became the central message of the continuing bonds model and is now regarded as a common aspect of bereavement in virtually all psychiatric and psychological models of grief (Klass and Steffen, 2018, p341). It was the emergence of a new paradigm that marked a sea change in the field of bereavement. The same change has not occurred in organisational studies (Bell and Taylor, 2011).

In 2006, Robert Neimeyer together with clinical psychologist, James Gilles, built on the continuing bonds model by advancing a model of bereavement as an *active process of meaning reconstruction* in the wake of loss. Neimeyer is a professor in the department of psychology at the University of Memphis, editor of the journal Death Studies and author of nearly 500 articles and book chapters. He has become one of the most renowned thinkers in the field of bereavement studies. Together with Gilles, he proposes that as human beings, we 'continually author our own life stories as we reflect, interpret and reinterpret what happens in our lives, and we tell and retell our stories to other people and ourselves. Meaning is embedded in our life stories' (Neimeyer et al., 2006, p38).

John Shotter, a professor of communication at the University of New Hampshire, would probably have agreed with Neimeyer and Gillies on this point. Shotter had a long-term interest in the social conditions conducive to people having a voice in the public discourse and argued that we construct life through language.

> We cannot avoid using narratives, metaphors or theories, but what we can avoid is becoming entrapped within their confines by claiming any one of them to be the single correct narrative, metaphor or theory. They are instruments, not depictions.
>
> (Shotter, 1993, p 132)

So, one interpretation of the ongoing prevalence of 'letting go and moving on' in organisation studies is that we are trapped within the confines of the spirit of capitalism. But what if we allowed ourselves to experiment with an alternative 'instrument' of making sense? Seeing an ending/beginning as a continuous process of meaning reconstruction, of narrating our lives and ourselves, may enable something else to grow from endings than what we currently seem to unconsciously cultivate.

Understanding grief and the narration of our lives as a *social* endeavour means that we do not narrate our lives on our own, we *negotiate* our stories with others (Neimeyer and Klass, 2014). From 2014, Neimeyer and colleagues, now Dennis Klass amongst them, have focused increasingly on the *social* dimension of the reconstruction of meaning. They propose that grief or mourning is 'not primarily an interior and individual process, but one that is intricately social' (Neimeyer and Klass, 2014, p 485). As such, they advocate a social constructionist model of grief in which 'the narrative processes by which meanings are found, appropriated or assembled occur at least as fully between people as within them' (Neimeyer and Klass, 2014). This means that in the process of trying to make sense of their loss and what it means in their lives is entangled in their relationships with significant others and wider social groups. In this way, the narratives we form in our attempts to make sense of our experience of loss arise from cultural, political and religious contexts; the meanings people find through the situated, negotiated sensemaking that is grieving must either be congruent with meanings that underpin the larger context – or, according to Neimeyer, represent an active form of resistance against them.

Drawing attention to the social constraints on meaning making, Neimeyer says, 'expressions of grief are policed to ensure their coherence with the prevailing social and political order' (Neimeyer and Klass, 2014, p485). This resonates with Bell and Taylor's (2011) argument as shown previously. 'The political question is, then, which collective – family, community, tribe, sect, nation – controls the meanings by which the dead are remembered' (Goss and Klass, 2005). Or more broadly, who controls the meanings by which the past is remembered.

Here are some examples of this phenomenon: in an organisation or in research, when a project comes to an end, who wins the battle of the history of the project? The researcher? Their commissioners or examiners? What changes if the project did or didn't achieve its aims? What about if the ideas developed through the project threaten existing thought collectives or power dynamics? The answers to these questions seem to turn on what might be at stake for whom in these decisions and what precedents they set for the future (see also Brahm on taking responsibility, in this volume). Much more broadly, if we think about our recent history, who gets to say which country had a 'good' pandemic, when and why? Was it Sweden which avoided restrictions or Australia which went hard? Was it about which countries were being politically led by men or women? Or by socialists or capitalists? In the plurality of perspectives, our common history is being continually renegotiated and in the case of the pandemic is likely continue to do so long into the future.

The Danish Professor of Psychology Svend Brinkmann argues that human social life presupposes practices of grief, 'which enable collectives to move into the future on the basis of the past' (Brinkmann, 2018, p1) and thus that we need to leave room for people to grieve as individuals and communities. Brinkmann underlines that if grief is fundamental to the constitution of society, 'we should expect much struggle and power politics' and suggests that modern societies in the West 'may be the first to leave it up to the individual to figure out how to navigate emotions of grief after a loss' (Brinkmann, 2018, p9). Brinkmann goes on to suggest that an individual focus on grief perpetuates existing power constellations and ideologies, which further supports what I have already argued. The current pathologisation of grief in response to endings may impact societal processes, as it works to switch off the symptoms that drive us to reconnect and restore our relations to the past, future, ourselves and each other.

To bring this to my own personal experience of ending a professional doctorate, what was negotiated was my professional identity. What was I expected to know, what were my fantasies about what was expected? What projects were I offered, where was I valued and given recognition and for what? My understanding of the world and myself in it had changed, but this was not yet visible or experienced from the outside. I believe this is quite similar to what some of the leaders go through when transitioning to a more executive role – or returning from leadership development programmes. They have to find themselves anew – in concert with others.

As we can begin to see, *power dynamics* lie at the heart of the work of dealing with endings. The prevailing social and political order might shift and people rarely let go of power, influence and privilege without struggle. And when things that matter to people are at stake, there is intense emotion, as I will show by drawing on the work of Professor of Management Ralph Stacey.

The emotionality of negotiated endings

Professor of Management Ralph Stacey came to a very similar conclusion to Neimeyer, but from a different angle. His approach was from complexity sciences. Together with colleagues he developed the perspective of complex responsive processes of relating and argued that patterns, including narratives that paint the history of what has happened and self-narratives about who we are, emerge from our everyday negotiated ongoings with each other. Identities emerge in the human communicative interaction and is 'an aspect of inclusion and exclusion and thus power relating' (Stacey, 2011, p328). We are continuously making sense of our experiences and our life stories, which means that who we think we are, our identity, is socially negotiated and thus political.

Arguing for this radically *social* understanding of individuals, Stacey (2011, p328) shows how negotiation for meaning, which happens in conversational processes, is closely linked to our sense of self and our identity. He underlines how deeply we are affected by threats to the continuation of this identity:

> Conversational processes having transformative potential, by their very nature threaten the continuity of identity. If a group of people

> have spent the past decades thinking and talking in terms of particular meta-psychological theories, for example, their individual and collective identities are inevitably closely tied up with that way of thinking. Conversations that challenge these theories hold out the potential for transformation but at the same time they threaten identity.
>
> (Stacey, 2003, p80)

When things end, whether it is a project or a job or a closure of a company or perhaps the end of an era of success, identities are at stake. And as we can see from the quote above, the threat of identity is not an intellectual or abstract concept. It is an embodied experience. The risk of being socially annihilated is intensely felt in the body, akin to the risk of being in physical danger; the pulse goes up, sweaty palms, knot in the stomach, muscles tighten, the usual signs of being activated and ready to fight or fly.

> Any sense that one gets of being about to be exposed to shame and exclusion can quite easily trigger some form of panic, which is the fear of the fear of being exposed. And responses to shame and panic can very easily take the form of aggression and other destructive processes such as envy and jealousy. [...] [C]onversations with transformative potential inevitably arouse anxiety at a deep existential level.
>
> (Stacey, 2003, p80)

According to Stacey then, in situations with potential for transformation, where identity is negotiated and where the stakes are high, there is intense emotion. When we as researchers introduce new ideas that challenge established ways of thinking and working, it is only to be expected that we won't meet open arms and acclamation. We must be prepared to enter a battlefield. The emotionality of endings can be complex with mixed feelings (Salzberger-Wittenberg, 2018, Larsen et. al., 2021), and the battle is fought over what is the 'correct' story of what has been, what is going to be, and who we are in all of this. It is very much about inclusion and exclusion, fame and blame. These battles can be fought in ignorance, eyes wide shut and with brutality. Or, perhaps there are ways to navigate this that result in fewer wounds and a soil that is not toxic but from which something healthy can grow. I will explore this later in the chapter.

In the above, I have explored the model of continuing bonds as an alternative way of making sense of endings to the ideal of letting go and moving on. I have done this by drawing on the work of Klass, Silverman and Stephen along with Neimeyer from the field of bereavement studies. I have shown that Stacey has come to very similar conclusions from the approach of complexity sciences in management studies and drawn on his insights into the emotionality of negotiated endings. The cultural beliefs and values that underpin the ideal of letting go and moving on described by Bell and Taylor above, put an effective lid on these intense emotions and render them invalid or inappropriate. What might be the implications of all of this to research practice, or to managers who experience endings?

Implications for practitioners

As we have begun to explore, there are consequences to an inattention to endings. Organisations are highly emotional landscapes, political 'battlefields' where not only history is continuously negotiated but also our sense of self, our identities. Covering over or denying these dynamics does not make them go away.

In the wake of our eagerness to get on with things, lies what we might surmise as 'unfinished business'. As I mentioned in the beginning of the chapter, psychoanalysis covers endings and terminations well and I will now explore two of the constructs from this field in particular; unfinished business and the principle of good enough.

'Unfinished business'

What happens if we don't do 'the work of grief' properly, if we get too impatient to 'move on' or even ignore it all together? In bereavement studies, a widely discussed risk factor in developing Prolonged Grief Disorder (PGD) rather than a more resilient path through bereavement is the construct of *unfinished business* (Klingspon et al., 2015, Holland et al., 2020). Building on the idea that we can experience grief with the loss of something as well as someone we value (Freud, 1917, Marris, 1974), I can argue that there is a similar risk of 'prolonged grief' or 'stuckness' with unfinished business in the field of research and organisational life more broadly. This is also in resonance with Freud's concept of melancholia. Unfinished business is constructed as comprising two factors; *unfulfilled wishes*, including missed opportunities and words left unspoken and *unresolved conflict*. Avoidance of painful emotion was considered in Gestalt therapy to be a key mechanism in the development and maintenance of unfinished business (Perls et al., 1951). In their research, Holland together with Neimeyer and colleagues conclude that unfinished business and meaning made of loss together account for 50–60% of the variance in prolonged grief symptoms (Perls et al., 1951). In other words, what keeps one out of two people stuck in grief is 'unfinished business'.

So, if we always rush on to the next thing, we might find ourselves or others, over time, wading in accumulated grief. What might a landscape of accumulated grief look like? As previously mentioned, grief responses include a range of emotions. This can be anger, loneliness, profound sadness, guilt and sometimes helplessness. A person in the midst of grieving may experience changes in eating and sleeping habits, easily taking to tears, a lack of energy, feeling withdrawn or isolated, having trouble concentrating and questioning their thoughts and beliefs about the world. To be stuck in grief (PGD) can manifest in a variety of symptoms including depression, emotional pain, emotional numbness, loneliness, identity disturbance and difficulty in managing interpersonal relationships (Lundorff et al., 2017). To borrow Norbert Elias' (1991) metaphor of society as a 'social fabric' of interwoven relational and interdependent bonds – our current predominant approach to endings, where we simply encourage each other to move on, makes the social fabric fragile, with loose ends and thin threads.

Relating this back to my personal experience of ending a professional doctorate, I can find resonance in some of this; the sadness, the loneliness, the withdrawal and the questioning of my thoughts and beliefs about the world. The gap between the real experience and an idea of a finishing line and of having becoming an expert is quite a big one. It has taken me some time to come to terms with the realisation that a 'professional doctorate' changed me as a person.

If we are more aware of the risks and consequences of avoiding dealing with endings, how *can* we cope? To explore this question, I will draw on the second construct from psychoanalysis: the principle of 'good enough'.

The principle of 'good enough'

The principle of the golden mean – the desirable middle between two extremes – was promoted by Aristotle, and in Shakespeare's King Lear, the Duke of Albany warns that in striving to better we often ruin what is well. But with the ideology of continuous improvement, always aiming for a better future state in both professional and personal lives appears to be the norm in modern western societies. The principle of good enough has become unfamiliar and confused with 'not enough' (Sidebotham, 2017). I can relate to this in my own process of finishing my doctorate. I have been habituated in my upbringing to aim for high quality and to always look for ways to improve. Even with the knowledge and awareness of the political dynamics in organisations I struggled under the idea that I should be able to give an 'executive summary' of my doctoral research in a way that people would understand and embrace. And even with the experience from a doctoral programme that takes a pragmatic stance to research arguing for a post-foundational position aiming for a 'good-enough ground for now' (Mowles, 2023) a part of me was expecting of myself to be more conclusive and better able to convince from firm ground.

In the field of psychoanalysis, the 'good-enough mother' was first described in 1953 by Donald Winnicott, a British psychoanalyst who argued that the good-enough mother was better than the perfect mother (Winnicott, 1953). If a perfect mother is one who immediately meets their child's every need always, then this may not benefit the child in the long run as s/he would linger in a world of unrealistic illusions, and be unable to deal with disappointment, frustration or sadness. I find Winnicott's thinking and the idea of 'good enough' helpful in dealing with endings. If I expect endings to be 'happy' where every need is met, I would probably 'linger in a world of unrealistic illusions' and would inevitably get frustrated or disappointed. What then might a 'good-enough ending' look like?

Psychotherapist Jill Salberg attempts to close a significant gap in the literature on ending therapeutic relations in her book, *Good Enough Endings* (2011). She describes how notions of perfect endings or prescribed ways to successfully complete an analysis are merely ideals, not realities. Rather, each ending has to be negotiated (Råbu et al., 2013) with both therapist and patient having to 'relinquish [their] desires for perfection' (Knafo, 2018, p13), the therapist coming to terms with not ending the treatment 'with a nice neat bow' and the patient giving up a fantasy of becoming complete.

Ending a professional doctorate, I was indeed influenced by ideals of completion and a fantasy of reaching a finishing line 'with a neat bow'. But I was at the same time increasingly influenced by the concept of 'good enough', gradually accepting my real experience of mixed feelings of relief and sadness, confusion and clarity, confidence and doubt.

The essence of 'good enough' is about taking the real world into account, coping with complexity and adjusting to what *is* rather than striving for what *should have been*. Something is good enough in a particular situation, all things considered, when further work to improve may be more harmful than helpful. The doctoral viva as I experienced it was not the delivery of a 'neat package' with a nice bow at all. And it was certainly not a finishing line – my work was far from 'complete'. But even though I was intellectually aware of this at the time, I still had to work with my fantasy that it should have been. The viva was a careful negotiation, not just about whether or not I had done the work and if it was good enough, but also a joint effort to be mindful of the personal situation of the examiner who had just lost a loved one. It was an attempt at a mindful weaving of ideas and considerations in concert with the examiners and my supervisor.

In her article on beginnings and endings in psychoanalysis, Knafo (2018) argues that loss and mourning are intrinsic parts of every analysis from beginning to end. For her, ending is not a phase, but a process that starts at the very beginning. Termination is always in the room. 'Beginnings foretell endings, and endings harked to beginnings. This is why the ending is always present in the first session' (2018, p8). Knafo explains further how the end is always present in the room, in every pause in the dialogue, in entering vacation, in finishing a single session or meeting. 'All of these moments suggest an ending and offer opportunities for rehearsal' (2018, p10). A successful termination, as Knafo describes it, 'brings with it a sense of having transcended the need for the relationship' with the very important point of the continuance of the work through the internalisation of the relationship. Matters live on past the ending. This is in line with the theory of continuing bonds.

Knafo ends the article by quoting her patient; 'I don't have to say goodbye to you. You're coming with me. What I'm saying goodbye to is being here, but not to the structure that has been built through dialogue'. She ends by saying 'we end an analysis but we never really terminate it'.

If matters live on past their ending and if bonds continue and we live on in each other, it becomes very important to make an effort to end well.

Towards an ethic of 'good-enough endings'

Guillemin and Gillam (2004) draw on the notion of reflexivity as a resource to understand the nature of ethics in qualitative research. They use Komesaroff's (1995) term 'microethics' to address the everyday ethical issues that arise in practice and argue that 'being reflexive in an ethical sense means acknowledging and being sensitised to the microethical dimensions of research practice' (Guillemin and Gillam, 2004, p278).

The term Responsible Research and Innovation was designated to be a key term in the European research framework Horizon 2020 and has received an increased focus since then (Bardone and Lind, 2016). Bardone and Lind take a phronesis-based approach and argue for responsibility as a duty of care. Often translated to practical wisdom, phronesis takes the complexity of social and human affairs seriously (Tsang, 2008) and is about 'cultivation and nurturement of a type of engagement with the actual practice of researching' (Bardone and Lind, 2016).

The phronesis-based approach acknowledges that research is lived and underlines its unpredictability and open endedness and sits well with the ideas of continuing bonds described earlier. Care is not understood as a moral disposition of good-hearted people. The act of caring is always attuned to the everyday ongoings, the here-and-nows and therefore deeply tied up to how a person makes sense of her engagements in the world. Bardone and Lind argue for the importance of developing reflexive abilities as key to cultivate practical wisdom.

Diochon and Nizet (2019) portray ethics as a fabric in the *Journal of Business Ethics Quarterly*. They explore the intrapersonal interplay of emotions and reflexivity in ethical sensemaking. The phenomenon of ethical sensemaking generally refers to processes triggered by disruptive events or a crisis of change, typically characterised by confusion, disorientation and ambiguity where people seek to understand. They argue that objectivist, rationalist approaches have long-dominated research on decision-making in ethics and that this 'neglects the emotional, intuitive and sensorial dimensions of ethical decisions' (p463). Ironically, when puzzled by a situation, an individual's anxiety, fear and frustration may 'deprive people of the ability to attend to cues that might fully support the sensemaking activity, thus leaving them to fall back on habituated and rigid responses' (p465). Finally, they also point to the performative dimension of ethical sensemaking: 'ethical subjects are produced by their sensemaking activity' (p481).

Being ethical then, according to the literature above, is about being attuned to or sensitive to our everyday ongoings with each other. It requires an ability to stay with a situation and cope carefully, even when there is intense emotion, or perhaps particularly when this is so. During times of ending, it seems that this practical wisdom is what is required of us to reknit the social fabric and to move on together without too many loose ends and unfinished businesses.

Weaving it together – caring for the continued bonds

We seem to tend *not* to pay attention to endings or to actively avoid dealing with endings by moving on quickly. This is influenced by a dominating focus on grief as a problem to be solved, to be handled effectively and by certain cultural assumptions that idealise stoicism, individualism and rationality, split beginnings and endings, and treat positive and negative emotions as a dualism with an emphasis on a positive attitude. The combination of these influences makes us rush on to the next thing, more or less oblivious of the relational and societal costs of leaving unfinished business in the shadows.

Coming to terms with not ending 'with a nice neat bow' where everyone's needs are met and giving up the fantasy of a perfect completion, we may find ways to grow on together and to begin again. Impatiently promoting 'letting go' can be tyrannical, and focusing on 'the silver lining' or 'fostering engagement' can be insensitive and highly offensive. It can be helpful to resist discursive demands to let go and move on whenever appropriate. The politics of endings can be messy and filled with emotion and we need an ability to tolerate the anxiety and distress that comes with meaning and identity reconstruction.

Introducing the theory of continuing bonds brings paradox to the fore. Beginnings and endings are two sides of the same coin and ever present. Relations never end and we continue to influence each other after we have parted, died even. We live on in each other. We carry the past in our bodies along with our ideas of the future and our stories of who we are. What has been and what is going to happen is continuously reiterated, enacted and negotiated, which brings power and politics at the centre of our experience.

Meaningful endings/beginnings entail mixed emotions and thankful sadness or melancholic joy can colour the transitional experience. It is not about letting go, but coming to terms with, integrating and finding or making helpful rather than hurtful ways to live on together – leaning into what emerges next. What has been becomes more of a sediment or a soil that we grow from, and that remains part of us rather than something we leave behind.

We always have to begin again, imperfect, unfinished, never quite ready, with our bruises and scars. This is what life demands from us. But how we choose to end together sets the stage for what comes next. Because in the end – there is always a new beginning.

References

Askeland, M.K. (2019). *Organisational change and the politics of identity: four reflexive inquiries into ordinary power struggles and their role in shaping organisations and individuals.* DMan thesis. University of Hertfordshire. Available at: https://doi.org/10.18745/th.22800

Bardone, E., and Lind, M. (2016). Towards a phronetic space for responsible research (and innovation). *Life Sciences, Society and Policy*, 12(1), pp. 1–18.

Becker, E. (1973). *The Denial of Death.* New York: Free Press.

Bell, E. and Taylor, S. (2011) Beyond letting go and moving on: New perspectives on organisational death, loss and grief. *Scandinavian Journal of Management*, 27(1), pp. 1–10.

Brinkmann, S. (2018). A society of sorrow: the constitution of society through grief. *Distinktion: Journal of Social Theory*, 20, pp. 1–15.

Charmaz, K., and Milligan, M. (2008). 'Grief.' In J.E. Stets and J.H. Turner (Eds.), *Handbook of the Sociology of Emotions*. New York: Springer, pp. 516–543.

Diochon, P.F., and Nizet, J. (2019). Ethics as a fabric: An emotional reflexive sensemaking process. *Business Ethics Quarterly*, 29(4), pp. 461–489.

Elias, N. (1991). *The Society of Individuals.* New York and London: Continuum.

Fineman, S. (2006). On being positive: Concerns and counterpoints. *Academy of Management Review*, 31(2), pp. 270–291.

Freud, S. (1917/2005). *On Murder, Mourning and Melancholia*. London: Penguin Books.

Goss, R., and Klass, D. (2005). *Dead But Not Lost: Grief Narratives in Religious Traditions*. Walnut Creek, CA: AltaMira.

Guillemin, M., and Gillam, L. (2004). Ethics, reflexivity, and 'Ethically important moments" in research. *Qualitative Inquiry*, 10(2), pp. 261–280.

Holland, J.M. et al. (2020). The Unfinished Business in Bereavement Scale (UBBS): Development and psychometric evaluation. *Death Studies*, 44(2), pp. 65–77.

Klass, D., Silverman, P.R., and Nickman, S.L. (1996). *Continuing Bonds: New Understandings of Grief*. London: Taylor & Francis.

Klass, D., and Steffen, E. (2018). *Continuing Bonds in Bereavement*. New York: Routledge.

Klingspon, K.L. et al. (2015). Unfinished business in bereavement. *Death Studies*, 39(7), pp. 387–398.

Knafo, D. (2018). Beginnings and endings: Time and termination in psychoanalysis. *Psychoanalytic Psychology*, 35(1), pp. 8–14.

Komesaroff, P.A. (1995). *Troubled Bodies: Critical Perspectives on Postmodernism, Medical Ethics, and the Body*. Durham, NC: Duke University Press.

Kubler-Ross, E. (1973) *On Death and Dying*. London: Taylor & Francis.

Larsen, J.T., Hershfield, H.E., Cazares, J.L., Hogan, C.L., and Carstensen, L.L. (2021). Meaningful endings and mixed emotions: The double-edged sword of reminiscence on good times. *Emotion*, 21(8), pp. 1650–1659.

Lundorff, M., Holmgren, H., Zachariae, R., Farver-Vestergaard, I., and O'Connor, M. (2017). Prevalence of prolonged grief disorder in adult bereavement: A systematic review and meta-analysis. *Journal of Affective Disorders*, 212, pp. 138–149.

Marris, P. (1974/1986). *Loss and Change*. Psychology Revivals, revised ed. London: Routledge.

Marris, P. (1996). *The Politics of Uncertainty: Attachment in Private and Public Life*. London: Routledge.

Mowles, C. (2023). https://medium.com/@chris_39461/leveraging-or-finding-good-enough-ground-for-now-31a7e8378f67

Neimeyer, R.A., Baldwin, S.A., and Gillies, J. (2006). Continuing bonds and reconstructing meaning: Mitigating complications in bereavement. *Death Studies*, 30(8), pp. 715–738.

Neimeyer, R.A., and Klass, D. (2014). A social constructionist account of grief: Loss and the narration of meaning. *Death Studies*, 38, pp. 485–498.

Perls, F., Hefferline, R., and Goodman, P. (1951). *Gestalt Therapy*. New York: Delta.

Råbu, M., Binder, P. E., and Haavind, H. (2013). Negotiating ending: A qualitative study of the process of ending psychotherapy. *European Journal of Psychotherapy & Counselling*, 15(3), pp. 274–295.

Salberg, J. (Ed.). (2011). *Good Enough Endings: Breaks, Interruptions, and Terminations from Contemporary Relational Perspectives*. New York: Routledge.

Salzberger-Wittenberg, I. (2018). *Experiencing Endings and Beginnings*. New York: Routledge.

Schumpeter, J.A. (1942/1994). *Capitalism, Socialism and Democracy*. London: Routledge.

Shotter, J. (1993). *Conversational Realities: The Construction of Life through Language*. London: Sage Publications.

Sidebotham, C. (2017). Good enough is good enough! *British Journal of General Practice*, 67(660), p. 311.

Stacey, R. (2003). *Complexity and Group Processes: A Radically Social Understanding of Individuals*. London: Routledge.

Stacey, R. (2011). *Strategic Management and Organisational Dynamics*, 6th ed. Harlow: Pearson Education.

Tsang, N. M. (2008). Kairos and practice wisdom in social work practice. *European Journal of Social Work*, 11(2), pp. 131–143.

Vince, R. (2020). Experiencing emotion in conducting qualitative research as a PhD student. *Journal of Management Education*, 44(4), pp. 508–523.

Weber, M. (1930/2001). *The Protestant Ethic and the Spirit of Capitalism*. London: Routledge.

Winnicott, D.W. (1953). Transitional objects and transitional phenomena; a study of the first not-me possession. *The International Journal of Psychoanalysis*, 34, pp. 89–97.

12

CONCLUDING NOTES

CHRIS MOWLES AND KIRAN CHAUHAN

A challenge to the orthodoxy

When Chris was relatively new to academia 15 years ago, he was keen to develop his experience as an examiner, and so responded positively to most invitations to examine. This had the twin benefit of building up his experience but also providing comparators of thesis quality and academic expectations to the ones developed on the DMan programme.

One such invitation was to examine a thesis of a young researcher at a university in the Midlands in the United Kingdom, who had written a thesis about complexity and leadership in the NHS. Chris had reservations about agreeing to examine having been sent the abstract, which described a predominantly statistical method adopted by the candidate. He had two sources of doubt: one was to do with his own competence at examining such a thesis when his own statistical skills were rudimentary, and the second was to do with what a thesis purporting to do with complexity could demonstrate from statistics based on linear relationships. On the first doubt,

DOI: 10.4324/9781003410522-15

and having provided a CV of his experience to date, Chris hoped that the university would choose the other external examiner (the candidate was a member of staff, so needed two externals) with the necessary expertise. The second concern was that he was intrigued to find out what case could be made for a statistical interpretation of complexity, whatever the candidate meant by this. And on reflection, Chris was convinced he could still evaluate the thesis on what it had to say about complexity and leadership and the strength of the candidate's argument irrespective of method.

As a note to potential doctoral students, or anyone else placed in a position of being judged competent by others, it worth noticing that the final doctoral examination is a test of everyone's competence, not just the candidate. Often examiners feel exactly the same kind of anxiety about performing to a good standard that the candidate themselves feel.

In the event, the other external was a qualitative sociologist, so both examiners struggled with the statistics, but they encountered a very well written and argued thesis which claimed to prove that certain leadership 'behaviours' were statistically more significant than others in coping with complexity and were thus generalisable to other NHS settings. There was little exploration of complexity theory in abstract or in practical form, except in the sense that the health settings in which the candidate had undertaken her research were deemed to be complex. The thesis was a good and highly competent example of what we might think of as orthodox research into leadership, and we were happy to examine it according to the expectations of the discipline in which it had been written.

When the examiners had brought both candidate and supervisor back into the room to tell her that she had passed with minor amendments, they explored with her what the thesis actually had to do with complexity, except in the everyday sense of meaning highly complicated, and whether an interest in complexity was really consonant with linear statistical methods. She agreed that on reflection that the reference to complexity was more stylistic than material, and that maybe she should either have said something in the thesis about meaning complexity in the everyday sense, or given the thesis a different title. As the conversation unfolded, it turned out that she had started as a researcher interested in ethnographic research wanting to interview leaders in the NHS about their experience of leading, but had been offered a job in a department where statistical analysis was the core discipline. Starting out as a qualitative social scientist, she had had to learn lots of statistical techniques in order to go on with her predominantly quantitative colleagues and to further her career. This seemed to both the external examiners as an interesting reflexive opportunity in the development of the thesis, and one of the amendments they asked of her was to write a short description of how she adapted to join a community to which she wanted to belong. This might offer insight into other 'behaviours', leaderly and otherwise, that take place in groups about which she had demonstrated academic interest.

Later and at lunch, the internal examiner and supervisor reflected with Chris on the changes they had experienced over the last few years in terms of questions from examiners about methodology. Previously the intellectual assumptions on which theses from this department were produced had been taken for granted. Now, increasingly examiners had begun to ask questions not just about whether the right statistical techniques had been applied but also whether statistics were applicable at all to the subjects which students were interested in pursuing.

There have been a variety of changes in the higher education sector in the last 20 years, including the expansion of business schools, which take in more and more students at every level. Additionally, there is a greater and greater compulsion to publish, which has brought about an increased rejection rate for submissions, and thus increased scrutiny of what counts as novel and relevant scholarship. There are a variety of different outcomes of the changing of the political economy of higher education, not least the challenging of taken for granted assumptions. What we think Chris experienced was an insight into the effects of the ongoing discussion in the academy which we refer to in the introduction, that relatively flat accounts of, say, what effective leadership looks like in complex organisations only partially answer what we really need to focus on to go on together sustainably and humanely in an accelerated and fragmented world. It was an indication of a slight shift in power relations, where those accustomed to understanding themselves as mainstream researchers began to have intimations of a different order of things.

It is important not to get carried away, though, because critical and reflexive research is still a substantial but minority tradition within organisational research. There is still a hierarchy of knowledge and research techniques, and it is not uncommon for researchers to be discouraged from using first-person accounts.

Two traditions

Our intention in sharing this story is not to highlight the importance of purism in all things complex but to bring into view some of the development, politics and assessment of research, which has been the topic of a number of chapters in this book, including in the Introduction where we produced a schematic of research methods, and which is often covered over. As we described in the Introduction, what we might think of as orthodox organisational research, the subject of the anecdote we tell here, is much less interested, by design, in exploring the origins of its own production or the social conditions from which it emerges. Instead, the intention is to investigate something other and often abstract, out there, and to say something about it which is objectively verifiable (Rasmussen, Chapter 9) that has little to do with the experience (Solsø, Chapter 6), identity (Larsen, Chapter 3; Stoltz Chapter 8) or social formation of the researcher or those researched (Chauhan and Mowles, Introduction; Wong Chapter 4). This position also is informed by an implied moral position that knowledge about human conduct is most helpfully increased by bringing the world into view independent of, and unmediated by researcher prejudice. It is positivist in the full sense of the word that we can improve ourselves and our condition with a more and more accurate representation of things as they really are, building towards a society based on scientific rationality.

Orthodox research makes necessary simplifications and cuts in social interaction, deliberately to narrow down the area of inquiry, but in doing so reduces questions about politics and power, as the moral philosopher Alasdair MacIntyre observed:

> Methodology then functions so as to communicate one very particular vision of the social world and one that obscures from view the fundamental levels of conceptualization, conflict, contestability, and unpredictability as they constitute and operate in the world.
>
> (MacIntyre, 1998, p64)

It came assomething of a surprise to Chris' hosts at the university in the UK Midlands that they should have to justify their methods, and in that sense, one might think of more orthodox methods as ideological in the sense that MacIntyre points to. They present the world not as a partial view, but as the way it is, the facts.

The chapters in this book, however, derive from traditions of thinking based on the philosophy of Aristotle, Hegel and the pragmatists in particular and are concerned with what people do in practice to maintain and develop the identity and values of the communities in which they work. Influenced by Aristotle, the chapters take an interest in practical judgement and the ethics and politics of community. From Hegel, they assume that society is constantly emerging through the interaction of thoroughly social selves. And from the pragmatists (influenced by both Aristotle and Hegel), they challenge taken-for-granted dualisms of mind and body, self and other and explore the deepening of experience. All of the chapters assume no separation between the research and researched, indeed they explicitly describe the process of forming and being formed while in turn the researcher strives to recognise their own eye (Chauhan, Chapter 2). History, particularity, acculturation (Wong, Chapter 4), politics (Brahm, Chapter 7; Stoltz Chapter 8) and feelings (Askeland, Chapter 11) matter, because they are the substrate out of which we weave our webs of meaning and value. These perspectives do not assume that we can necessarily achieve a more and more complete understanding of the world as it really is, but that there is no end to inquiry into making the most of experience. So, while there may be no nice neat bows with which to tie things up, any conclusions we draw are likely to be good enough to go on together for now.

To assume that we make and are made by the world that we are studying is not the same as saying that we cannot reach more comfortable accommodations with each other and with ourselves. The pragmatic project involves squeezing more enjoyment and fulfilment out of experience, while accepting that we can never master it, instrumentalise it or fully understand ourselves.

In Chapter 5, Mowles posits, drawing on Lash (2003), that in the early years of the new millennium, there was a reflexive turn in sociology consistent with the emergence of the digital revolution. Instead of reflection, which mirrors back the more stable institutions and political economy of the 20th century, reflexivity enables self-constituting subjects better to understand themselves in a more fragmented, accelerated and non-linear world. If we accept one of the central premises of this book that subjects become subjects because of the objective social conditions into which they are born, then how subjectivities arise can also offer important insights into the human condition. Reflexivity is central to this inquiry.

And nor are these subjectivities of an ideal type. In more conventional organisational research, there is often an emphasis on paying attention to affectual aspects of employment which seem to us predicated on developing compliant organisational citizens: staff are encouraged to bring their best self to work, to align with the values, to be authentic, to become vulnerable for better team working and to remain positive. In the chapters in this book, we see more flawed human beings struggling with the full spectrum of what it means to be human. The chapters portray dilemmas which call out conflicting goods that break down artificial divides between, on the one hand, what being 'professional' demands of us in our working lives, and on the other, the themes which preoccupy us in the rest of our lives. There is no requirement to leave our bad selves, and our politics at the door.

So, a more intensive reading of the chapters reveals that Chauhan (Chapter 2) writes about sociality, but also about the experience of shame and the resistance he experiences to threats to his identity. Meanwhile, in exploring the presentation of the self in everyday life, Larsen (Chapter 3) notices his feelings of competence and adequacy. Wong (Chapter 4) describes how culture informs and inhibits what we pay attention to and what we miss, but at the same time, she tells us about what it means to belong amid feelings of rootlessness. Solsø (Chapter 6) discusses the centrality of doubt to inquiry and also points out how the experience of breakdown can be destabilising and shaming. Exploring agency refracted through human and non-human agents, Brahm (Chapter 7) is provoked by embarrassment and feelings of having let his colleagues down. Stoltz (Chapter 8) writes about the interconnectedness of compromise and time, but also explores confidence amid the inevitability of social hierarchies. Rasmussen (Chapter 9) explores the assumed hierarchy of research methods in the Academy, but her inquiry also brings up rivalry and the desire for recognition. Askeland (Chapter 11) discusses the creativity and destruction involved in endings and beginnings, but in doing so opens up a discussion about loss and grief.

This tradition of research places feeling human bodies front and centre while trying to develop an involved detachment about why and how we feel what we do. Equally there is a requirement in each case to say something about the movement of each scholar–practitioner's thinking and their practice. The point of this kind of research is to notice differently with the assumption that this leads to a difference in practice; one of the central insights of the pragmatic philosophical canon is that there is no separation between thinking and acting. Thinking is a form of action.

Limitations

So far, we have made an argument that the methods explored in the chapters in this volume are more consonant with organisational life as we experience it at work. They try to do justice to flux and change and events and persons in their becoming and assume that we are just as human at work as we are anywhere else. The emphasis is on exploring the complexity of experience in all its plurality and incompleteness, where there is greater inclination towards understanding rather than control. There are of course limitations to this set of assumptions.

First, organisation and management studies are predominantly instrumental disciplines where n-step models, tools, techniques, tips and tricks proliferate. The intellectual traditions from which the methods in this volume derive are mostly uninterested in reducing complex phenomena to schemata. So, there is a gulf between what most people are taught in today's business schools and the kind of material that this approach to research generates, along with an assumed hierarchy of research methods which we referred to earlier. This may leave hard-pressed managers wondering what they should do with what they read here: if complex accounts are given of complex experience, then it is a legitimate question to ask – so what? As editors, we have tried not to leave the burden of interpretation with managers. To make these ideas more accessible and useful in organisations, we asked the contributing authors to work hard at spelling out the consequence for managers, at least in terms of what they should be paying attention to and the possible consequences for them. This encourages a different way to notice what is going on with the intention that a more complex attitude may offer novel ways of responding in the unique contexts readers find themselves. Put another way, the contributors have tried to make their practice implications explicit so that they can become implicit for the reader.

Second, and linked to the first point, this tradition of research makes a virtue out of contingency. If context, history and particular people doing particular things matter, then do the research methods show up anything more than the particular scholar–practitioner's unique experience? In order to address this limitation, authors in this volume have had to explore the paradox of the particular and the general. In writing more sociologically, they have had to demonstrate as clearly as possible how the subject of their studies, including themselves as researchers, is a particular example of broader social trends, which will always be unique, but can nonetheless say something about the societies we live in and how they might impact us. The nature of the struggles described may be relevant to author and reader if they are plausible, resonant and useful.

Third, the chapters in this book need to be cautious about the project of reclaiming subjectivity (Chauhan and Mowles, Introduction). It seems to us that, especially in the Global North, we may experience a particularly extreme form of individualism and idealism which privileges the autonomous and sovereign individual as self-making and world-making. There is a difference between solipsism, a preoccupation with self and its concerns, and the mobilisation of subjectivity to understand something more about social interaction. The research tradition we adopt is sceptical enough about the idea of 'truth' and even more so the idea that one could claim 'my truth', the world of alternative facts based on what people feel – or can persuade others – to be true. So first-person narrative research always carries with it the risk that it is of much more interest to the researcher than the reader. The two poles of objectivity and subjectivity are always in play. MacIntyre recommends, we should be critical of the ways in which bureaucracy and particular methods can meld to cover over contestation and politics ideologically. But this is not the same as declaring that we have had enough of experts, rather to see that expertise only takes us so far, and may not answer the practical and political questions as to what to do about expert insights. Equally, while our lived experience may make a difference to humanising the homogenising tendencies of bureaucracies, this is not the same as saying it trumps the more objectifying tendencies of science and systematic inquiry. The chapters in this book aim to be more systematic about the social; to draw on experience, feelings, the unconscious and identity but to subject these deliberations to the review of a broader community of inquiry and to locate it within broader social trends and scholarly discourse.

Finally, the chapters in this volume privilege critical reflexivity but it is important not to be co-opted by the contemporary ideology of self-monitoring and self-making linked to the extreme form of idealism in currency today, which we allude to above. In the Global North, ideologies concerned with individualism, competition, marketisation and instrumentalisation predominate, which imply that individuals can achieve the life they want if they set their mind firmly enough towards it. Sets of ideas prevail precisely because they are adapted and changed to meet new circumstances, and it comes as no surprise that reflexivity too is in danger of co-option. Although critical reflexive inquiry, the ability to think about our relationships with others and explore just how helpful our habitual ways of responding are, is one of our key resources in complex times, nonetheless we should be conscious about how these exact same processes can make us anxious, hypervigilant employees who self-monitor only for the good of the organisation, and in the process, once more lose ourselves. In the digital age, we are monitored and surveilled more than ever before, but we should also be wary of how we surveil ourselves.

What next for this tradition of researching practice?

In the spirit of the method we have been describing in this volume, what comes next in developing our approach to researching practice will very likely depend on the people who are involved, and the breakdowns we encounter in trying to do and share meaningful research. Some of the problems we have found ourselves grappling with recently are about how to make sense of and respond to the assimilation of central concepts in the complexity sciences into the managerialist paradigm over the last 20 years. Of course, we think it is, in general, helpful that more people are engaging with the potential implications of social complexity in organisational life. However, if that happens without acknowledging the incoherence of, for example, thinking emergence or self-organisation can be manipulated to particular ends, we risk missing important opportunities to think again about what we are doing with and to each other at work. So, one direction we are pursuing is to articulate the radical critique that is still offered by the complex responsive processes perspective when complexity has been mainstreamed – what could a post- or neo-complexity research stance look like?

In addition, like other programmes offering alternatives to more orthodox organisational research, we can find ourselves on the margins of our business school. And we are aware that there are others working in, for example, critical management studies, process organisation studies, organisational ethnography, practice-oriented educationalists and even social psychologists, who share similar interests, theoretical foundations and stances, even if they don't use complexity as a foundational concept. So, what would activism to diversify the possibilities for researching organisations look like? And what would be the benefits of a more collectivist, inter-disciplinary practice-based movement?

In keeping with one of the premises of our method, that whatever happens does so as a result of what everyone is doing, it's worth reflecting on our contribution to the feeling of being on the margins. Perhaps in developing an interdisciplinary perspective that brings together complexity theory, process sociology, pragmatic philosophy and group analytic theory, amongst others, we make ourselves inaccessible and hide behind a thicket of exotic terms and concepts. In contemporary society, there is a great deal of discussion about elites, where elite groups (who are so by any reasonable evaluation and definition) pretend not to be and point the finger elsewhere. We in our turn make a claim that we are writing about every day experience and yet may be making the ordinary extraordinary to the degree that it seems unrecognisable to ordinary managers and leaders. Does it really have to be so complex? As a research tradition, we should be alive to the requirement to do justice to our key theoretical tenets while making our ideas accessible as possible, always conscious of the dynamics of inclusion and exclusion which many of the authors in this volume write about.

To that end, we noted earlier that we asked the authors in this volume to work hard to make the movement in their practice explicit so that the implications for the readers are implicit. But there are also questions about who we think might benefit from the insights described, compared to who might actually engage with the volume, and the ideas more generally. In the introduction, we suggested that we were writing for anyone curious about understanding their experience at work more deeply informed by a complexity perspective, with first-person research methods being one way of exploring it. If we take as examples the people who want to come on the Doctor of Management programme at the University of Hertfordshire, or those who respond positively to things we have written or talks that we give, overwhelmingly the most enthusiastic are those who already have questions about their own practice and a degree of dissatisfaction about what they have been taught or what their organisation expects them to do. In this volume, we point to the centrality of doubt, so another way of putting it is that our invitation seems to be most fertile where respondents already experience it. Scholarship in its more affecting form reaches out a hand from the page and grasps the hand of the reader as an affirmation of and in solidarity with the particular doubts they have experienced. We might conclude, then, that the encouragement to reflect on whether current practice is helpful resonates most with the dissatisfied, who may be in the minority.

Where we do encounter enthusiasm, this sometimes leads to the desire that somehow the perspective of complex responsive processes should be made more 'mainstream', imagining that by doing so, the chances of making organisations more humane and sustainable increase. And, of course, if we were not convinced of the relevance and value of thinking differently, then we wouldn't continue to develop the discourse; in doing so we reveal our own ideological leanings. While possible in principle, critical contemporary sociological accounts of late modernity (Jaeggi, 2016, Rosa, 2021) suggest that discourses offering certainty, stability and positivity are much more appealing than those that emphasise the implications of social acceleration, fragmentation and alienation. In emphasising processuality, uncertainty and emergence, we differentiate ourselves from the mainstream because of the matters we attend to, appreciating that our distinctiveness may change over time. More significantly, the complex responsive processes perspective arises through critical engagement with the mainstream or taken for granted, so as the mainstream continues to evolve (for example, by assimilating complexity as noted earlier) our tradition seeks to continue to critique and problematise it. Valuing the emergent is like trying to catch the bird on the wing, in flight; and if there are no permanent points of stability, then the most we can achieve is what the pragmatists think of good enough ground for now. As CS Peirce said:

> [science] is not standing on the bedrock of fact. It is walking upon a bog and can only say, this ground seems to hold for the present. Here I will stay till it begins to give way.
>
> (Peirce in Misak, 2004, p176)

Lastly, the perspectives in this volume are radically decentring and play with the paradox of the imperfection of human beings and their finitude, set against the infinite plurality of experience. One of the central premises is that we can never quite get on top of ourselves and what we are doing, and that there is no privileged position or god's eye view to orchestrate everyone else. The universe is constantly opening up and is manifold. For the editors of this volume at least, human fallibility, the crack where the light gets in, is a source of hope. How bleak would the future be if we could cover it over with our designs and grand plans? We hope that in suggesting that there will always be an element of the ineffable and mysterious in being alive does not come across as creating another exclusionary and esoteric dynamic; this stance does, however, contrast to the aspirations of more positivist research which posits that, in the end, human ingenuity will eventually unlock the secrets of the universe with a theory of everything. While agreeing with C.S. Peirce that truth is theoretically realisable if we can weave together enough strands of the rope, this is only practically possible at the end of inquiry. For us at least, inquiry may only bring forth more inquiry.

We started this volume outlining how researching practice in ways that try to take experience – in all its blooming buzzing confusion – seriously, could help to remoralise workplaces; the current global context suggests this is needed now more than ever. The chapters explore how we might go about doing this: instead of rushing to evaluate and fix problems we encounter in practice, we aim for a careful and thorough look into social patterns and how they shift. We take an interest in the rhythms of interaction, the currents of conflict, bureaucratic pressures and people's motives and emotional responses, all entangled in a complexity that demands to be elucidated. This elucidation requires a sense of both history and proportion for explanations to be compelling. For all the contributors, while they are no longer students, they have continued these habits of inquiry after completing their doctorates, not because they have been told to, but because it is hard to go back to seeing social life more simply, once it has been understood as entangled and uncontrollable. We hope that readers will have found ideas in the chapters about understanding organisational life that helps them see their research practice and working worlds in new lights too. Moreover, we hope readers find help in reflecting on what responsibilities they can take, as researchers or managers, for themselves and their colleagues in creating new capacities to act, together, into the unknown future that stretches out before us.

References

Jaeggi, R. (2016) *Alienation*, New York: Columbia University Press.

Lash, S. (2003) Reflexivity as Non-linearity. *Theory, Culture & Society*, 20(2), pp49–57.

MacIntyre, A. (1998) Social Science Methodology as the Ideology of Bureaucratic Authority, in Knight, K. (ed.) *The MacIntyre Reader* (pp. 53–68), Cambridge: Polity Press.

Misak, C.J. (2004) *Truth and End of Inquiry: A Peircean Account of Truth*, Oxford: Oxford University Press.

Rosa, H. (2021) *Resonance: A Sociology of Our Relationship to the World*, Cambridge: Polity Press.

INDEX OF NAMES

Note: Page numbers followed by "n" denote endnotes.

INDEX

Note: **Bold** page numbers refer to tables; *italic* page numbers refer to figures and page numbers followed by "n" denote endnotes.